P9-CCG-749

*An Exposure
of the Heart*

An Exposure of the Heart

by
Rebecca Busselle

W.W. Norton & Company
New York • London

Published simultaneously in Canada by Penguin Books Canada Ltd.,
2801 John Street, Markham, Ontario L3R 1B4.
Printed in the United States of America.

The text and display type of this book is composed in Garamond Light.
Composition and manufacturing by Arcata Graphics.
Book design by Charlotte Staub.

First Edition

Poem on pp. 97–98 credited to
Judi Arentsen

Library of Congress Cataloging-in-Publication Data

Busselle, Rebecca, 1941–
    An exposure of the heart
    / Rebecca Busselle.
        p. cm.
    1. Wassaic Developmental Center (N.Y.)   2. Wassaic Developmental
Center (N.Y.)—Pictorial works.   3. Mental retardation facilities—
New York (State)   4. Mental retardation facilities—New York
(State)—Pictorial works.
HV3006.N692W372   1989
362.3'85' 09747—dc 19   87–23938

ISBN 0-393-02547-0

W. W. Norton & Company, Inc., 500 Fifth Avenue, New York, N.Y. 10110
W. W. Norton & Company Ltd., 37 Great Russell Street, London WC1B 3NU

1 2 3 4 5 6 7 8 9 0

For Sam
and
Wynne, Katrina, and Max

Foreword

In 1983 I spent a year photographing at Wassaic Developmental Center, a large institution for the developmentally disabled in upstate New York. With over a decade of professional photographic experience, I planned to make aesthetic images of what I knew would be a difficult subject. But from the first day I felt my camera would not be sufficient to record the impact of the huge grey stucco buildings and the people within them. I needed words. I needed to write down what I saw and heard, and explore what the shapes and motion, the noise and silence meant in my life. Even with words, the year was more than I could put in this book.

The people on these pages are the residents of the institution and the staff who directly provide services for them. The administrative perspective, both locally and on the state level, is only represented by the impact it had on the residents through its policies and decisions.

Because of their disabilities, the residents of Wassaic have been exiled to an institution. In order to protect their privacy, as well as the privacy of their families and the staff, I have changed all names and many identifying characteristics, background information, and incidents. I have, however, represented the people of Wassaic with all possible truthfulness.

Developmental disability means a disability of a person which:

1. is attributable to mental retardation, cerebral palsy, epilepsy, neurological impairment, or autism;

2. is attributable to any other condition of a person found to be closely related to mental retardation because such condition results in similar impairment of general intellectual functioning or adaptive behavior to that of mentally retarded persons or requires treatment and services similar to those required for such persons;

3. originates before the person attains age eighteen;

4. has continued or can be expected to continue indefinitely;

5. constitutes a substantial handicap to such person's ability to function normally in society.

New York State Mental Hygiene Law
Chapter 978, Section 1.03(22)

An Exposure
of the Heart

Winter

1

A boy with an enormous head lay on a bed. I tried to look away out of the politeness I'd spent my lifetime practicing, but the size, the heaviness of his deformity held me. His temples and forehead bulged, his skin stretched tight over the swelling like a polished granite boulder And how could a neck so thin lift that head? At the end of his small torso lay skinny stick legs with broken ends for feet. At last I turned away. But now he was staring at me, his eyes large and melted at the edges. His lips pulled up over yellow horse teeth.

"You coming to see me?" he gargled in a voice as brittle as broken egg shells. "You coming to see me?" he croaked as I fled down the corridor.

Steam boiled from a bathroom into the hallway. Two attendants—in plastic aprons and high, black rubber boots like workers in a meat-packing house—held a hose and, under the running water, a teenage boy. He lay on his side on a plastic tray, a bony hip jutting up sharply under thin-veined skin. The men rinsed lather from him in bubbly sheets; the slick, white-soaped body was still as a carcass under their hands. I saw this in a flash and moved quickly by, my oversized white camera bag knocking against my hip.

On Ward B a dozen women and girls waited for lunch in wheelchairs. Some had tiny, spider legs drawn up in strange positions. None could speak. Aides fastened towels around them for bibs. A stainless-steel steam cart rolled lunch in, and a cabbage smell took over. Flesh-colored plastic plates were piled with mashed potatoes, topped with a red-brown mixture that looked like dog food. Aides fed the women, pushing food back in when it dribbled from their mouths.

One girl had been rocking, slamming her head into her wheelchair, but she stopped to eat. Another wouldn't swallow. Another laughed silently, her eyes crinkled, while food was poured down her mouth.

A girl was carried in unconscious from a seizure and put on a mat on the floor. Her face was deathly white, her body toneless. The staff took her pulse, checked her responses. She was in a hospital gown, and they changed her diapers. I caught a glimpse of dark pubic hair and developed sex. I turned away, my camera heavy and useless in my hands.

"That's my baby," said a voice behind me. A wrinkled woman with blonde finger curls dwarfing her face wedged a toothpick firmly into the corner of her mouth. "I'm her foster grandma—the state pays me. That's my baby," she repeated, leading with her toothpick as she nodded toward the pale body on the mat. "She gets the fits from time to time, but don't worry, she'll be fine in a couple of hours. I'll be home by then, so I won't see her 'til tomorrow. And she'll be Grandma's sweet little girl again." She gave a suck on the toothpick, shifted it to the opposite corner of her lips.

"You gonna take some pictures?" another grandma feeding a child called out. "Well why don't you come over to the hospital and photograph my darlin'? This here's one of them." She swiped at a wayward glob of mashed potato resting on a pocked and purple chin. "But the other one's been in the hospital for a couple of months now. They feed her through a tube in her stomach." She gave me a plump, satisfied smile.

In physical therapy, children lay on mats or were strapped into special wheelchairs, heads lolling. One cried a little in exhausted, irritable coughs. I didn't look at them for long. I barely glanced. There were things to study on the wall after all—charts and lists of names I did not know, did not want to know. The basement smelled like a hospital emergency room; sweat slid from under my arms and crawled toward my waist like a slow, irritating fly.

"These are the most severely and profoundly retarded clients in the institution," the head therapist said, his voice quiet, as though one of the lifeless creatures could overhear and be offended.

"Oh I see," I nodded wisely. The words came from a hole in the back of my head and seemed to float in front of me, like word bubbles from a comic-book character.

I circled the room, camera ready, strobe clamped on its side. Several times I lifted it to eye level and looked through the viewfinder, but each time I lowered it without having made a photograph. I dreaded the flash of white light, the distraction it would cause, the attention on my presence. And in this basement I felt the uneasiness I'd had in other places: intruding on a mosque in Mali, invading the privacy of veiled women wading on a Moroccan beach. I might as well have been across an ocean. I put down my camera and turned off the strobe battery pack.

Photographing seemed silly and irrelevant. I didn't want to photograph these people or infringe on their helpless lives. Their handicaps were their own, no concern of mine or anyone else's. I would have to give up this project immediately, return the grant to the Arts Council. If I could get out of this, I could continue making portraits of friends and my children, printing in the golden tones of palladium and platinum.

I left Wassaic. I had not made one photograph. Outside, I stared at the bare trees, listened to them shush against the wind, and felt oxygen come back into my lungs. I knew I'd made a very big mistake. It had proved impossible for me to spend a few hours—much less the year I'd planned—taking pictures.

As my car bucked off a frost heave, I imagined my camera smashing against the sides of the trunk, the lens shattering. In the rearview mirror the snow-patched country highway streamed behind me, and in the corner of the mirror I glimpsed the untameable top of my graying curls. I pushed myself higher and met my eyes, green and steady, yet unfamiliar as a stranger's. If only I could expose my brain for inspection as easily as my face, it would look soft, vague, no more formed than runny scrambled eggs. I was frightened. I'd gotten myself into something larger than I could manage.

Twenty minutes later I was home. The day was dazzling clear and bright, the wind now still. My daughter Katrina was back from school, and our cross-country skis were propped up against the porch. An eighth grader, she had done well on a math test and was very pleased with herself. We carried our skis up the hill to the old railroad bed; Katrina clipped her Walkman on her belt, put the earphones firmly over her ears like muffs. She wore her fuzzy lavender cap, blonde hair streaming below it, and her face was a fine healthy pink. I remembered a pale, twisted face with closed eyes lying on a mat after a seizure. Katrina shot me a grin and took off through a trail in the woods, pumping her agile body and singing.

2

Three days later I forced myself back to Wassaic. Pride would not let me quit so easily. I wandered through Juniper Hall, my heavy, old-fashioned Speed Graphic pulling at my arm. It seemed a waste of effort even to carry the thing around. It was time to admit I would never be able to turn this sadness into images; even when I saw a photograph, I was unable to take it. I thought of myself as a photographer who recorded intimacy, who was unafraid of pain, yet I also knew I sometimes backed down when I found things too emotional.

We once had a neighbor, a woman in her seventies, whose beloved cow, Bright Eyes, was dying in a snow-covered field after calving. Anna borrowed blankets, swaddled the cow like an infant, and sat cross-legged in the field, Bright Eyes's big cow-head on her lap. When I saw them isolated against the white background, I knew it would be a fine photograph. Both looked up at me with dulling eyes that knew death. I could not appropriate their pain. I hid my camera under my parka and didn't make the picture.

Why then, had I wanted to photograph Wassaic?

For years the sight of Wassaic had repelled me. To see twenty-seven huge cement buildings in our gentle farm and woods landscape was as jolting as the sudden shape of an adult in a baby's crib. Like most upstate institutions, it was built along the railroad tracks; the poor, the homeless, the mad, the retarded, the crippled, the unwanted were shipped from New York City to asylums along the line. If there wasn't room at one, there would be at another. At Wassaic, in 1968, almost five thousand people had been warehoused in wretched, overcrowded conditions. Five thousand is twice the population of Millerton, the small town fifteen minutes away where I live.

People in Millerton have had an intimate, uneasy relationship with Wassaic. Most have been employed, or have had parents or grandparents employed there; it is the second largest employer in Dutchess County, surpassed only by IBM. At the lowest end of the pay scale, Wassaic has provided jobs for food-service workers, housekeepers, launderers, and stenographers. While entry-level salaries are low for therapy aides—the direct-care staff who bathe, dress, and feed the residents—raises are automatic and benefits are considered to be good. Jobs are available in middle-management positions, such as building supervisors, nurses, and social workers, as well as for doctors and upper-level administrators. My husband, Sam, has worked as a planner for Wassaic during the decade we have lived in the area.

Everyone from Millerton to Dover Plains has friends whose lives are bound by "the hill." And so dark tales have been carried up and down the Harlem Valley—of the "zoo" on the hill; of "the way we used to keep order up there"; of night-shift exhaustion and sleeping employees fired; of employees assaulted; of escapes by the "retards," the "dummies," the "animals." I had heard these things.

After the Willowbrook scandal of 1972, which focused national outrage on New York State institutions for the retarded, conditions at Wassaic changed—had to change. When reporters exposed the Staten Island institution, TV cameras swept over naked residents lying in their own urine and feces—images from torture chambers and concentration camps. A three-year court battle resulted in the Willowbrook consent decree, and with the threat of litigation against other state institutions, reform began. Massive improvements were planned at Wassaic; the huge gray buildings became less crowded as released residents moved to state- and privately-run group homes in nearby communities, of which Millerton was one.

A few years later my family and I moved to the area after three years in West Africa with the Peace Corps. Sam, an architect and educational consultant, found a job at Wassaic planning the substantial changes that had to be made. We bought a dilapidated eighteenth-century house that had been added to and stuccoed over, and began renovating it on evenings and weekends.

On a nearby farm, five women and one man sat outside under the giant leaves of a catalpa tree, from afternoon to nightfall, spring through fall. Their tidy row of blue metal chairs faced the road. Occasionally a car went by. The women wore straw sun hats, white ankle socks, and flowered house dresses. This was a "family care home" for those released from Wassaic—a way to provide foster care and supplement community incomes.

When I drove by I'd slow and peer; they'd cheerfully wave and sometimes hold up a little yapping dog that was their only visitor. One day I stopped my car and photographed them as they sat. I came back on Saturday morning, when the women did each other's hair, and photographed them in their thick, pink, sausage curlers.

For me, photography has been a way to gain intimacy. Not only am I given time with my subjects, but a photograph gives a moment a chance to stand still. With my camera I learned what happened in the lives of my "retarded" neighbors. I photographed other family care homes—retarded people shucking corn and feeding goats and dancing together at Saturday night socials, much as other community members do. The difference was that they had grown up inside the cement walls of an enormous institution. Though some of them stuttered or left ideas undeveloped, though some cackled or spoke shrilly, though others were turned inward, none seemed handicapped enough to demand incarceration.

I began to ask myself these questions: What could their lives have been like before they were released from Wassaic? Who were the people left there? What could I learn from photographing them? And how would I do it?

Lewis Hine, an unflinching documentarian of the early twentieth century, pioneered frontal portraiture and eye contact with his subjects, yet photographed retarded children in profile, unable to face them. Diane Arbus had presented her subjects in harsh detail so we could gawk. Geraldo Rivera had rushed into Willowbrook to expose the horrors, his fast-moving TV camera making shadowy, frightening images. I didn't yet know what I wanted from my own photographs, but I knew what I did not want.

A hand moved toward me and instinctively I jerked the camera from it. A girl stood against the corridor wall—a girl with hair cut straight below her ears and thick bangs that boxed a small face. Her skin seemed new and tender, stretched over fragile bones, and a faint blue tinted the hollow beneath her eyes. She was thin, angular, dressed in baggy slacks bunched at the waist by a belt. Her hand hovered, groping for a place to land now that the camera was gone, then settled on my forearm.

"I see you've met Emily," said a curly-headed aide coming out of Ward C. "She'll latch on to anyone that comes by, so in the future watch out if you don't want company."

I looked warily at the girl holding on to me—the knobs of her wrists and elbows poked from her arms while her bent legs and rounded shoulders skewed her body into a question mark.

"My name's Vera, and this is Emily Benedict, one of my five kids," the young aide announced, squeezing Emily's shoulder. Emily's hand slid to my wrist and gripped it, her fingers pressing firmly enough to take my pulse. We were linked, as though I were someone she'd been waiting for.

"Come on Emily, leave the lady alone. Get back in the ward," Vera said, her voice edging down. Emily clutched my wrist. "Emily just wants to be on the go, up and down the halls. You'd think limping like she does from her cerebral palsy she'd want to stay still sometimes, but no luck. The whole group's a piece of work. It's like being with a bunch of two-year-olds, only they aren't, you know. Emily's actually the baby here—there are only a few kids under fourteen left. She's only twelve."

"Twelve," I repeated, trying to take it in. I knew twelve-year-olds. Emily's head came to my shoulder, at exactly the same spot as my own twelve-year-old, Max.

"She's got a funny face, doesn't she? Sometimes she looks like a baby, and sometimes she gets so serious she looks old. Compared to most of the kids around here, she looks pretty normal. But how normal can you be with an IQ in the twenties? And she does a bunch of strange things—for one, she's always humming."

I looked down and listened. A little noise came from Emily, the hum of an electric wire in winter, just a faint buzz. She was smiling as she hummed, a wide, joyful grin stretched across her cheeks, as though her noise were telling a secret no one else could hear.

I saw my first photograph.

Pulling my wrist gently from Emily's grip, I backed off and focused the camera. She began to twist from the waist, her feet firmly spread. I adjusted the focus for the front swing of her twist, waiting for her to loom into range. When the strobe went off Emily squeaked and clapped, and I put down my camera and clapped for her, this girl who'd given me my first Wassaic photograph.

In the physical-therapy room eight wheelchair clients were positioned on mats. The head therapist, Bernie, wore a wide leather belt with brass rivets; keys packed tight as a fist hung from his belt loop. He raked sinewy fingers across the top of his head, through hair closely mown to his scalp.

"Things have really changed since I started working here twenty years ago," Bernie said in a surprisingly soft voice. He knelt and gently massaged a client's arm.

"First, you have to remember this place didn't always have a fancy name like 'Developmental Center.' It used to be called the 'State School.' And there weren't any 'aides,' just 'attendants.' As for the 'clients,' that's the latest fancy word they've put out. Before we were supposed to call them 'residents,' but most of the time they were still 'inmates.' "

I realized then how troubled I was by the official terminology. There ought to be a better word than "client." It had the coldness of a business transaction.

"Another thing that's changed is the way we classify the clients. We used to call them 'morons' or 'imbeciles' or 'idiots,' depending on how severely they were retarded. Now we designate their handicap by different labels: mild, which means they can be educated; moderate, which means they can be trained; severe and profound, which means they are totally dependant.

"When I started here I was assigned to M building," Bernie continued. "M was the building for juvenile delinquents. Some of them were probably borderline retarded, but most of them were normal kids from the city who had gotten into trouble. They'd be convicted by a judge for skipping school, or their parents would have them declared unmanageable. They'd be sentenced to three months in a detention center, they'd serve two months, then the place would get over-crowded. So with one month to go, they'd be transferred up here. That would be it. They'd be up here for years and years. With one month left to serve." He unclipped the keys from his belt and swung them on their leather thong as he spoke.

"The main thing you could say about this place was that it was clean. I mean spit-polish clean. You could eat off the floor. Of course, the residents did all the work. The attendants didn't do anything but organize them. The toilets were scrubbed two or three times a day with stiff brushes. Same with the floors.

"And once a week we waxed the floors. We lined the guys up on their hands and knees with bars of paraffin, and then raced them down the length of a room, waxing. Then we'd pick out the littlest guy and set him on top of the buffer. We'd tell the other guys they were going to build their muscles, and they'd push the weighted buffer around the room. Everyone was happy—the little guy getting his ride and the big guys building muscles. And we were happy too, because we'd gotten our job done."

Tenderly, Bernie lifted a tiny ball of a woman as though he were picking up a huge kitten. Her wide, thick, bright red tongue hung down like an enormous, swollen lip; her withered knees were drawn up to her chin.

"Every day we'd go to a central dining hall for meals.

We'd line the boys up according to size and march them over while someone inspected them. You had to use a lot of discipline in those days. Taking away privileges, that sort of thing." Bernie cradled the twisted, scrunched up woman as though she were a nursing infant.

"And we'd reward them with a piece of candy, though we were told not to be too nice or we'd lose control. Sometimes I'd be the only person in charge of a hundred and twenty guys for three or four hours. You had to be on top of it all the time, 'cause they sure could have overpowered any of us."

I could imagine Bernie standing, arms crossed, feet spread, ready for trouble, the heavy bunch of keys at his belt.

"Most of the boys graduated out of here. Lots went into the army. They held down jobs and became members of the community. Years later I saw one of them working at the supermarket. Of course there were some that didn't make it—bright guys, too. They started going downhill as soon as they were put in here. Quit talking. Quit walking, the works.

"Those years were tough on everybody. For years I worked nights and babysat for my own kid during the day. I was a zombie, I can tell you." Bernie shook his head and laughed, but his hand passed over the top of his crew cut in a gesture of renewed fatigue.

"Guess who's wet again?" He looked over at the woman bundled by her own flesh. "I don't mind the clean up—she's my baby now. She has Down's Syndrome—what they used to call 'mongoloid' in the old days. She's a lot different from the clients we used to have in here—then we'd have *them* clean up, but it's our turn now."

3

A bed sheet covered a table. A huge slab cake was swirled with rosettes and "Be My Valentine" iced in red. "Look at those things," the recreation aide said, gazing up at the droopy red and white streamers that criss-crossed the basement ceiling. "They look like they've been up there in the rain for a week. Every damn time I decorate for a party I forget how much they're going to sag. But check out the best part!" She pointed to a freestanding cardboard cutout painted with life-sized bodies of a man and a woman, arms around each other, two holes in place of the heads. "You get it? We pick a boy and a girl and put them in side by side. Then they can be valentines!"

She looked at me expectantly, waiting for my response while I struggled to keep my face neutral. Surely she couldn't mean they were planning to pair off profoundly retarded people as mock sweethearts?

In each hand she held a styrofoam bowl filled with scraps of paper. She gestured down with her chin. "You guessed it—the boys' names go in this bowl and the girls' in that. Without looking—absolutely random—we draw two names, wheel them up, get them in place, and take their pictures."

The room was filled with wheelchairs and the noise of babbles, isolated screeches, and howls. I looked around for faces I could recognize. There was the boy I'd seen the first day, with the huge hydrocephalic head; barely able to sit, he reclined covered to his waist with a blanket that made him look legless.

"Who is that boy?" I asked, pointing into the traffic jam of wheelchairs.

"Which one?"

Desperately I sorted through possible descriptions. The one with the huge head? The one with no legs? The one lying down? "The one with the plaid blanket."

"Why, that's Dwight. Everyone knows Dwight."

Across the room Dwight slowly rotated his swollen head until his eyes were solid on me. "You coming to see me?" he called in his cackled voice, and there was no doubt that he was addressing me. I smiled, embarrassed to have been caught staring at him again. "You coming to see me?" And then came giggles like hiccups, fast over each other as though he'd made, or seen, the greatest joke imaginable.

I moved through the party making photographs. A boy, twisted in a wheelchair, beamed when he saw me. He couldn't speak, but he knew the body language of posing: he flung his arm around the nearest person to lure the camera— then held dead still.

I photographed a plump girl who did endless sit-ups from her chair. She said things to me in elongated, moaned sounds, a speech I couldn't understand. I bent closer, straining for a few words.

Something—someone—zoomed into the room on his belly; his body was on a wheeled platform, his arms had huge biceps, and little useless legs trailed behind. Though I moved away from this alligator-boy, he was always nearby. His eyes followed me in a sullen, hostile stare.

I remembered a photograph I had made in a small village in Sierra Leone. A man with the same powerful torso hauled his withered, dwarfed legs around using blocks of wood as arm-shoes. He watched me photograph everyone in the village with eyes that scorned my embarrassment and fear of his deformity. Just before I left, when there was nothing to risk but his discomfort, I turned to him with my camera. His stare was silent, unsmiling permission. He raised a cigarette to his mouth, and as I pressed the shutter, he posed for me, disdainful and uncompromised.

Then across the room I found Emily Benedict in the crowd of wheelchairs and jerking, rocking kids. I was unprepared for my pleasure when I saw her sharp, little face. She looked so normal. I raised the camera and through the viewfinder saw her slowly recognize me as though she were taking the picture and I were coming into focus. She stood, and with one hand shading her eyes as if saluting, she lurched toward me.

"Settle down Emily. We're going to send you back to your room if you don't calm down," a shrill voice said. Emily twisted from her hips in big corkscrew turns, her fingers on my forearm. "Leave that lady alone, I told you." A hand took her wrist, pulled her fingers from me. "Get on back here and eat your ice cream." Emily sat obediently, focused on her bowl of ice cream and mashed-up piece of cake, and began to rub her hands over it, as though over a warming fire.

"I said cut it out, Emily. Do you want to go right back to your ward?" I looked directly into the sallow face of a young woman, her cheek muscles pulled tight, her chin firmly dimpled with years of bad temper.

Drawing out an empty chair, I rested my elbow on the table, and propped my chin on my fist. "Don't you think it's sweet she gets so excited over a party?" I asked tentatively.

"Sweet, my ass." She shot me a disgusted look. "She's being a nuisance, that's what."

Then I was angry. Emily is so thin her bones show; why should she be chided for showing pleasure over food? I watched her react to the scolding voice: her small, bony hand folded into a fist, four fingers gripping her thumb, and she straightened her arms, her wrists pointed forward.

Then with teeth clamped together, she began to hum, the sound building like a motorcycle whining towards me. Her face was rigid.

Emily was twelve years old. She was the same size, the same age, as Max. But if she were a normal twelve she'd be learning algebra and playing softball. Next year she'd be thirteen, the age now of Katrina who made snow ice cream, played the flute, and studied American history. My oldest son, Wynne, was twenty-one. When Emily reached Wynne's age, she should drive a car and go to college.

I looked around the basement room, at the sagging crepe paper, the remnants of the cake, the wheelchairs lined up for sweetheart polaroids—faces of severely retarded young people behind normal cardboard bodies. What was this party about? No one seemed to be aware of the decorations. Why the elaborate, Capital Bakery cake and punch bowl full of ice cream like a Park Avenue birthday party? Cake and ice cream were mashed together on the plates.

"You are *not,* you are *not* going to have any ice cream if you don't say 'please.' " The same aide who had disciplined Emily had her hands on a boy's shoulders. "Now say it, 'please,' and you'll get some." Her pinched, angry face was close to his blank one. Her lips spit out "please"; his did not move.

Did this boy know the word "please"? Could he be taught to say it, to value it as a way of getting what he needed? Or did "please" just reflect the aide's insistence on some recognizable word in a place where words were garbled or nonexistent?

That was the only thing that could explain this party: It was the staff that needed to have things "normal." A party—even if they were the only ones who understood and appreciated it—made life in Juniper Hall seem whole. Never mind that heating pipes supported the crepe paper; never mind that bed sheets doubled as tablecloths; never mind that the guests moaned or rocked or shrieked. Never mind that college was out of the question for Emily. So was first grade. Never mind. Bring out the cardboard lovers and let's take a picture.

When the party was over Emily sat in a corner of Ward C, absorbed in "Pop! Goes the Weasel" on a baby's plastic music box. Finger across my lips for silence, I nodded to Vera, then photographed Emily—two shots. Her dark eyes squeezed shut, then opened wide at the sharp strobe light, while her cheeks mounded up in a smile.

I watched her beaming at me. "Vera, is her personality always this placid? I saw her angry a while ago at the party, but it all seemed turned inside. Does she ever blow up?" I asked.

"Only when she comes back from an outing," Vera said, lighting a cigarette. "And then she can really blow. The worst is when her grandmother brings her back. See, Emily is smart enough not to like just sitting here all day. When she goes out she's really sad to get back. So she'll take that silly music box she likes to carry around and throw it on the floor. Why it's never broken, I don't know. But that's it. That's how she gets mad."

I asked how often her grandmother took her out.

"Quite often, more than most parents."

"What does that mean? Once a month?"

"More like once every three months," Vera said grinding out the cigarette she had just begun. "Most parents don't take them out at all. I'd guess—and this is only a guess—that out of seventy residents in this building only ten of them go home."

As though to compensate for saying such a harsh thing, Vera went over to play with the kids. "You better get to know all these kids if you're going to be around a while," she said boring a tickle-finger into a girl's stomach. "This here is June." The little girl in the chair whimpered, her face was tomato red, the skin on her ears raw and cracked. "She's the oldest of the group. She's almost thirty." Nothing about June looked thirty; her torso and skinny legs belonged to an old woman, while her face was a big, red, drippy-nosed baby's.

"And over there is Wonder Woman." A sturdy body was draped over the couch, now and then letting out a holler without moving. "That's not her real name of course, but that's what we call her, because believe me, she's strong. Don't be fooled by her being female. She likes to come on like she's lazy, but when she gets going, stand back."

Vera then peered under the couch where two sneaker soles stuck out like big rabbit ears. "That's Louisa under there. She'll come out when she's ready, and you won't see her quiet again for another week.

"And where's that Vincent gone to?" Vera demanded. "He's not officially in this ward, but a couple of kids just got transferred out, and he likes this room, so I let him hang out here. He's supposed to use crutches, but he scoots around on that overgrown skateboard and escapes into the hall all the time." I realized that this was the alligator-boy I'd seen at the party.

"Then there's Carrie," Vera said, with a nod at a girl in a wheelchair. "She's a stitch—the only one in the group that talks. And what a mouth."

"Our name is Carrie," the girl drawled, pronouncing "r" as "w," just as Max had done when he was two. I smiled, amused by her first-person plural. "We're gonna be a good gi-wl. We gonna be good, we pwomise. Then Momma's gonna come see us." But as she droned on in her pokey way, I realized some adult had taught her that speech pattern—someone who also found that stereotypical "we" of nurses a cute trick.

Vera tickled June's belly again; Louisa appeared from under the couch and began crying. Wonder Woman gave me a hungry look of joy and lunged; she pulled me toward her with an iron-strong grip on my arm. Emily held tighter to my other arm. "That's the problem—they all get jealous. Things will even out in summer when the weather's better." Summer? It was February. "Meanwhile, things are going to get rougher because the foster grandparents are being laid off. There's funding for a few, but most of them—including Emily's—are going. Too bad. She's real attached to her."

So Emily had a real grandmother who saw her every few months, and a foster one who was about to be fired. Where was her mother?

"These are all good kids," Vera continued as she pried Wonder Woman's hand off me. "Wassaic does the best it can for them, but it is what it is. If you ask me, Emily shouldn't even be here."

I looked at the child by my side and thought of Max again, healthy and normal in every way. "And if she were mine she wouldn't be," I blurted out. "She'd be at home with me." I meant it, yet as I said the words, I felt awkward and false. If Emily were at home with me I wouldn't be standing in this room—or anywhere—with my camera. I wouldn't have had the time and emotional freedom to pursue an artistic career. I would have devoted the last twelve years to this severely retarded girl. I would have been stuck.

I could not think of it another minute. "I'm late for an appointment," I said to Vera sliding my arm from Emily's hand at the same time. "Perhaps I'll see you later in the week." Once again, I fled.

4

"Smile, you're on Candid Camera!" a voice rasped close behind me. "Are you planning to make us all famous? Put us on the television?" On one shoulder hung my camera bag loaded with 4 × 5 film holders, a light meter hung around my neck, my battery pack hung from my other shoulder, and I gripped the Speed Graphic with both hands.

I turned to a woman with brassy hair knotted so tightly on her head that the corners of her eyes pulled up. Beneath lids of iridescent turquoise, steely eyes looked me over. "So, why are you taking pictures in this building?" She spoke distinctly, pronouncing each word, each syllable with the force of a slap.

"I'm going to be photographing all over Wassaic."

"No," she said as she waggled her index finger and shook her head, "why are you in *this* building?"

"Because I was told Juniper's one of the best," I answered glibly. I was eager to be on my way.

"Who told you that?"

"Well," I said, stalling under her hostility, "lots of people. The building supervisor for one." Indeed he'd said it was the very best building at Wassaic; others had told me the same.

"Of course he thinks so. He makes forty thousand dollars a year. For him this is easy street. He and all the other administrators. They rake in money while we do all the work." She blocked my way in the corridor; angry washboard lines creased her forehead and her nails gouged into her palms. "Look at that girl over there lifting. We all lift from wheelchair to mat to toilet to bath to bed more than fifty times a day. Is that the building supervisor lifting and changing diapers?

No. He sits at his desk making forty thousand a year and saying the building is great. It *used* to be great. Now it's a zoo."

I felt confused. From what I knew of the history of the institution, conditions had vastly improved over the last decade. This woman had everything backwards. And her intensity frightened me.

Calmly I asked her how long she'd worked at Wassaic.

"Twenty years." The answer choked out of her. She didn't look old enough to have worked anywhere for twenty years; she must have been a young girl when she began this job she so resented. "And believe me, if I had known what it would be like, I'd have ended it all before I started."

"But you must like your work somewhat to have stayed in it so long," I said, though I feared I sounded naïve and patronizing.

"The job used to be okay. You could do what you wanted. Now there are too damn many bosses everywhere. All the time they are just looking around for some way to trip you up. It is terrible." Her mouth set bitterly at the end of each sentence. "So take your camera around, make pictures of these animals. Then tell me what a good building this is."

A few days later I looked in Emily Benedict's dayroom as I passed by. Emily recognized me immediately; she put down her music box and linked her arm through mine. Limping slightly, she walked out the door of her ward. She wanted to roam the halls, touching the cool, tiled walls, tracing a finger down the frosty windows.

In Ward D the angry aide was setting up for lunch. "Look everybody, it's Allen Funt." The overlay of jolliness did nothing to erase the anger from her voice. "You haven't broken your camera yet photographing the zoo?"

"No," I said, keeping down my own anger. "By the way, is your name Marge?"—a name I thought I'd overheard.

"Marge? Of course that's it." She snorted laughter. "The administration sent you with your camera to spy on me, didn't they?" she roared. "Well, I won't tell you my name. To you, it's Marge. Isn't that right? Isn't that my name?" She winked at an aide.

Several men moaned as they waited for lunch. Shrieks came from one of the bedrooms. "Happens every day," the angry aide shouted. "We don't pay attention to it."

"Roger doesn't like to eat anything but sweets," explained another aide as she fed a young boy, whose body seemed to fold in on itself. "That's why I started with the pureed fruit salad." She popped in a spoonful of a pasty-looking main course, then as he tried to spit it out, she dribbled in milk from a baby's training cup. The next time the spoon came near he clapped his lips firmly shut. "Come on Roger, open up," she said gently, wiggling the spoon between his lips. "Every mouthful is an effort. He makes himself gag on it, so I never know if I've succeeded or not."

Could my camera ever show what an agonizing chore eating was for this young man, and what a trial for the person feeding him—three times a day, every day of his life?

As I photographed, a man began to howl. And a few seconds later, another resident had an outburst, slamming his head repeatedly against his cushioned chair and shouting.

It seemed that this lunch hour was difficult enough, and I asked the aide if perhaps the strobe agitated them. "It startled me," she said frankly, "so it must be unnerving for them. I've heard of clients having seizures because of flashing lights."

The angry aide called across the room. "No, it doesn't bother them. They don't think the same way we do. They don't have the same reactions. That's why they're in this place."

I asked the name of a client I remembered seeing at the Valentine party: a big, handsome teenager who looked as though he should be head of a student council, not wheelchair bound and unable to speak.

"That's your son, isn't it, Loretta?" The aide howled with laughter and slapped her hand on the angry aide's shoulder. "Whoa, that's a good one!"

So, she was Loretta.

"Of course you ask his name," Loretta said turning her venom back to me. "He's one of the pretty boys. You're all alike, you only want the cute ones. They're the ones who get taken home." She glanced scornfully at Emily who sat quiet and composed, her face turned up to mine. "I can tell your kind. You've come here to see them vegetate." She waved a hand in front of my face. "Don't worry, that's not my word. I learned it from the management. If you're not always agitating them, they vegetate." She leapt from the table alive with energy. "But come with me. Here's a picture you should take."

I stood still with my distrust.

"Come on, I thought you wanted to see everything in this place."

Reluctantly I followed her to a back bedroom, leaving my camera on the table.

One client was masturbating. I looked away. Two other clients lay inert in bed-cribs, their tiny withered limbs, lifeless, their eyes, open. "There you have it," Loretta said. "The dregs. The scum. They're not the pretty ones. Go get your camera."

I only half looked. The same veil that fell on my first visit lowered itself again. I left the room. "Hey, she's going to do it!" she shouted after me. "She's going to take their pictures, but only because I dared her."

I had had no intention of doing it, but now I feared Loretta's ridicule and scorn if I did not. I returned with the camera and made one photograph.

"So this is it, now you have it," Loretta giggled as she followed me back to the dayroom. "You've taken pictures of the dumping ground. The bottom of the barrel."

Emily was agitated; I tucked her hand under my arm. Loretta blocked my way. "Oh Allen Funt, you don't leave Ward D so easily. Here's another picture for you," she said and stepped aside. A man sat naked in his wheelchair, legs drawn up. I'd seen him the day before blindly removing his clothes as he lay waiting his turn in physical therapy.

"I've seen him do that trick downstairs," I said coldly. I wasn't afraid of making strong photographs, but I wouldn't be bullied into objectifying or degrading anyone again.

Because Sam and I worked in different parts of the institution—Sam in the administration building while I roamed the wards—we didn't have a chance to talk until evening. It was a relief to be home with him, doing normal dinnertime chores. Sam's handsome, craggy face is still young, with gentle lines that deepen when he smiles. He is well over six feet tall; as we worked next to each other, peeling potatoes at the kitchen counter, his shoulder seemed an inviting resting place for my head. I began to tell him about my day, my encounters with Loretta.

His forehead tightened, and he stopped working. "You could have her brought up on charges for that behavior. That's clearly client abuse."

I stood at the sink, running water over the potatoes and thinking. If I actively campaigned against an injustice, I would ruin what I wanted to do. Wassaic would no longer be open to me. I thought of the great photographer W. Eugene Smith and the images he had made of mercury poisoning in the Japanese city of Minamata. He had taken an active, partisan role in that struggle—and was almost beaten to death for it. It was not physical fear that kept me from reporting Loretta, but the fear that I'd lose permission to photograph and to talk to whomever I wanted.

5

My studio, a separate building on our property, has two rooms: a darkroom and a cheerful workroom where I write. For the first time since I began the project—though I'd taken over sixty photographs—I went into the darkroom. The 4 × 5 negatives are tray-developed in batches of ten—a process that takes about fifteen minutes in total darkness. Then the lights can be turned on while the film is washed for another twenty minutes.

I developed the first batch of ten. Six negatives were well exposed, but to my horror, the next four were absolutely blank. I rushed to develop the second batch. In blackness I carefully shuffled negatives through the developer, begging the minutes to hurry. I transferred them through a quick rinse to the fixer and began timing again. Though I'm usually comforted by this time alone in the dark, now I felt the tension of the past weeks grinding like gravel under my breastbone. At last the phosphorescent hands of the darkroom timer clicked to zero. I turned on the room lights. The black fixer tray looked empty; all the negatives were blank.

I felt unsteady with disappointment. Could these be my negatives? I sat down to think, but within seconds I knew the answer: the synch was off on the strobe. It had remained off for all the shootings. A little switch can be accidently knocked from X to M with disastrous results; it was one of the equipment pitfalls I had been unable to conquer over the years. It seemed as though one part of me was working against the other part—as though through mechanical errors I was saying "no!" when work became too emotionally difficult. So, except for the few pictures I had taken with available light, the only images I had of the past weeks were the words in my journal.

I drove fifteen minutes to the top of Silver Mountain for lunch with Martha. She was the first friend I had made when we moved to Millerton, and the bond between us had proved enduring. I often photographed her; we skied together; we traded garden plants; our lives seemed to mesh in an easy intimacy. For many years she'd had a satisfying, productive career as a weaver and designer; now, in her late thirties, Martha was preparing for a change. She was two-and-a-half-months pregnant with her first child. I loved to hear her talk about the baby she was expecting, for while she spoke of it with the same circumspection she gave the rest of her life, there was a new tenderness that seemed to make her complete. Sometimes it would burst out in flashes of joy. Yesterday, she had made her first maternity dress.

Lately we'd not had much time together, partly because Martha had been spending a few days each week in the Manhattan apartment she and her husband owned, and partly because I'd been so consumed by my days at Wassaic. Now, at last, we could have an hour together.

Winter light poured through her greenhouse onto the brick kitchen floor and across the Shaker trestle table set for two. A fat loaf of homemade bread waited on the counter. Whenever I had problems, large or small, I could count on Martha to listen. While she ladled hot pumpkin soup into ceramic bowls, I ranted about my latest technological mistake. As always, she empathized.

Then I began to talk about Wassaic. I wanted to see if I could put into words what I had seen. "Being in that building is the most difficult thing I've ever done," I said.

Martha was silent, and when I looked at her face, her mouth was set into a straight, thin line. Her hands were clasped over her still-flat belly. Abruptly, I stopped speaking.

"Please Rebecca, don't talk about this today. I can't listen. It scares me too much to think about birth defects. I don't want to know about children who've suffered oxygen deprivation. Please, have some pumpkin soup and let's talk about something cheerful."

If I couldn't see my own photographs, I could at least see the official slides from the Wassaic New Employees Department, taken over the past thirty years. A mid-level supervisor agreed to show them to me since it was a slack time in the department; no new employees were being hired. She sat at her desk and munched a fried chicken breast, working delicately around the bones. When she finished, she touched her fingers with her tongue and ran them through a tissue.

"I've seen a lot of changes in the thirty years I've been here, not all for the best, I'll tell you," she said, wadding up the remains of her snack in tin foil. "But when a place goes from 4,500 clients and 1,500 staff, to 1,500 clients and 3,000 staff, there have to be some big changes. I'm going to show you the slides I show at orientation, because they're already in order in a carousel." As she pulled a curtain across her window, the room darkened to twilight.

In the first slide it is autumn on the Wassaic grounds. Burnished trees surround a graceful white clapboard New

England house, large and rambling with green wooden shutters, glowing in late afternoon light.

"This is Berry Cottage, where many years ago old Dr. Albers lived alone with his wife and one child. Can you believe it, in a house that size? And he was only assistant director for the girls. Those people had it easy. They were entitled to a working girl—one of the higher-functioning residents—to do the cleaning."

She clicked through several slides of well-tended staff houses, now all residences for the clients. "It's no wonder these people came into the state system and didn't leave! They had a house servant, they had their yard work taken care of, the state even paid their taxes!"

The slide changed to a particularly sumptuous house, formerly the director's residence. Now it was a respite center—a hostel where handicapped people living in the community could stay for short times when their families needed a vacation. "When Dr. Hampton lived here this place was run like a tight ship, and he was here almost twenty years. See that tree in the corner of the slide? It was a *crime* to pick a pear off that tree. A crime. All the men from Dogwood, which was next door, would steal pears as soon as they were ripe. And Dr. Hampton would have them locked up in P-5 for doing it."

I hesitated to probe further. The details of Wassaic life were painful.

"That was solitary maximum security," she volunteered. "There were nineteen cells each with a bed. They got thrown in until they calmed down."

"A padded cell?"

"My goodness no, cement and tile. If the resident took the bed apart—and many were so upset they did—then we called the campus cops to take the bed away and he slept on the floor with a blanket." We gazed at the landscaped lawn and tidy pear tree still on the screen. "There were no sedatives in those days. We used to give them a dose of paraldehyde. You know what that is? It's a strong drug they give alcoholics for the dt's. That stuff smells awful. Once I decided to taste it, just to see if it was as bad as it smelled. So I stuck my finger into the rim of the big jar and put it on the tip of my tongue. It made my entire tongue numb, completely numb. And I thought, my God, think what it must do, a big injection of that inside the body."

The next slide was a rustic lodge, shaded by huge maples and overlooking a still, green pond. "That's Cherry Valley park, on the north end of the grounds. Oh, we had parties and picnics there—it was so nice," she sighed. "There was a life guard on duty all summer, and a roped-off area where the little ones would wade."

"This was for both staff and clients?" I asked.

"Oh no," she said, horrified. "Staff and their families *only*."

The old club store flashed on—a commissary for employees only. "You could bring something out to a resident, but they weren't allowed in there." Next came the bowling alley, the poolroom, the library—all segregated from use by the handicapped.

"Now here's one of the dorms in the sixties." The screen filled with white—white bare walls, row after row of white iron beds packed tightly together. "When you needed to see if a client was wet or something, you'd have to pull the bed out into the center island, check the client, then push the bed back. This place was a dumping ground. Anyone that wasn't wanted for any reason was put here.

"I remember one month, in 1963, we admitted sixty-seven children between the ages of five and sixteen. One night I heard a child sobbing and sobbing. I asked someone why she was crying, and they said she'd just been admitted. You weren't supposed to get too close to the clients then, and I'm not naturally partial to kids myself, but I went and picked up that little five-year-old girl and held her and sang to her and rocked her until she went to sleep hours later." She hugged her own ample arms and rocked. "My supervisor found me with her and gave me hell.

"Oh my God, there was overcrowding and overwork then. I can't believe it when I hear people complain now. They don't know what overwork means. You see the next slide?"

Two male clients with fuzz-ball hair stood in an empty dayroom, backs to the camera. They wore pajama bottoms but no shirts. "Those draw-string pull-up pants were the easiest to get off and on. And you'll notice they have no shoes. It wasn't because they didn't have shoes, but because there wasn't enough staff to put them on."

Next slide: Wall-to-wall wheelchairs packed together as tightly as the beds had been. "That was taken in the early seventies. The wheelchair clients were tied in these hard, wooden chairs, and there they sat all day. The best part of the day was being taken out of line to the bathroom. We tripped them"—the term for taking them to the toilet—"every two hours. That was their day."

She began a series of slides showing the physical changes in the buildings brought about by the Willowbrook consent decree. Wardrobes appeared serving as makeshift partitions for privacy. Furniture changed from hard, plastic-molded chairs to stuffed furniture. Curtains went up. There were pictures on the walls. Yet, I'd heard there were units that still reflected the old way.

We switched to the employees' dining room. "The clients eat there now. Very few staff do. It's easier to change the clients than to change the employees. They're the ones that cling to the old ways. They don't want to let go and I understand why. When I worked on the wards we had working girls do everything for us. We were worked to death keeping order, but in all the time I was there I never lifted a patient, and I never mopped a floor."

I thought of aides I'd seen with pail and mop cleaning up feces, of aides in Juniper Hall lifting eight clients a day, six times each day. Many of them had back injuries and went out on compensation. But for the "working girls" there had been no compensation; if their backs hurt they went on working.

"And I'll tell you something else," she continued. "In all that time I never saw a bedsore. Never. Never saw a cockroach either. I had seventy-five bed patients, but I supervised them. I did not change beds, and I did not wash soiled sheets. Never. That's why it worked. That's why employees were happier."

Specks of white dust danced in the light shaft from the empty projector.

6

Emily became withdrawn when told to sit down and wait. If she had her music box, she would wind up "Pop! Goes the Weasel," holding it to her ear and jumping back each time the "Pop!" came around. If she were anxious or bored, she would hum, as though to hear herself were to be assured of reality. When she was excited but trying not to show it, she punctuated her hum with little intakes of breath. Often she let her agitation out in a high-pitched buzz, standing with her toes turned in, twisting back and forth from the hips. Every day she greeted my reappearance with the hope and disbelief of someone who had crossed a desert but didn't yet know whether the lake was a mirage.

Sitting with her, I showed her how to rotate the focus knob that extended the bellows of the Speed Graphic. Her delicate hands were on top of mine, directing me, and she stared intensely at them. I put my arm around her; she disengaged it, putting my hand back on the focusing knob. There was no humming then, or twisting, just sheer concentration.

"Hey, don't you even say hello to anyone any more?" Vera asked as she watched us.

"Didn't I? Sorry. Hello Vera."

"No, it's not me—it's the rest of these guys. Emily's not the only one in the room, you know."

I looked over at Wonder Woman lying on the couch picking at her socks; Louisa twirling around the room, scratching her arms. I saw June rocking in a chair, rubbing her scabby red nose.

"Don't take this the wrong way," Vera said, "but I've noticed something. In here you mainly take pictures of the ones who give you feedback. You need to look at the other ones too. They're all equal."

I knew Vera was right: I had to learn to look at everyone and learn to look harder. That evening, when I arrived to photograph Juniper's evening shift, I went into the bathroom I had rushed past on my first day at Wassaic.

The T-shirt sleeves of the aide giving baths were rolled over his shoulders, the strings of his plastic apron doubled around and tied in front. "You love your whirlpool, don't you Roger?" he asked. Roger didn't look especially happy.

A strap around his waist and another under his arm held him upright in the seat. The aide poured in bubbly skin-softener soap and the aerator foamed it up. After fifteen minutes a hydraulic lift raised the seat, swung Roger over the edge of the tub, and he was dried off.

Then I saw his entire body for the first time. At the bottom of his rib cage there was a crater-like indentation, as though a meteor had landed on his stomach. His limbs were tiny, drawn up and knotted into painful-looking positions. On his back was a lump the size of a cantaloupe.

"He's my favorite," said another aide as she put clean pampers over mature genitalia and blonde pubic hair, and pressed the pin tabs over frail, pinched hips. "Aren't you, buh-buh?" She tweaked his cheeks. "Give us a little smile now darlin', come on." His mouth stayed drawn and sullen. She put his emaciated limbs into clean pajamas and covered up the hollow chest.

The next man to be washed had been placed on a slanted plastic tray, the one I had glimpsed my first day. "He doesn't like this much," the bath aide said, and I saw why. He was soaped, then hosed off with a fine spray. Because his body was darkly hairy and his lower legs retracted against his thighs, he looked like a little, old monkey being readied for an experiment. He was a grown, human man.

James came next. "He's a tough one," the aide said. "Start with the fact that he's deaf and blind—and self-abusive. See those lumps on his head? He bangs it on anything he can. Wears a football helmet. And wears a life preserver to protect his chest. Still, you'll see bruises on his legs because he can get to those. Just knocks himself against anything he can, hard." As if to demonstrate, James jerked his head against the side of the tub. "See? He doesn't even like the whirlpool."

"Do you think he has any pleasure in life?" I asked.

"I think he's happy when he's knocking his head."

Emily sat naked on the toilet, a small pale figure in a gleaming white room. She stood when she heard my voice. Because her nipples were flat against her chest, and she had no trace of pubic hair, her pre-adolescent body could support my illusion that she was a small child.

"She really should be doing this herself," Vera said as she put Emily's pajamas on. Vera was so proud of her girls' accomplishments she wanted them to perform constantly—not only for applause, but because she didn't want their skills to slip. Then Emily was ready for bed, clutching her music box like a small child with a stuffed animal. "Pull back the covers," Vera instructed her, and Emily did, staring at us all the while.

When she was in bed, I resisted the urge to give her a good-night kiss and stroke her forehead as I do with my own children. I knew that soon I'd have to leave Juniper to begin photographing other areas of Wassaic. I wouldn't always be able to spend as much time with Emily; now that her foster grandma was going out of her life, I didn't want Emily becoming too dependent on me. But that was a rationalization: I didn't want to become too dependent on Emily. More and more I seemed to be relying on her to ground this experience for me—a lot of responsibility to put on a speechless, profoundly retarded child.

When I got home Sam had supper waiting—fresh asparagus with parmesan cheese and roast chicken. Max gave me a hug, wrapping a leg around mine with an extraordinary display of balance that almost toppled me. Katrina came downstairs. "Mama-pajama!" she exclaimed, giggling over her latest nickname for me. She gave me a kiss. For months she had been conserving her affection: A kiss freely given at thirteen is a gift.

7

My little orange Volkswagen was stolen in New York City. I'd spent three solitary days with my typewriter in Martha's West Side apartment while she and her husband Murray were in Millerton; it had been a break from Wassaic, a break from the kids, a break from the winter. I'd been astounded and elated to find a parking place valid for three days, and several times had walked by to check on the car. When I had gone to my parking place to drive back to Millerton, the car had vanished. Panicked, I thought I must have parked on another street. I walked up and down the adjacent blocks, questioning my memory. It was no use: I knew exactly where the car had been. Then I prayed it had been towed.

In tears I called a friend, who cancelled his evening plans to accompany me to the precinct station. The police told me that vintage Volkswagens are usually carved up quickly for parts; I should not expect to see it again. Being robbed is an assault, and I cried myself to sleep.

The next morning I called my friend to thank him for his support the night before, still sniffling angry little tears. While we talked, Martha and Murray let themselves into the apartment. I saw immediately that they both looked distracted. Murray's eyes were rimmed with pink. As I hung up and told them about the car, I began to cry again. I tried to pull myself together. "Well it's not really that huge a thing," I said. "I shouldn't carry on so. It's not like losing a child."

"I know," Martha said. "I lost mine yesterday."

It took me a second: Martha had no child. Then I read

her devastated face, empty and grieving. Martha had had a miscarriage.

We clung together and sobbed. We made tea and talked in the tiny, dark kitchen. She told me of the spotting, the painful cramps, her fear. "I know the baby wasn't a person. It was only an idea," she cried, "but it was a big one. I'm stunned by the loss. I don't know what I'll do next."

I borrowed a car from another friend and drove back to Millerton in pouring rain, the broken wipers making watery streaks on the windshield. My eyes were puffy, my head hollow. One phrase of Martha's repeated itself: "The doctor said it wasn't a viable baby."

It is estimated that only 31 percent of all egg and sperm unions result in a living birth. Dr. Virginia Apgar and Joan Beck, in their book *Is My Baby All Right?*, list the many possible chromosomal abnormalities that can occur, the primary reasons for not having a "viable baby." The most critical time follows conception, often before the first period is missed. During the early weeks growth is so rapid that a mistake within a single cell can cause a chain reaction. All true malformations occur during the first three months while the body structure and major organs are formed. Most chromosomal errors, however, are too severe to survive to birth.

And what about those errors that do survive—those that don't end as they had for Martha, in weeks of grief, but cause a lifetime of grief? Were Emily's handicaps the result of a genetic error? The severe birth defects W. Eugene Smith photographed in Minamata were caused by mercury-poisoned fish eaten by pregnant women. Nor will anyone who read *Life* magazine forget the photographs of Thalidomide babies. Viruses can cause severe malformations—deafness, heart defects, retardation. My mother had had rubella during the first three months she was pregnant with my sister Kathleen, almost forty years ago. She had agonized over getting an abortion, then spent the pregnancy desperately trying not to think about the consequences of her decision. My mother had been very fortunate. Kathleen was normal.

The chromosomal abnormality of Martha's baby had not slipped by. Even in her pain she knew she was lucky.

Emily wasn't as thrilled to see me as she was to see my camera. The classic choice of the press photographer through the 1950s, the Speed Graphic has the solidity of a view camera and the portability of a folding hand camera. She remembered the strobe button and the focusing knob. I let her hold the battery pack, showed her how to turn off and on the blinking light. She discovered a red button and gave it a jab.

Vera wasn't in Ward C today; a blank-faced woman seemed to be in charge. She stared at a soap opera while absently reaming out her nose with her thumb. Loretta had told me that there's an institution-wide rule: no daytime television. She adhered to it rigidly—not because she agreed with the rule, but because she considered no TV a deprivation for the clients. Vera, on the other hand, ignored it. She seemed to have TV on all the time, though the set was placed on such a high shelf the kids couldn't see it.

During a commercial, the aide looked around the room for the first time. "You!" she yelled, hauling Louisa out by her leg from under the couch. "Why did you do that? Take off those pants this minute and get clean ones." She yanked Louisa to her feet. "I'm not going to do it for you. I didn't pee all over myself."

A giant black man wearing a football jersey under a leather jacket, and a blue-jeweled earring in his left ear, came in the dayroom.

"About time you got here," yelled the aide from the bathroom. "These kids are driving me nuts peein' all over the place. You take over—I'm goin' back to B Ward!"

The male aide glanced at me as Emily went over to him. "Hey Emily—you just sit there with your mother until I get myself organized," he said taking off his jacket. "Now go on, sit back down with your mother. I'll be right there."

Her mother? He couldn't really believe that I was Emily's mother? He must mean it, if not as a joke, as a familiarity he extended to any maternal-looking woman. When he came back I introduced myself. "My name's Rebecca . . ." I began.

He cut in politely. "How do you do, Mrs. Benedict."

I had no words. He did think I was Emily's mother. He thought this sad, handicapped girl was mine.

"Oh no," I said. "I'm just . . ." But I didn't know how to finish the sentence. Just a mother of someone else. Normal, healthy children. Just a photographer doing my job.

Emily looked at me curiously, as though she heard my suspended thoughts. I looked at her: This child I was now so eager to deny had impressed me a few minutes before with sustained curiosity about my camera, showing me how well she remembered what she had learned, how fearlessly she tried new things like poking a red button.

"An admirer," I finished. "I'm just an admirer."

At dinner I told Max and Katrina about Emily for the first time.

"She can't talk at all?" Max said, stirring rice around his plate. "How old did you say she is?"

"Mom, can you bring her home sometime? Do they let them out of there?" Katrina asked.

"I'm sure she could visit for a day, maybe in spring."

"Doesn't she have parents?" Max asked. He had stopped

eating. He didn't look up from his plate. "Don't her own parents take her home?"

"I don't know anything about her parents. Her grandmother comes to visit now and then, I think. But it would be fun to have her here for a day, don't you agree Max?"

He looked at me then, his twelve-year-old eyes honest and clear. "I don't think I could handle it."

Max loves kids. He would zoom toy cars around the floor with a two-year-old, show a six-year-old the secret path to the raspberry patch. He loves animals. When three corn-eating raccoons were treed by our dog, it was Max who wanted to call the wildlife center instead of the farmer who would have shot them.

"Why couldn't you handle it?"

"I don't know. It just makes me feel weird to think about her in our house, that's all. She sounds so retarded and stuff." Quickly he cleared his plate—an unusual gesture.

"Max," I called to his back as he went toward the kitchen. "I don't understand your attitude."

As he turned I saw the clarity gone from his eyes. *He* didn't understand his attitude. His face darkened with the same confusion I felt when I had been mistaken for Emily's mother.

"Max, think about it, okay? There's still lots of time until spring."

8

"You better take some pictures of this disgusting place," hissed an aide sloshing water from a pail in the Butternut Learning reception hall. "It doesn't matter how much I clean. Nothing helps." He scrubbed furiously at the floor, driving the mop handle like a bayonet. On his T-shirt huddled a vulture, drool dripping from its beak: *Patience my ass. I'm going out and kill something.*

It had been hard to leave Juniper Hall. I felt protected and safe there; I knew what to expect from the staff—even Loretta—and if I didn't feel comfortable with the residents, I had at least become accustomed to them. For a month Emily had been my escort; when I felt overwhelmed I could focus on her. Yet I knew Juniper was different from other buildings on the hill. The residents were younger; most were physically disabled; there were few behavior problems. In other learning centers and residential halls I would start to photograph a different Wassaic.

The hall was sweltering. A swamp stench of rotten vegetation and stagnant water rose from the floor. I stepped back toward the outside—fresh air—but the door was closed.

Unless ill and medically confined to a ward, each client must spend six hours a day, five days a week in a program center like Butternut, the same way children are required to attend school. For the physically fragile young people in Juniper Hall, the learning programs were in the same building, but other Wassaic clients attended programs in separate buildings, transported from their residential halls by a blue bus that took them across campus.

"You want to see something? I'll show you the bathrooms—but hold your nose 'cause they're awful, they're always awful. Take pictures of them, I dare you." Mechanically, I followed.

In 1972, following the Willowbrook scandal, Wassaic undertook a twelve-million-dollar renovation. The interiors of buildings had been made clean and new with plaster and paint. Huge open wards had been partitioned into living units and classrooms. Elevators had been added, new bathrooms installed. A decade later, Butternut was the last building scheduled for renovation at Wassaic.

"You won't believe what it's like in here." The aide swept his arm into the bathroom, an impresario introducing a vaudeville act. "Don't worry, it's empty, lady. Go ahead and take some snaps."

The smell of excrement was old, ground into the cracked floors for decades, yet sharp and uncontrolled. Gang toilets were exposed to the room; one stall had a sheet pinned up for privacy, but even that hung in tatters. A bare light bulb dangled from the ceiling. The wash basins looked stolen from some ancient hand laundry.

"That's it, you've seen it. Now come to the place where I spend the rest of my day. Then get a full-time job here and see how you like it."

The small room for behavior problems had once been an office. I tried to imagine someone sitting sedately at a desk as I looked at the cubicle jammed with residents. A bumper sticker had been plastered on the olive-shiny walls: *"I'm like freakin' out!"*

"Sha-bam bam bam! Sha-bam bam bam!" a client screamed. "Sha-bam bam bam!"

The aide—Ronald—leaned his mop in a corner. His red hair fringed out below a red bandana cap, and his face was puffy in little hills, like punched-down bread dough. "I stopped smoking by regressing myself to a pre-smoking age, then living in that skin," he wheezed, his fingernail gouging at a cuticle. "But I think I'm going to have to start again. The teacher's out sick today and there are only us two aides to take care of these clients."

"Sha-bam bam bam! Sha-bam bam bam!"

An old whiskery woman began to howl. She yanked off her shoes and socks, and when Ronald came near her, hit out at him—hard.

"She certainly is angry," I remarked inanely.

"Oh that's nothing," Ronald said. "Watch this. Agatha's something else." He ducked as Agatha hurled a shoe above his head. "Some aim, huh? What's really neat about it is she's totally blind."

"Sha-bam bam bam!" screamed the client, his voice guttural and grating. Over and over, "Sha-bam bam bam!"

"That's one of Manny's two words. Get ready for the other one."

"No! No!"

The frustration and anger stunned me. I recognized my own voice as a young mother. When I listened to myself in those days I wondered what damage that outraged voice could do. Manny confirmed my fears, for he was stuck on "No" and reproduced it with awesome emotion.

"Sha-bam bam bam! No! No!"

"No! No! No!" Agatha screamed high and desperate, contrapuntal to Manny. Suddenly she sat down, only her toothless gums whacking together.

"Mondays are always a bitch," Ronald sighed as he walked to the window and looked out, clocking the morning. Mud patches dotted the snow. "The clients don't go to program over the weekend and they unlearn so much. I really don't know how we make it through."

There were two aides, eight residents, two wheelchairs, and one photographer in the tiny behavior room of Butternut.

"If Earl comes at you, get out of here," Ronald called across the room, his voice an octave lower than the screeches and shouts. "He's a hepatitis carrier. And he'll bite anyone."

I didn't know who Earl was, and I didn't know how I'd get out.

The open wards in Butternut had been subdivided with metal lockers and plastic milk cartons, partitions flimsy enough to be knocked down by noise, let alone someone falling or pushing. The walls had giant spider-web cracks and blistering paint. Electrical circuitry and switch boxes were exposed.

In the corner of a make-shift classroom, someone had draped a red and white parachute; it was oddly whimsical, as though a circus tent had been set up in the middle of a bombed city. Sherry—a teacher wearing an efficient jumpsuit, her gray-streaked hair tidily drawn back with combs—bent from the waist to show me the straight chair and mirror under the parachute.

"I sit someone down there, then flap the parachute around him," she said flapping her arms like chicken wings. "It makes a swishy-noise and a lot of visual commotion. A few clients really react to it, really wake up. They look at themselves." She put her elbows down and folded into a teacher again, while she gave a rueful snicker. "I'm not sure it's really a brilliant teaching tool, but it does make the room look better."

"That's Gregory," Sherry said nodding at the resident who sat staring in the mirror. A skeleton man in baggy clothes, Gregory's eyes were glazed under thin, pink eyebrows. His forehead, crinkled in a look of perpetual surprise, was uninterrupted by a hairline and slid into his bald pate. "He's only been here a short time. Transferred out of an upstate developmental center. Seems he was always being knocked around by other residents. They had him in a unit with the least behavior problems and he was still getting beat up all the time. When he arrived he had a fractured wrist, and he hadn't been here a week before what was left of his hair fell out."

As I aimed my camera at Gregory he rose, growling from his throat.

"Sit down there boy, she's not going to hurt you," said a young aide as he eased him back in front of the mirror. "I've been one-on-one with Gregory for six months and I've really become attached to him. He's got a degenerative brain disease. He's got to have someone watching him all his waking hours, and probably that's not enough." He drew his index finger over the top of Gregory's dome.

"They sure run things different here than they used to. One-on-one wasn't something they did in the old days. When my dad worked here forty years ago everyone wore striped pajamas. He was one of three attendants on a ward of two hundred men, all in one big open room."

Three attendants for two hundred men?

"And you know what their protection was? A big old bar of laundry soap. They'd put that soap in a pillow case and swing it around their heads."

I looked at Gregory staring at his own drained face in the mirror. I imagined a bar of soap cracking against his skull.

"But someone like Gregory, he would have been easy to take care of. You'd just tie him up in a camisole," the aide continued.

"Why? What does he do?"

"Eats. Everything. Shovels anything he can find into his mouth. It would be one thing if he just ate food, but no. He eats towels and sheets. A few weeks ago I saw it for myself, and I couldn't believe it. He had a bowel movement and it was a towel, a whole towel right there in the toilet. And see this pillow?" The aide crossed the room and came back with a pillow covered with heavy plastic. "He's figured out how to rip these open and then eat the fiber glass. That's like eating insulation or something. Can you imagine what that does to your insides?"

I could hear no more. I turned away from Gregory and the aide to a client who sat rubbing his hands.

"Jacob speaks twenty languages, none of them intelligible," Sherry said looking up from the charts she was filling in. "There's this theory that he got off the boat from Russia and was abandoned. You can get him to talk by opening his left hand," Sherry said. "Go ahead, try it."

I looked at Jacob's hands, large, red, and scaly, hands I didn't want to touch. With all my courage I slid my knuckles down his palm and pried my fingers between his. His oily eyes rolled around but as his fingers straightened, words came. They were strange words, but I leaned forward and listened. His language had cadence; his eyes darted around as though flashing back into memory.

It was easy to imagine the immigrant Jacob, dirty, exhausted from the trial of Ellis Island, lost in New York, trying to explain himself, confusing words and dialects while an incomprehensible and uncaring New World rushed around him.

"Has anyone who understands Eastern European languages listened to him?" I asked, but the aide was restraining Gregory from eating a book, and Sherry was nowhere around.

At the end of the program day, coats were being put on the behavior-room clients. Ronald looked exhausted and ragged. "I'd go nuts if my two days off weren't coming up," he said. "Sometimes I just don't see the point of any of this programming."

It was hard for me to see, too. In Butternut the clients ranged in chronological age from twenty-seven to seventy-five, though in many ways they had not developed mentally beyond what they had been at three or ten. Many were still in diapers. In their classrooms they were being trained—for what? Life outside the institution? None of them seemed able to function in any real way. A few could comb their hair and brush their teeth; a few could feed themselves without a terrible mess. But what did that really mean? Wassaic seemed to be their final stop.

Everyone was buttoned in overcoats and ready for the bus, waiting patiently in the hot room.

"Sha-bam bam bam!" Manny yelled and dumped a container of small blocks to the floor where they exploded like shattered glass.

Ronald got on his knees. "Come on Manny, help me clean these up," he said in a voice ground to a whisper; Manny sat on the floor, picked up a few blocks.

Ronald finished and stood. Manny stayed on his knees and began kissing Ronald's feet, his lips loudly smacking the shoe top in a grotesque parody of subservience. Ronald looked at me pink-faced, his eyes drooped with sadness.

"Some very cruel person taught him that a long time ago."

9

The evening paper said seventy-five hundred pink slips had gone out state-wide. Mario Cuomo, the new governor elected in part by the staunch support of New York State employees and their unions when he ran against Lew Lehrman—a man who wanted to cut drastically the number of state workers in prisons, hospitals, and developmental centers—had now come up with a large list of cuts himself. It was said that over two hundred jobs at Wassaic were scheduled for elimination. There was talk about "bumping from the top, both laterally and downward." I did not understand those words.

But I did understand that provisionals would be the first to go.

Sam was provisional; after eight years of working for Wassaic, his job description still had not been finalized, and he had not been assigned a permanent "item." I put down the newspaper and asked him if he were worried.

He was quiet before he answered, his right hand twisting his gold wedding ring. He seemed to be looking inward, stirring words around. "It's the level of anxiety I can't decide on," he said at last.

The next morning I managed—after cleaning the house, delivering a forgotten book to Katrina at school, going to the hardware store to exchange a can of paint—somehow, I managed to get to Wassaic before the programs started. I wanted to spend a few minutes with Emily before I began photographing in Butternut. Two teachers were discussing the layoffs as I hung up my coat.

"We worried day to day and now it's hour to hour," said one teacher.

The other pointed to the bulletin board announcing a daily Alcoholics Anonymous meeting. "We're all going to need that if this keeps up much longer."

I attached my strobe to the Speed Graphic, plugged it into the battery pack, put a film holder in the camera back, and quietly walked to Emily's room. I wanted to surprise her with an early morning visit.

Emily was actually laughing out loud. She was with a white curly-haired woman in a blue smock, her foster grandma. She was physical with Emily in a way I'd never been, tickling her and kissing her cheek. She put her nose to Emily's. "Say hi!" she whispered.

And Emily did, clear as could be, "Hi," with a long breathy

H sound. Grandma rewarded her with a big hug, and she laughed again, hugging her back. "Now put both arms around Grandma," she told her.

Emily did. A big two-armed hug that meant love and happiness.

A sign drawn in multi-colored felt markers directed everyone down to the basement for a farewell luncheon the staff was giving for the foster grandparents. The grandmas were dressed to the nines, sporting shoulder corsages of one carnation and lots of ribbon and tulle. The goodbyes were emotional; strong feelings had developed among them, as well as with the staff. The room was full of hugs, corsages and bosoms colliding.

"There were a lot of problems with this program at first," the building supervisor confided. "Most of these grandparents are very poor. For a lot of them, the best thing this program did was give them a hot meal every day, nicely prepared, and almost balanced. God knows what they eat at home. And when this program started, we had to get rid of a lot of them for different reasons. Child abuse was one. Another was the opposite: A kid would be involved with some obsessive behavior, say twisting a piece of string, and the grandparent would bring him a string!"

He looked down at me with conspiratorial astonishment.

Oh dear, I thought, I probably would have been dismissed on just those charges. There would have been a moment with these profoundly retarded kids when I'd give in and provide them with whatever made them happy.

This morning, when I'd stopped by Sherry's classroom in Butternut, I saw that the beautiful, fanciful, red-and-white-striped parachute she had set up was gone. It had been removed because Willie, a man who was always being told to put his hands in his pockets, wouldn't stop flicking it. I could imagine how pretty it looked when he hit the corner, the red and white lines blurring, and how it made a whirring noise. Were I Willie's teacher, I couldn't order him to put his hands in his pockets all day. Why shouldn't it be the responsibility of the state to provide him with parachutes and silver foil to shake and flick? But I wasn't going to tell anyone I felt that way, certainly not the supervisor who looked into my face so expectantly for my horror.

The buffet table opened and a line quickly formed. The staff had prepared a feast: lasagna and ziti, cold cuts artfully rolled, salads and pickles, chopped liver and brown bread, hard rolls, soft rolls, a cherry cheese cake, and the crowning glory, a huge chocolate cake with "THANK YOU" inscribed on it. Everyone loaded up, the line moved slowly.

"Next week I'm going for an interview. I sure hope I can come back here to work," a grandma with a Dolly Parton hairdo said. I smiled and told her I hoped so too. But when I had asked the supervisor how many of those who had been let go would be restored to their jobs, his answer had been definite: none.

I saw the grandma who always mouthed a toothpick; I saw Selma, the skinny black grandma whose wig sometimes slipped to one side. I saw Emily's grandma, alone and looking sad. I sat next to a grandma with a pouty mouth who silently alternated a bite of potato salad with a drag on her cigarette. When she broke the silence, it was to lean over and stage whisper, "Look at Dolores. See what she's doing? She's taking food home with her, and she don't even work here now."

Indeed Dolores had pulled foil from her purse and was tucking it over a plate. In fact, now that the daily hot lunch was no longer available, most of the grandmas were exiting with whatever food they could carry. When the staff claimed their casserole dishes and serving trays, there were no left-overs.

I went back to Ward C in the late afternoon, and Emily was instantly at my side. She ran her hands over my arm and down my back to assure herself I was really there. Even though the table was set for supper, she wanted to walk the halls.

"You're going to spoil her," Vera chided, winking as she said it.

"I'll take that risk."

"In that case we have several others that would benefit from your spoiling too. I'm serious. Everyone needs attention. There's just not enough staff to go around, and now the grandparents are gone. But if you think it's bad now, wait a couple of weeks until they make these budget cuts. A lot of people are slated to get the ax. I *think* I've got enough senior-ity to stay working, but you never know."

The director had issued a statement that the direct-care staff—therapy aides like Vera—would not be affected. Yet, since they are blue-collar workers, who are usually laid off in a time of penny-pinching, they could hardly believe their invulnerability.

Emily did not know that layoffs were important to her. She did not know she was losing her grandma. She did not know Vera's job could be in jeopardy. She just knew she wanted her walk and pulled at my wrist.

"Ah ha, Allen Funt, now I know what you are doing in this building with your big camera," Loretta said as we passed her ward. "You are going to help the governor decide who should stay and who should go. Well, take pictures of every-one, but it won't do any good. They will always can the work-ers first. Do you think they are going to fire the chiefs?"

□   □   □   □

The *Millerton News*—our ten-page weekly paper—reported that Wassaic morale was at an all-time low because of the layoff threat. It began to hit home for me as well. Even Sam admitted his job did not look as secure as it had a few weeks ago. "There's a general meeting at three tomorrow to explain the cuts," he told me, and I heard the edge in his voice. Our car had been stolen; we were trying to make decisions about changing schools for Katrina; this was no time for Sam to be unemployed.

The next day I went to talk to Martha, as I often do when there's something troubling in my life. We sat in her studio, mugs of hot tea chasing away the late afternoon cold. The sun faded, but lining the walls I could see the bins of soft yarns, the looms, the finished lengths of heavy, shimmering fabric. She turned on the lamp above the couch, illuminating her face still pinched and raw from the ordeal of her miscarriage. As we talked, her hand stroked a square of wool lying on her knee as though she were petting her cat. I asked her how she was.

"I've embarked on a new sewing project," she said smiling, but looking out of practice. "It's the best way I know to take my mind off my troubles: make something really complex, something harder than I can easily manage, something that makes me follow directions exactly. So, no more maternity clothes for me. This time I'm making a tailored, fitted jacket, size ten. Lots of seams and details. And very snug around my waist."

After supper, while the kids were doing homework, Sam and I sat in front of the fireplace and put another log on the embers. It was a chance to talk alone at last. He had changed, as he does after work, into soft corduroy pants and his favorite chamois shirt. His hair is dark blond and combed to the side, but sometimes by the end of the day it moves across the part and curls down on his forehead. He pushed his glasses up, massaging the bridge of his nose with two fingers.

"Today there was a steady line of people through the administration building being given pink slips," he said. "I wasn't one of them."

My breath caught. I had tried not to talk about the possibilities, for Sam's self-assurance and positive attitude had seen us through anxious situations before. This had been no time to undermine his confidence.

"One of the Learning Center supervisors was in the lineup, quite distraught—as anyone would be waiting to be fired. I took her to my office to talk, and when noon came around I shared my lunch with her. She does have, however, a 'back-up item'—meaning, if she were fired from her supervisor's job she could go back to the social worker's job she was promoted from two years ago." He leaned forward in his chair and jabbed the new log with the poker.

"I don't have a back-up item," he said slowly, "but I figured it was time to cover myself somehow. So I went to the personnel office and took the therapy-aide test."

The requirement for a therapy aide was a high school diploma. Sam has a graduate degree in architecture. A therapy aide made half of what he earned. Yet I knew his thinking: If he were fired, the therapy-aide position would allow our medical and dental benefits to continue while he looked for another job.

Sam leaned back as the fire blazed up. Locking his hands behind his neck, he looked in my eyes. "I passed the therapy aide test with an 82. The more intelligent you are, the worse you do on the test—because you want to help the clients, not just obey orders."

10

Elaine, the petite music therapist, pounded big progressive chords on the piano and sang, "Delmar, hello; Delmar, hello." A tall lanky black man caught up with the phrase ends, ". . . 'ar, . . . 'lo," as he smacked a snare drum aggressively with open palms. An aide leaned against the piano watching.

I looked at the schedule on the music-room door expecting to see Delmar's name in the early morning time slot, but the only name was *John Doe*.

Elaine never stopped playing. When Delmar quickened the beat, she followed; when he slowed, she slowed. He stopped hitting the drum and began rocking. Elaine gave him a drum stick. Boom-boom-boom-boom, he was off in the same determined rhythm until Elaine changed the tempo and confounded him. He stopped, sucked the drum stick, then sucked his fingers.

He beat the drum again, face intense, then reached forward and hit Elaine's hand as she steadied the drum. An accident? The drum stick swirled back and smacked the aide's arm. Not an accident. The music slowed and slipped into a minor key. "It's almost time to go now, Delmar, goodbye." And he was there, his melody the same as hers, on tune, and words lagging slightly behind. "Delmar, goodbye."

"Come on, John, let's go." The aide clamped a hand around his wrist and pulled him to his feet, unfolding him like an accordion hinged at knees, hips, waist—until he stood a head taller than the aide.

"Is that his name, John Delmar?" I asked staring at the man who swayed like a lone palm tree in the wind.

"No," Elaine said. "His official name on the records is John Doe Number 11."

It was the name for fill-in-the-blank forms.

"There already were ten John Does at Wassaic when he came years ago. The police picked him up for heaving rocks through store windows. He told the police his name was Delmar Tate, and that was the last word he spoke. They brought him here, but they never were able to find any background on him, not even if that was his real name. So he was listed as John Doe Number 11."

I had never heard of anyone so anonymous. No past, no future. I followed him to his program room to see his present.

Delmar Tate, a.k.a. John Doe Number 11, sat dazed in an easy chair, singing tunelessly and repetitively, "Lu lu lu, lu lu lu."

"He's usually out of it the rest of the day after his music," Fred Law, his teacher, told me. As he spoke, Delmar got up. Though he and Fred Law were the same height and build, Delmar looked larger and alarming, his long arms reaching stiffly out from an overhead swing as though swimming. His balance was poor and he staggered with each arm stroke. "We really have to watch out for him. When he's up, everything else stops, and it's one on one."

Delmar looked drunk, staggering and swinging. I could imagine rocks being catapulted through windows.

"Want to go for a walk?" Fred Law asked Delmar. "I'll take him down to the gross motor area and let him work some of this off."

As I packed up my camera to follow, an aide said this: "He's really trouble, Number 11 is. He's even raped."

"Raped?" I repeated.

"Yup, on the back wards. And he usually busts heads open when he does it."

I was silent with images. Someone I love dearly had been raped while she walked on an East River island where New

York City mental patients are incarcerated. I was in Africa when it happened, and even a year later she could not speak about it.

While Delmar slept in the easy chair, Fred Law and the aide who told me about the raping went on a break.

"He be with me in my unit almost three years now," said Clay, the energetic, savvy black aide who watched the room. "You should see him when he come on, man. He got into his feces. He cleared the table with a sweep of his arm. The food workers be so scared of him they just dumped food in a tray and slide it down to him. He'd smear food all over the place then steal it from everyone else.

"Well, I spent two weeks just watching him," Clay said folding his arms and settling into his chair. "Pretty soon I watch him so much that I knows him. I *be* him. Like I be completely inside him. So I figures I'd treat him like we was down South. Show him some good ol' down home discipline, just like he be one of my kids. So I say, 'John, I know why you acting this way. You just want attention. But if you keep it up, I'm going to tell your mama.' And he stops dead and say, 'Mama!' I know I had him then—I could get through to him. Then one day when he be acting up, I say, 'Son, the way you acting people gonna think you no better than a dog.' I looked over at him and water be just running from his eyes. I know I had him for sure then.

"I worked on him for two years. Trouble be, after two years I ain't had no vacation. So I take three weeks, and when I come back everything has slipped. The food people be scared to death and John Doe be into his feces again."

Fred Law was back in the room and Delmar woke, ranging and bellowing. I felt my own tension. "What about this rape business?" I asked Clay.

"What rape? I never heard anything like that, did you Fred?"

"Where did you hear that?" Fred Law asked.

Wasn't it an hour ago in this room? Wasn't it the blond-haired aide who told me?

"I've never heard about any rape," Fred Law said. "It hasn't been mentioned in any case review."

Why would the aide have said that? Was it to frighten me—an inquisitive woman photographer? Was it a fantasy of his own? Was it a rumor he'd heard and repeated sincerely? Whatever his reason, the effect on me had been powerful.

After supper I told Sam and the kids about John Doe Number 11.

"Why won't they call him by the name he gave them?" Max asked, outraged. "Or if they have to make up a name, why can't they pick one that ten other people don't have?"

Then I told them about the aide who said he had raped, and the others who had denied it.

"I believe it's true," Max said, "because of other stuff I've heard about that place."

"Like what?" Sam asked.

"Like David's mom works there." David was Max's classmate and best friend. "She said there are all kinds of weirdos up there. There's a guy who walks around giving everyone the fist and saying, 'You want a knuckle sandwich?' "

"I know who that is," Sam said. "He's a big bluffer."

"David went up there once and saw him. He says he's never going back, and I don't blame him." Max's eyes were defended, looking steadily at the paper napkin he tore into small pieces. "And there's another guy that played with his penis until it almost came off."

"Max," Sam said, "Look at me. Some terrible things do

happen. And there certainly are people at Wassaic who need professional help with their problems. It's important that they get it, and it's important that we think of them as real people, not as caricatures."

"Maybe." His eyes were straight on Sam's. "But don't ever ask me to go up there."

Delmar Tate's music therapy session was scheduled first thing in the morning. For days I had thought of this John Doe, the troublemaker, releasing his aggression on the drum rather than on cars or other people. It was reassuring to know his "Lu-lu-lu, lu-lu-lu" could be sung in a room where it would be applauded.

At 8:45 the door to Elaine's little room was closed. I heard no music.

In his classroom, Delmar sat quietly in his recliner. His long arms were still. I asked his teacher when he was going to music therapy.

"He isn't. They've stopped all that. It just didn't seem to be getting anywhere, and Elaine couldn't handle him."

I fiddled with my film holders, making myself busy to let the shock go by. The one thing that seemed hopeful for Delmar was no more. I knew there was a thin line between being merely inquisitive and prying for details or explanations; stepping over it could make the staff wary of me. But I felt involved. I asked whose decision this was.

"Elaine's and mine." Fred Law sounded definite, yet there was an edge to his voice that told me he wanted to get on with his week, not rehash old decisions. "Since he's so big and hard to handle I've always had to have an aide go with him. And I really am understaffed, although"—he looked around at his two aides—"I suppose he could have gone this morning. But I don't know why it should be John Doe.

I mean why waste that on someone who needs three men to hold him down when there are others who ask for little and could use it?"

He nodded to a client passionately sucking his thumb. "Take him, he's good as gold. Never causes any trouble. Why couldn't we give that half hour to him?" Through the irritated voice I heard guilt, then dismissal. "I don't know, we just couldn't deal with it any more, that's all."

11

"It's about time you told me what you're taking all these pictures for." Fred Law flicked his head and challenged me with a strong jaw covered by the silver-blue shine of a stubborn beard. "What's the point of all this?"

"I want to document the institution as it really is. I want people to see what's happening in here."

"You can't do it," he interrupted, his words blasting out. I recoiled, for at last someone had voiced what I dared not even think. "You see a picture of a normal child standing by a lake, baiting a hook, and when you look at it you have a whole story. You see a picture of a normal child on a swing, pumping to the sky, and you have a whole story. But a picture of Lisa would tell so little." He pointed to a diminutive woman, rocking in a corner. "If you took a picture of her smiling no one would ever know how much work it took to get her to that smile. You can't photograph progress."

As he talked, a deaf, blind woman unbuttoned her shirt and removed it, exposing withered breasts. Fred put it back on, kneeling in front of her like a kindergarten teacher doing up snowsuit snaps. "And how would you explain this in a picture?" he asked. "A grown man putting a shirt on a grown woman?"

He rose to his feet. "And how could a picture say anything about this room?" He held out his hands in a helpless gesture. "Or the noise level?"

The program afternoon was over at Butternut. Through the Dutch door of the behavior unit I saw a pale and exhausted aide, hair streaking over her face, like the migrant mother in the Dorothea Lange photograph.

"Calm down, Hattie. Don't do that, just calm down." She held the arm of a client who writhed in her wheelchair, football helmet askew. "You've been pinching me all afternoon and now you've got to calm down before I can let go of you. There Hattie, nice Hattie."

Hattie twisted and pulled at her arm. The aide's grip was firm, and Hattie could easily have hurt herself thrashing around. Maybe if the aide let go Hattie might calm down. Doesn't everyone have a tendency to hysteria when upset and restrained?

Then Manny, who had been sitting quietly, leaped up and pushed over Hattie's wheelchair. The chair and Hattie were sideways on the floor; now the aide had to restrain Hattie and fend off Manny while righting the wheelchair.

I was outside the Dutch door, my hands full of my large camera. I knew I should drop it and help, but I was afraid for myself and my equipment.

Another aide came to help. "I'd hate to be on duty with her tonight," she said as Hattie tried to bang her head against the chair, increasingly excited. Both their grips on Hattie were strong, their knuckles white.

I moved inside the behavior room. The camera was in

my hands, shutter cocked, black slide removed. I estimated the camera-to-subject distance and focused. And then the moral question was there, as it had been so many times before. To take a photograph at this point would not only objectify a difficult situation, but might possibly make it worse. I knew these aides didn't need Hattie agitated further by the strobe. I also knew it would make them anxious, for the anger they were feeling and trying so hard not to show would be clear on film.

I took my hand from the shutter cable and left the behavior room. I could not take the picture. In the hall I found I was shaking. God, I would scream and kick and flail and bite and hit if I were made to sit in that tiny, hopeless room all day, with Earl flipping out and Agatha screaming and throwing shoes and Manny screaming, "Sha-bam bam bam!" and pushing over my chair. I would bang and bang my head. Self-inflicted pain would feel good after a day like that.

I had looked forward to it all day; at last it was four o'clock, and Emily would be back in her room.

"Well, look who's here," Vera said, and Emily looked, her dark eyes foggy at first, then clearing. I was so glad to see her, and she let me hug her wiry little body and run my hand over her straight, fine hair.

Louisa emerged from under the couch and flew around the room, twirling on her toes. Wonder Woman lay sluggishly on the couch. Vincent scooted into a corner and glowered. "We've been a vewy good gi-wl today," Carrie said.

"I don't know about this place. And things are going to get tougher around here in a couple of weeks," Vera said. "There's another vacation coming up—Easter. That means the teachers will all be out. That means long, long days."

"What will happen to these kids?"

She shrugged. "Depends. If I can get help maybe I can take them out somewhere, but I can't imagine where the help would come from. There aren't any more foster grandparents in this ward. If the weather's nice maybe we can play outside. Otherwise they'll just sit here."

Emily tugged at my wrist, letting me know I'd ignored her too long.

We walked to Ward A, where the most handicapped clients had been put under special care. These bedrooms were cheerful and homey, with bright patchwork spreads, crib mobiles, and stuffed animals on each bed; yet there were no babies on this ward, only teenagers and young adults. They wore pampers, they were fed, they were totally helpless.

Watching as Emily limped over to each bed and touched the stuffed animals, I thought about what childhood meant to the staff. As long as the clients could be seen as childish, the staff could show parental love. Many had "babies"—Bernie had Naomi, a little rolled up kitten-like woman with a big, red tongue; Clay was a stern parent to John Doe Number 11.

And so I toured the rest of the wards with my beautiful child, indulging the things she liked to do. Turn on the light in Ward E. Push the elevator button. Look out the window. And then she led me to the front door.

"No Emily, we can't go out there. It's cold and we don't have our coats."

She dragged me into her bedroom. When she tried to move faster, her limp turned to a lurch. She groped inside her cubby for her coat.

What a liar I was. It was cold, but not that cold. That wasn't the real reason I couldn't take her out. It was five o'clock and I had to go home.

□   □   □

Supper was turkey, homemade stuffing, and garden beans from the freezer. "What would you think if we had some of the Ward C girls over during Easter vacation?" I asked looking around the table, but knowing the question was mainly for Max.

"Great," Katrina said, flicking her eyes at Max.

"It's okay with me," he replied quickly, "because I won't be here. I'll be sure to be out of the house that day."

I spoke to him calmly. I told him I too had felt fear and bewilderment at Wassaic, but this was his own home.

"I just don't want those kinds of people in our house," he said.

"You wouldn't say that if they were black or Chinese," Sam said, and though he was trying to sound reassuring and educational, I could feel his anger. Those were strong words Max had used.

"I don't know what it is about me," Max said, "but I've always had a hard time around retarded people. Twenty or thirty people can walk by a retarded person and not be bothered, then they see me and grab. They want to touch me, and I don't like it. I only weigh ninety-eight pounds."

Again I told him it was his house, and I would never put him in danger.

"Would there be people to guard them? How many?"

I listened to him, and I felt for his distress, but I had questions. How could two children a year apart in age, raised by the same parents, have developed such different attitudes of acceptance? Because he is the youngest, had we somehow overprotected Max? How should I proceed in order to lessen his fear, but not shelter him? This much I knew: I couldn't give up some form of this Easter idea.

Spring

1

Emily heard my voice and lunged from the dayroom. When I hugged her small body it stiffened, her muscles as tight as winched cables. Her hand clamped onto my wrist. She knew what she wanted. I was her ticket to freedom, a walk around the halls, someday a walk outside if she were lucky. But then her mouth opened and a cough rumbled up and hacked out. She coughed again and again. I took her down the hall to the nurse.

The nurse was unconcerned; they'd already made a culture on it. The results would be in the next day.

I heard myself say in a firm voice, "I'm planning to take Emily home with me for Easter. I need to know if this cough is just a cold, or something more serious."

She shrugged. "Wash your hands thoroughly, that's my advice."

She hadn't heard. She didn't care. But I had said it: I was going to take Emily home with me for Easter.

Two days later Emily's cough was greatly improved; a mere cold, the nurse said. Had it been bronchitis I'd have canceled my plan, but a cold—my family was exposed to colds all the time. That was no excuse not to take her home. I tracked down the Juniper Hall social worker to ask permission for Emily's Easter visit.

"You want to take her home?" he asked, leaning back in the conference-room chair and twirling a pencil between his palms. "This must be the big day of the year. Two other staff people have asked to take clients home for Easter. It's Emily Benedict, you say?" He reached back and pulled a thick, red spiral binder from the bookcase.

I watched with interest as he opened it, for this notebook represented a clinical biography of Emily. It contained her admission papers, performance charts, evaluations, medical reports, court orders. As he flipped through it I asked him to tell me something about Emily's background and diagnosis.

"Her tests put her retardation in the severe catagory, which means her IQ is between thirty-five and twenty."

IQ does not take into account creativity, motivation, or social skills.

"She also has a mild CP—cerebral palsey—," he continued, "with some ataxia—which means balance problems—and a monoplegia—which means only one limb is affected. In Emily's case, her leg. It was braced for years, but she's walking well without that now." He looked up from the record. "Multiple disabilities are very common with mental retardation. Every case is different. It's estimated that about half the people who have CP aren't retarded at all; in fact some of them are exceptionally bright, but lack the coordination to communicate. I guess one way to look at it is that Emily's a lucky girl, really. She manages to get her needs known. And she could have been blind or deaf or have seizures."

He read on silently, his index finger traveling across the page. "Her grandmother is her correspondent—the person we keep informed of her progress and communicate with when a decision needs to be made for her." He drummed his pencil on the table. "Oh yeah, I remember the grandmother. She comes to see Emily from time to time. Doesn't seem like there's any parent around. I guess that's how she managed to get in here. She's one of a very few young kids left in Wassaic, and all those kids are in Juniper. The mother is someplace in Arizona, and the grandmother lives a couple of hours from Wassaic." He closed the red notebook.

"So, what's the next step to get Emily home for Easter?" I asked.

"I'll call up the grandmother—Mrs. Benedict—and see if she's got any objections. Check back with me in a couple of days."

"Hey! Hey, you!" Emily and I were walking slowly; she trailed her hand along the wall, watching her fingers jump from tile to tile. I stopped and turned. The social worker marched down the hall waving his pencil as though it were a flag. "I talked to the grandmother, and she asked me who you were. I couldn't give her much information." He hiked his shoulders to his ears and flopped open his hands in a who-am-I-to-know? gesture. "Anyway, she says she wants to talk to you herself. Come to my office, and we'll give her a call."

"Mrs. Benedict?" I asked, tucking the phone under my chin so I could use both hands to straighten Emily's twisted sweater sleeves. Somehow having her grandmother on the phone made me want to tidy her up. I introduced myself and told her I wanted to take Emily home for Easter. "But maybe you want to take her home yourself," I ended. I heard in my own words both disappointment and relief. If—for reasons beyond my control—Emily couldn't come home for Easter, I wouldn't have to deal with Max's negative reaction.

The voice on the phone was old and weary. "I wish I could, I really do. It's just that I'm not—I'm just not up to it," she said. She broke off phrases in breathless puffs, and her voice quavered a little at the end of sentences. "However I'd be very pleased if you'd take Emily for the day."

I looked at Emily. She was purring her low sound of happiness, rolling it in her throat. I wondered if she knew who was on the phone.

"I love Emily dearly, but it's been hard to see her these past few years. My eyes aren't what they used to be, and though I drive, I don't dare go far from home. I'm afraid I have to rely on others; sometimes my nephew drives me over, and sometimes a neighbor does. My daughter—Emily's mother—doesn't live around here, so she can't be of much service."

Guilt. I too had lived far from my parents my entire adult life.

"But if you want to take Emily for Easter, you must know something about her. Tell me, is she doing all right there?"

I hesitated. What could "all right" mean? That her physical needs were being met? Yes.

"I'll tell you why I'm asking," Mrs. Benedict continued. "A letter from Wassaic came last week. It says they've located a community residence for Emily and want to move her there as soon as it's renovated."

A small current of fear ran through me. Could I continue photographing if Emily were not here? Would I be able to face Wassaic daily without her?

"I've hoped for years something like this would happen. But now that I actually have to give my permission to move her, I have some doubts. Emily's settled at Wassaic. It's her home. Don't you think a move would be disrupting and confusing?"

"Perhaps a little." Then I caught myself. My own feelings had to be separated from Emily's welfare. I turned my back to the social worker, who seemed engrossed in paperwork. "But it seems to me Emily could use a little disruption in her life now. Most of her time here is pretty flat." I looked at Emily, who had begun twisting her hips and stamping her feet in an impatient little war dance.

"The residence is very near my home, by country standards," Mrs. Benedict continued. "I'd pass by the street every time I leave the farm and go into the village. I'm afraid I'll feel guilty if I don't stop in to visit."

Yes. I often felt guilty popping in for a mere ten minutes when I knew Emily really needed large blocks of time.

"And what if she figures out how near she is to home? What if she wants to be with me all the time? I can take her occasionally, but not often, unless her mother is around"—her voice twisted—"which won't be likely."

In the pause after her grandmother spoke I felt the responsibility to say something on Emily's behalf.

"Mrs. Benedict, you asked if Emily was doing all right at Wassaic. That's a hard question to answer. I think the majority of the staff are wonderful, especially Vera, who has most of the direct care for Emily," I said slowly. "But Emily is bored here. I think her life would be better in a good community residence."

From what I knew, these homes in the community for six to a dozen clients were served by a staff able to focus their energies with less distraction. During the weekdays

Emily would be enrolled in a day program. In the evenings and on weekends, she would be walked to her fill, played with, loved, and hugged more in a community residence.

"I'm not an employee here, you know, and I certainly am no expert." That hedge again, covering myself in case I were misunderstood, or blundered into an area where I didn't belong. "Because it's such an enormous place, it's too easy to become anonymous. No matter how hard they try, Wassaic's not a home. I think Emily will grow old better outside the institution."

"Grow old," she murmured. "That's one thing I do know about. I never dreamed that in my old age I'd be the one making decisions for a grandchild. And if Emily lives to be old, someone will *still* have to make decisions for her. You know, some days the nightmare of Emily's first year is as vivid as it was twelve years ago, and so is the horror of the decision to put her in Wassaic."

I was silent against problems I could not understand, a history I could not imagine. Emily was here, was real, was pulling at my wrist in little tugs now, her hands opening and closing like pincers.

"But yes, take her out of there for Easter. Even with her enormous handicaps, she's always been quite a companion." Mrs. Benedict's voice had lost its quaver and gained authority. "Enjoy your time together. Maybe we'll meet one day so I can thank you in person."

I hung up the phone. "So it's all worked out?" the social worker asked, as though he'd overheard none of my conversation.

Emily had me halfway out the door. This was our time together.

"You know, an interesting thing happened," he called to me. "I told you two other people wanted to take clients home for Easter? Well, when I called their families to get permission, both families decided to take the clients themselves. I guess someone else wanting their kids made them more desirable."

"Emily's coming for Easter," I told Katrina and Max.

Katrina groaned. Then she examined a contact print of Emily sitting in bed, winding up her music box, and she changed her mind. "I think she looks adorable," she pronounced. "She'll be kind of like a sister."

"One sister's enough," Max said. "I don't want her to come."

I tried to reason with him. "Emily can't talk. She won't grab you. You can ignore her if you want. The only person she'll want to be with is me, unless someone else tries harder with her and shows more interest. You can both be as involved or uninvolved as you wish."

"I want to get her an Easter basket and a solid chocolate Easter bunny." Katrina said.

I suggested we make the traditional Easter lamb cake in the metal mold Sam's mother had used during his childhood.

"Would she like that better than a circle cake?"

"No, it's just to amuse ourselves," I admitted. I remembered my disdain of the elaborate Valentine cake at the Juniper party.

"But are we going to have an Easter like we've always had?" Max asked, glancing anxiously at Emily's photograph. "I mean even if she's here, can we still have ham?"

"Of course we can, Max."

"I just don't want her to wreck it for all of us."

He looked as though he wanted to say something else, but I cut him off. "Don't make any judgments until you've had the experience." I watched him go upstairs to his homework and knew I was not handling things well.

2

We awoke on Easter Day to cold and rain and hemlock branches wind-whipped against the window. So much for playing outside. I immediately began to worry about how she would fare inside. Would it be safe to light the wood stove? Should I move small objects off the tables? Our house was not set up for a two-and-a-half-year-old.

On the way to the car Emily seemed bewildered: She swung her head from side to side as though asking if she'd really accomplished it, the longed-for turn out the door, the walk down the ramp. Was this really a car she was being put into? And then we were off through the grounds, down the hill, and she hummed loudly, leading with her chin as though her sound were taking her out of Wassaic. She groped for my forearm, so I steered with one hand. I told her where we were going and who would be there. I told her what we would do at the house. Even though I knew there'd be no answer, I asked her how it felt to be free.

It was drizzling as she limped over the uneven flagstones to the house, clutching my wrist. I opened the door; Emily stumbled a little on the doorstep, then we were inside. Licorice, our big black dog, came up and nuzzled Emily's knee. Strange sounds, strange smells. She looked up at the skylights in bewilderment, holding me desperately. I told her the name of everyone: my Aunt Pat, who peered at her with welcome; Max, who smiled through his wariness and said hi; Katrina, suddenly shy; Sam, who greeted her heartily. Emily looked at each person with dark, unfocused, eyes.

Bach was on the radio and a nice, steady fire burned in the fireplace. As Emily shuffled to a chair, a piece of uneven floorboard threw off her balance, then her sneakers caught on the fringe of the Egyptian rug. When I eased her into the chair, she was startled by the creak of the rush seat. In Ward C she sat in a molded plastic chair. Katrina called off Licorice, who had a green tennis ball in his mouth. Emily looked ready to cry. I sent Max to the car for my camera bag; perhaps if she saw an object she could recognize she'd be happy. Katrina ran upstairs for the soft, cuddly bear she'd had since she was a baby.

Emily focused intently on the strobe and set it off to great cheers. She ran her fingers over the bear and smiled. But when she saw a half-inflated old balloon she purred her delighted sound. She put it to my mouth, puckered hers, and blew. There was something I could do—blow up the yellow balloon and slowly let the air out.

When I got up to start lunch Emily lunged for me, but Katrina took over and soon she was all hers, screaming with laughter while Katrina blew and blew the balloon. Max watched from a chair across the room, his chin propped in his hand while he jiggled one foot. When Emily tired of the balloon she brought Katrina over to a table lamp. Katrina tipped the lamp shade and there was another instant hit. She did it again and again and again, then when her patience had run out, she toured Emily around the dining room.

At lunch Emily wasn't interested in the ham at all. She liked the homemade bread, which we gave her without the hard crunchy crust. I worried about her choking, for she put big hunks in her mouth, then chewed with tiny, mincing bites, barely moving her jaw. She looked at the salad, and Katrina gave her a lettuce leaf. She spit it out, disgusted. "Give her some milk, quick," Max said.

Emily saw the large, multi-flowered Easter lily Aunt Pat had brought and pulled it toward her. Eyes half closed, she smiled as she leaned her nose into the open petals, then giggled as a pistil tickled her skin.

"Two-and-a-half doesn't seem such a bad age to be fixed in," Aunt Pat said, raising her glass in a toast.

After lunch we piled the dyed eggs back into their cartons, agreeing it would be too ambitious to hide them. While this had seemed a good idea when Emily was in Juniper, I could tell that here she'd never have the discrimination to find them. There are African masks and sculptures around the rooms. There are two life-size mannequins that look real at first glance. There are skylights and incandescent bulbs and orange fires. There are surfaces at random heights and unpredictable chairs. Who would care about a pink egg?

At four o'clock Aunt Pat left. "I've never had such a touching Easter," she said, kissing us all, kissing Emily.

I too put on my coat and pulled Emily gently from the table where she sat with the Easter lily, running her finger up the long stalk. It was time to go back.

"Can I come with you?" Katrina asked, slipping on her parka.

I hesitated.

"Mom. She's my friend too. I have a right to see where she lives."

Emily was thrilled to be back in the car. She bounced and hummed; occasionally she put her fingers on the steering wheel.

As we turned into Wassaic her pleasure drained. She knew where we were. We were returning her. I had to lift her feet from the car to the parking lot. In the hall she let out a sharp cry. We went into the dayroom, and she gripped Katrina's arm. The Ward C kids were in their usual places, Louisa twirling around the room, Wonder Woman draped on the couch. We'd brought the Easter lily from our house for Emily, and I put it on the table. A few days later I would find it brown and withered, placed high on a room divider where she could neither see nor smell it.

I took off Emily's jacket and put it in her closet. A few minutes later she had it on again. The aide who once mistook me for Emily's mother came in; when Emily released Katrina and reached for him, we fled.

"It's the saddest place I've ever seen," Katrina said.

At home, each of us were exhausted from the emotion of the day. As I left with Emily, Max had said he was going to take a nap. I yawned the whole drive home. Sam was collapsed on the day bed. Katrina rushed up to her room. I went to the chaise in my studio, put in ear plugs, and pulled a quilt over me.

After we slept I found Max in the kitchen, rolling a boiled egg on the counter to crack the shell. "What was the day like for you?" I asked.

"It wasn't the greatest. I felt pretty strange the whole time. But I wasn't scared of her, I don't want you to think that." He picked away at the egg shell, exposing the slick, firm white. "I really felt sorry for her. I couldn't think about anything else."

As we were talking, Katrina came yawning downstairs and watched Max peel his egg. "Max, you know we're going to have Emily over again," she said, almost as a threat.

Max didn't object; I even thought he might welcome the opportunity to try again with Emily when he had digested this experience. I realized it had been only two months since I had walked into Wassaic. That first day I could see nothing, could not look at the people. I remembered feeling as though I were under water for hours afterward. How could I expect more of Max, considering my own experience? How could

I ask for more than that he keep an open mind and an open heart?

The next morning I awoke painfully from this dream: My mother, Martha, and I are all pregnant at the same time. First Martha loses her baby, as she had five weeks ago. Then my mother, who is very pregnant, also loses her baby. I am shocked and grieved for her, but I am still pregnant. I remember what my father, a doctor, has told me—you know things are well with the fetus if you feel it kick twelve times a day. I suddenly fear the movement I've felt is mere stomach gurglings. I go to my doctor, a white-suited man, and ask him to make an X ray of the baby. "I don't want to have another stillbirth," I tell him. He does the X ray and says the fetus is not viable, it must go.

Then he is holding a little thing in his hand, all white and vernix-covered, my baby. "It wasn't quite dead, but it certainly would have been no genius," he tells me. I cannot bear to look. "See this curve in the spine? That's a pocket of retardation." I force myself to look. "And see how the hand is crossed over the chest," he continues. "It would never straighten out. That's your fault. You should have known better than to have a baby at your age. Let's look at your charts. You've been going downhill for years now." My grief is unbearable.

I could hardly open my eyes in the morning, for though the dream was terribly sad, I sensed its importance and wanted to stay in it.

But as soon as I was awake I thought about Emily. Sam had told me yesterday she would definitely be moving into the residence near her grandmother. The move was planned for July. It really would happen and was undoubtedly a good thing for Emily. But . . . But it left me little time with her.

I had a clear perspective about what was right and responsible, but I knew it would be a loss for me.

I added that component to my dream. Josh Greenfeld, in his book about his autistic son, *A Child Called Noah,* suggests we all secretly long for a child that won't grow up and leave us. Though that idea is hard to accept, I know it's a truth deep in my unconscious. In my dream Emily was the damaged fetus, crippled and retarded, that I did not give birth to. She was the child I would never have, the child who would never grow up.

3

Evergreen Transitional, a program center across the campus from both Butternut Learning and Juniper Hall, could be reached either by walking leisurely around the horseshoe-shaped drive, or, more quickly, by cutting across the lawn. It sat long and low connecting two older residential buildings, its yellow brick from a more recent but less substantial era, much like the trailers—"portable classrooms"—in the yards of once spiffy schools. Inside, bulletin boards had been used to partition the vast Evergreen space into rooms, leaving open a large dining area in the middle which accommodated dozens of formica tables, and at one end, a gleaming installation of stainless steel counters and steam trays. On a clothesline above the entrance hung a construction paper cut-out, the letters looking like faded laundry, "Welcome to Evergreen Transitional."

"Transitional to what?" I asked the program supervisor.

"Okay," she began, taking a deep breath, "usually transitional means pre-vocational or on the way to a workshop situation. In this case our clients are all geriatric, so most of them will be here forever."

Until the great, ultimate transition, I thought.

One basement classroom was like a kindergarten room with bunnies and shamrocks on the walls, though St. Patrick's Day had long passed, and Easter was five days behind us. Old ladies were leafing through ragged catalogues of household items and knickknacks. Fluorescent light glared from the ceiling, beating back what natural light seeped in from the ground-level windows.

A client leaped up from a chair like a sprung clothespin. "I'm Sybil. What's in that box?" She put her hand on my Speed Graphic. "You gonna take my picture?"

"Sit down, Sybil," the teacher commanded. He was a tall, loose-jointed man, with trousers gathered by a belt high above his waist. He shuffled a stack of 8 × 10 cards. "Ok, what is this?" he asked holding up a card with a garishly colored drawing.

"A horse," Sybil declared.

"Sally, what do you think this is?"

"A cow."

He turned to a third old lady.

"An elephant."

"Come on now," he sighed. "What's gray and has a trunk?"

Silence.

"A mouse with a suitcase," the teacher snickered.

Several of the clients tittered. It seemed they had heard it before.

"Let's try another one." He held up a card with a drawing of a woman's garment.

"A raincoat," someone suggested. Shabby, but still it could pass.

"A dress." Shapeless, but it could be a dress.

"No, no," said the teacher, uneasy at his pupils' poor showing in front of the visitor. "What do you wear to bed?"

"Pajamas!" Sybil screamed triumphantly.

"Look, there are no pants." The teacher pointed at the formless garment. "What do you put over your head to go to bed?"

"A nightie."

Relief.

He turned to other matters. "All right, we have some religious days coming up, let's talk about them." He looked around the room expectantly, as though someone else might offer to lead the discussion. "What holidays did we just have?"

"Thursday, Friday, Saturday, and Sunday," said an old lady promptly.

"Well, what was last Sunday?"

"Hanukkah," said Sybil.

"No, it was Easter."

"Yeah."

"And what do we think of when we think of Easter?"

"A bonnet," Sybil announced, clearly the star and all-around ham of the class. She patted her gray curls and flapped her toothless jaws. "I'm gonna get me a bonnet." She came over to me and gave me a very strong hug. "I like you. Are you a streetwalker? Do you stay with the other streetwalkers?"

"I went to high school," a client named Emma told me in a small, stuttery voice. "I can read and I can spell. I didn't do too good in school, but I went. I have all these arithmetic books, see?" Grade-school notebooks and workbooks bulged from a frayed shopping bag on the footrest of her electric wheelchair. With the back of her bent, palsied hand, she pushed the joy stick that drove the chair, maneuvering herself face to face with Gertrude Healy. I took my camera and a film holder out of my white bag.

Gertrude wore a housedress covered with forget-me-nots.

Over her lap, a gray blanket outlined tiny legs that dangled in the wheelchair. Her hands were serene in her lap. Because of her stunted legs her body and head looked disproportionately large; with her close-cropped gray hair she resembled Gertrude Stein.

The two old women talked to each other while waiting for their lunch shift in Evergreen Transitional. I photographed them side by side; being in front of the old press camera seemed to please them, as though it were something remembered from their past. When I finished they looked at me expecting conversation, but I could think of nothing to say. The questions I really wanted to ask about their lives seemed too intrusive.

As though she knew what my questions might be, Gertrude Healy began to speak in a voice that sounded more like recitation than spontaneous speech. "I was born on St. Patrick's Day, 1900." She smiled and looked satisfied, paused a minute, then leaned forward to tell me more. "I was six when my parents put me away on Randall's Island. I can remember the horse-and-buggy ride to the landing and the ferry over. That's the only way you could get there in those days."

At the turn of the century, Randall's Island and Ward's Island, in New York's East River, were grim homes for the unwanted. During the eighteenth and nineteenth century both islands were used for potter's fields, garbage dumps, and almshouses. In 1906, when Gertrude went there, Randall's Island was dominated by the sprawling "House of Refuge," a punitive detention home for juvenile delinquents, and the New York City Children's Hospital, another dumping ground for abandoned and "defective" children.

"I spent all my time on Randall's Island except for two months when I went to Ward's Island. I cried the whole time there, because I would wake up and I wouldn't be at my home. That's what I thought of Randall's Island, it was my home.

"I couldn't walk, I never could," Gertrude continued. "But I could crawl on my hands and knees. At Randall's Island I got knee pads and that made it easier."

I glanced again at the blanket that covered her lap. Under it were knees that had scraped along the cold and splintery floor of a tenement house and only felt relief when she had been *put away,* that chilling phrase. And in her head was a brain that could recall events and dates three quarters of a century ago.

"How did you feel . . ." I began and stopped. I could not shake the phrase *put away* from my mind. I leaned towards her, wanting to ask, but wanting to ask in a low voice so we would not be overheard. "How did you feel when your parents put you away? Were you very angry at them?"

"Oh, no!" Gertrude looked shocked. "I loved my parents very much. They lived on the West Side and they always came to see me, every three weeks. They never forgot about me."

The resiliency of the human heart.

She told me more about Randall's Island, entertaining me as though I had come for tea. She described the circus they went to on the first Tuesday of every April; she said how lovely it was to sit on the wooden porches of the buildings in summertime. "Then I came to Wassaic in 1934. They tore down our place on Randall's Island to build the Triborough bridge, you know."

Wassaic had been built to relieve overcrowding at existing upstate institutions and to accommodate people displaced when the Randall's Island and Ward's Island buildings were demolished. Nearly 950 inmates were transferred from the metropolitan setting to the hurriedly built, isolated, country one. Gertrude was among them. The population of the four-year-old school—still under construction and struggling to organize—was already 2,900. *The Annual Report of the Wassaic State School, 1934,* admits, "It became evident that a certain amount of overcrowding was unavoidable, and extra beds were placed in every ward."

"All the girls wore the same dresses, blue, the color you have on," Gertrude said pointing to my faded jeans. "The men all wore these striped suits. Monkey suits, we called them. Each building had its own dining room and we'd all walk over. Except for the cripples. And that's what I liked best about the new place. I got my first wheelchair here in 1935."

After twenty-nine years as a ward of the state, Gertrude finally got off her hands and knees.

Emma broke in, her jaw moving for several seconds before words came out. I strained to hear her soft, stuttering voice. "I came here from upstate. My mother put me away when I was seventeen because she couldn't lift me no more. I had polio. I loved my mother so much. When she told me she was going to put me away I cried my eyes out."

"I wish I had one like Emma's," Gertrude said nodding at the electric wheelchair, "then I could get around more. It's too hard to wheel myself in this one."

Emma looked at Gertrude and shook her head. "It ain't nothing," she said. "It don't get you out of here and that's what counts."

Later I found out some facts of Emma's history. Her parents were German immigrants with no retardation in the family.

There were three girls; the older two were twins. Emma weighed twelve pounds when she was born, but she contracted measles and her weight plummeted to four pounds. Later medical examinations showed she had probably had spinal meningitis and polio at an early age. This left her crippled and mildly retarded with an IQ of 68. (I wondered how the testing was done. Surely her speech difficulties might make her intelligence seem lower. But I had not yet discovered that IQ points were routinely shaved to enable residents to keep federal funding, 70 being the cutoff point.) Cerebral palsy had not only made it difficult for her to sit up, but had cramped her hands into a claw-like position.

Ever since she was transferred from an upstate institution to Wassaic thirty-five years ago, she had been deeply lonely and depressed. A psychologist reported that she had talked of suicide. She felt embarrassed being at the mercy of others for all her physical needs; she was sensitive to slights or unkindness from the staff. Her spirits were reportedly lifted when she received a motorized wheelchair. She also seemed comforted by having been taken, as she requested, to visit her mother's grave. Medication helped her spasticity and improved her emotional outlook, though she was still prone to terrible depressions. There seemed to be general agreement that she did not belong in Wassaic but in the community, though they had not been able to find a place that would take a spastic quadriplegic.

The speech teacher worked in a space partitioned with flimsy portable walls. She had been on vacation all last week and was back with determined energy. Like the little iris that pushed through the mud and ruled alone in the April garden, she was dressed head to toe in purple—purple suit, lavender blouse, purple high heels, and most startling, deep eggplant-purple fingernails.

She put a tray of plastic fruits and vegetables in front of a tiny old lady. "All right Tillie, identify these," she said, raising the level and pitch of her voice. "I want a banana, a plum, an onion, and a tomato. Banana, plum, onion, and tomato."

Tillie looked blank. Then tentatively she picked up the plastic apple.

"Tillie. Banana, plum, onion, and tomato." Her voice had a weary edge, and I could see the vacation wearing right off.

Tillie's hand floated above the tray and landed on the plastic banana.

"Good Tillie! Now I'm going to peel it and eat it, I'm so hungry!"

The ladies laughed.

"Now, plum, onion, and tomato."

The ladies stared vacantly beyond hearing or memory or interest. I was fascinated by the purple nails touching the plastic fruit.

"Plum, grapes, corn, apple, and orange." The speech teacher became more dispirited as the tray progressed around the table. Soon she even forgot what she had asked for.

4

A week passed without sun, and then we had the kind of day that gave spring its name, with a clear sky and warm breeze. When I'd finished my morning darkroom chores I did not go to Wassaic but instead cleaned debris from my perennial garden, making space for new shoots to push through. My fingers were dry from scraping at the earth, my hands were thorn-scratched from pruning roses. I raked last fall's oak leaves down the hill until my shoulders ached. At lunch I read about mulching and double-digging, and reacquainted myself with lupine and digitalis.

"It's really nice out there, isn't it?" Emma stammered. She slumped with her head almost on her wheelchair tray, her large, wrinkled breasts pushed up against the open neck of a sky-blue dress. Her hands were pincers twisted back on themselves.

I looked across her room in Birch Hall—the residence which housed many of the women who attended the Evergreen Transitional program—and out onto the green. Emma's head was down so low she couldn't see out the window. I was tongue-tied with my freedom. Finally I said, "It's lovely. I guess you'd like to be able to go outside."

Emma nodded. In the bedroom she shared with three other clients, the heat was on full blast as though it were January.

She directed me to the bottom drawer of a small bedside dresser where a photograph album lay on top of folded nightgowns. The first two pages were color shots of staff, whom she described as friends, or if they were young handsome men, boyfriends. One picture was centered in the third page. In it Emma sat outside on a day as lovely as this one. The hills in the background told me she was at Wassaic. Her hair was dark, long and loose; her arms tan and firm in a sleeveless print dress. Her face was handsome, and she smiled a big, crooked smile. She sat behind a table, her body so straight and aligned I had to look closely to see she was in a wheelchair.

I asked her when the picture had been taken, but she

was not like Gertrude Healy, precise in her dates; she was more like me, vague and unmindful of the years. "A few years ago," she said dismissively.

The last photograph in the album was her mother's grave, stark, gray granite softened by daffodils.

I closed the album and Emma pointed to a miniature chest with three tiers of drawers. "Open the top one," she directed. In it was a small box with a crucifix on a chain. The price tag—$2.98—was still on the lid.

"Take it," she said, "Go on, take it."

I could not. I felt as embarrassed as I'd been in Africa when people who had nothing gave me all they had—a calabash of rice or a bunch of bananas. I had accepted only because I knew it was unforgivably rude to refuse, but I had felt humiliated by my clothes, my watch, the landrover that brought me to a village.

Emma accepted my refusal. But on top of the dresser, she spied an emery board. "There," she cried. "Take that! I don't need it."

And I did. An hour ago, my fingernails ragged from pulling leaves and stones from the garden, I filed my scratchy nails with a metal file and wished for an old-fashioned emery board with a rough and smooth side. Emma could see I was delighted.

Then she was once again a shy and nervous hostess. "Sit down," she said. But I was restless and kept looking out the window, anxious to be outdoors again, to go home, to work in my garden.

The next day I followed a fluffy gray and white cat ambling down Birch Hall, with a tail like a feather boa. "That's Homer, the cat," an aide explained. "He belongs to Samantha and he's even certified by the Board of Health. Samantha gets special favors but after all, she's been here fifty years, longer than anyone else."

Samantha's room was a marvel. Double-tiered lace curtains were tied to form graceful swoops as though adorning the windows of a Boston townhouse. The walls were covered with framed photographs; knickknacks and artificial flowers cluttered the dresser. In the corner was a small refrigerator with a lock.

An old lady wobbled unsteadily into the room on two canes. Straight white hair hung past her shoulders; her face was smooth and pale, unaged by sun, and her eyes were cataracted like gray sea-washed stones. She wore a pink baby-doll nightie. Samantha. The resident who'd been in Wassaic longest.

My eye caught a calendar on the wall: a bronzed nude man waded into the ocean, a triangle of white flesh marking his buttocks. Samantha saw me looking at it and giggled.

"We just don't know where she gets these things," the aide said, winking. "Our team leader doesn't like her to have it, but every year she gets another Buns calendar and we just don't know from where. She's the scandal of the building. Somehow all the new employees find their way over to this room."

Next to the calendar, framed, was a poem.

Samantha's Poem

Forty-seven years ago a young girl came to stay.
She was just 19, had reached the third grade when she came
* this way.*
She has some trouble walking; in school she learned quite slow.
Her father had remarried, there was nowhere else to go.

Her family's loss became our gain—a friend she did become.
And we became her family; she was liked by everyone.

As we look back we realize she never should have come,
But that was many years ago and that's how things were done.

To overcome the guilt some felt all moved PDQ
And Samantha got the word quite fast—the community's for
you.
But after being here for years, her home this had become.
To move her out at this late date—that should not be done.

She got a job and did real well and some began to say,
That if she wants to stay right here that she should have her
way.
So Samantha still lives here with us, is working every day.
She gives us all a real hard time in her own fantastic way.

She keeps up on all the gossip, she keeps us on our toes.
She even entertains us with poetry and prose.
So Happy Anniversary is our wish today
And thanks for all the fun you brought to us along the way.

"I never want to leave here," Samantha told me, beaming. "Some people think I could start over, but I don't think so. I don't think I could do that.

"I wanted to be a nun. I lived in a convent and went through all the training. At the end of it they told me I couldn't be a nun. That was the saddest day of my life. I cried and cried. If only they had told me before I started, I wouldn't have gone through it all."

So even as a young girl Samantha had wanted a cloistered life. She had wanted in rather than out from the beginning.

She blinked several times, cleared her eyes, then nodded toward the picture of the nude man wading into the ocean. "But what do you think those nuns would say if they could see that calendar?"

While it was required that all clients go to programming regardless of age, there were some medical exemptions. A few old ladies were allowed to stay in the ward, though the paperwork that gave them their rest was slippery and dangerous. There were "steps" and "stages"; it was possible to lose the exemption.

Marybelle was ninety-two, white-haired and stooped. Around her neck were several strings of beads made from painted macaroni shells. She had no teeth and talked constantly. Though I couldn't understand her words, her actions and gestures communicated clearly; she was busy as could be. She scuttled around hurrying an aide who wasn't changing Lottie's clothes quickly enough.

Marybelle loved Lottie, who alternated between bed and a recliner. Lottie was incontinent and needed frequent changing. The aides removed her wet gown revealing a sadly bald pubis and prolapsed vulva that hung down like udders. Gently the aides cleaned and lotioned her almost nonexistent buttocks. And ninety-two-year-old Marybelle tugged at the wet sheet, muttering toothlessly, telling them to hurry and make Lottie comfortable.

"Are they old friends?" I asked.

"No, Lottie's a new love. They've been together for five years, ever since we moved into this building."

I'd heard about these loves, one old woman tenderly caring and providing service for another. Is it just the female spirit that so needs to love and nurture? Often when the "bright" women have no one to care for, they have dolls.

In the same ward I sat beside another very old, white-haired lady who spoke slowly and with difficulty, but with a great need to be understood.

"How old are you?" I asked.

She shrugged and laughed, as though that were very much beside the point.

"Eighty?" I persisted.

"More than that. I'm eighty-seven."

An aide raised her eyebrow and shook her head slightly.

The old lady, who certainly looked eighty-seven, inched her wheelchair toward me. "My family pushed me out, just pushed me out. I don't know why."

"Could you walk then?"

"Sure. I don't know why they did it." Her eyes looked steadily into mine. "I think about it all the time. They came to see me once, then they never came again. I always think about that. I had two babies, both born at the same time. A boy and a girl. Oh, that was something, two at once."

"What happened to them?" I asked.

"I don't know. The people here would never tell me. I asked and asked, but they'd never tell me. I remember when the boy got sassy. He was four then, and I told him to come to me. 'No,' he said. He wouldn't come. Don't you think that's fresh?"

As she spoke I imagined this picture: Sixty years ago this woman was in her twenties, pretty. She'd gone to school for a few years, but could never learn to read and had been labeled "slow." Or perhaps she never went to school but worked making fancy hats in a sweatshop. She became pregnant. Her family, desperately poor, was enraged and ashamed by her pregnancy. They said anyone could take advantage of her because she was "slow."

When she gave birth to twins, she could not return to work, and her family was even angrier. I could imagine that they shouted at her continually and sometimes her father hit her. And she, in turn, was outraged at these twins who had brought her misery and shame. She neglected the children. The neighbors discovered this, and her place—and her family's—slipped lower in the social order. Her parents must have feared she would become pregnant again. They decided to send the children away, perhaps to a cousin who had a farm upstate, and to put her away in an institution for the feeble-minded. They told her it was for her own good. They told her they would come to see her. They came once.

I took her photograph, but it would not be the young, pretty, bitter face Lewis Hine had once photographed in sweatshops; in this old face, history and grief would be hidden in wrinkles carved by an adult life in Wassaic.

When the strobe light blazed the whole ward applauded. I took another photograph and again everyone clapped and yelled "Hooray!" So I went around the ward, not really taking pictures, but setting off the strobe until all the old women were satisfied.

"You're beautiful," I said impulsively to a woman sitting at a dayroom table, smoking. "Let me take your picture."

"I'm not beautiful." Her voice was soft and thick. "I used to be, but I'm not now. I used to be fat too, but now I'm thin."

In fact Rhoda Alexius was magnificent, silver hair swooping from a cow lick, clear skin, a dignified face with high cheekbones. She sat in a wheelchair, "because one of the people in this building pushed me over and it broke my hip."

Her low, husky voice made me bend to hear her. "I hate this place. It's so noisy I can't stand it. I've hated this place since I came here. When I was fifteen my father was run over by a streetcar, and my mother saw it, and she had a heart attack. I was left all alone with my cousin. She didn't know what to do, so she brought me up here and said she'd come for me in two months. That was it. I'm fifty-six now. I came here when I was fifteen, in 1941."

The year I was born. My lifetime in Wassaic.

"And what did you think when you first saw this place?" I tried to sound as neutral as possible.

"I thought, 'Oh my God.' " Her eyes could not meet mine. "The director came up to me when I got here and asked me, "Rhoda, do you know you're in the state school now? Do you know this is an institution? And I said, 'Yes. I know it now.' "

This was the stuff of literature, of Solzhenitsyn and Kafka. A person is brought to a vast, impersonal institution. The door slams.

There were shrieks throughout the building, but on this ward there were constant screams. I looked around the room. A client sat naked in a chair, while another walked off with her clothes. I also saw a brown pile on the floor which could only be excrement.

"I used to have two boyfriends when I lived at home," Rhoda Alexius was telling me. "One used to look at me all the time as I helped my mama. Oh yes, I went to school until fifth grade. I can read and write and count to a hundred in English and Greek. And I used to help my mama cook and clean."

An aide came into the ward and groaned. I looked back at the naked woman and saw she had brown on her mouth. She was eating shit. I tried to keep the conversation with Rhoda Alexius going and not look.

"One day the boy is standing there watching me and he says, 'I'll bet you are a hard worker.' "

The aide picked up the pile on the floor with a paper towel. He hurried from the room.

" 'I work all the time,' I told him, and he winked at me. Later he asked me to marry him."

The aide returned with another wheelchair with a potty

seat. He loaded on the client, her legs and body smeared in feces.

" 'Why would I marry you?' I said. 'I don't even know you.' 'Well you can get to know me after we're married.' " She paused, looked straight ahead past where the soiled client had been sitting, and said in a low and bitter voice, "I wish to God I'd done that, married him whether I knew him or not. I wouldn't be in this place if I had. I would have money and a house and children."

I sat in my car, too unnerved to turn on the ignition. I was free to walk out and I had. The staff were paid for all they had to go through and went home at the end of the shift. Rhoda Alexius had to stay, had to listen or shut down. How many of these women had simply shut down over the years? Not Samantha with her "buns" calendar, but all those other silent and unintelligible women? They had been put away because they were orphans or "slow" or physically disabled or sexually active. They were at the end of their lives, with so little to show except maybe a visitor now and then, and occasional talk about how it used to be before they had been put away.

5

Because it was the children's spring vacation, we planned a five-day family trip to Washington, D.C. With our bags in the car, Katrina, Max, and I stopped by Wassaic to pick up Sam for the six-hour drive.

As we drove in the parking lot, Max looked around apprehensively. "Are there any retarded people in the building where Dad works?" he asked.

"No," I said.

"Are you sure?"

"Max, there's nothing to worry about."

"In that case I'll go in and get him." He left the car but headed the wrong way.

"It's through the other door," I called.

"What's wrong kid, you lost?" A resident stood watching us, hands jammed in his pockets.

Max was polite and collected. "No, I just got confused for a moment." He ran back to the car. "Mom," he whispered anxiously, "*what* door do I use?"

"You need some help?" the man yelled over.

"No thanks." Max understood my quick instructions and went in the right door.

Katrina sat in the back seat; I was behind the wheel. The man approached the car. A few inches from the open window his fists popped from his pockets. Each knuckle sported a gaudy ring—rhinestones, day-glow plastic, fake emeralds. "See these?" He grinned a semi-toothed smile which crinkled his eyes. "I won't be happy until I have ten more." As he cocked his head a wave of copper-streaked hair fell across his forehead. A waterfall of necklaces glinted under his collar.

"All your jewelry's very pretty," I said.

"Well, look at this." He held out two earrings in the shape of feet.

"How can you wear those without holes in your ears?"

"I just freeze my ears and stick a pin through them and hang them on," he said.

"That's nice," I said limply.

"I've got a dress at home. I wear it in the summer."

I didn't turn around to see how Katrina, silent in the back seat, was reacting to all this, but I knew I wanted to distract him. I changed my tone and took charge. "What's your name?"

"Benjamin," he said with great finality and pleasure, before a cloud of possible doubt crossed his brow. "That's a girl's name, isn't it?"

"No, that's a boy's name."

"But it's got to be a girl's name because there's a girl here named it and she's not my sister." He leaned in the car window, giggling, and spied my camera. "Hey, you gonna take my picture?"

"Sure. Sometime I'll take your picture."

"Oh goodie! I can wear my dress! And I can wear my wig!"

Sam and Max came out the door, and I saw Max hesitate. Benjamin bounded off.

"Max! you miss all the good ones," Katrina said as we drove off. "I almost cracked up—wait 'til you hear what he does to his ears!"

I was absent from Wassaic for five days, yet it could have been five weeks, the break was so complete. Katrina and Max joined hordes of other vacationing kids at the Air and Space Museum, while Sam and I wandered around the Hirshhorn, the National Gallery, and the National Portrait Gallery. I rarely thought of Wassaic. This was the real world, the normal world that oohs and ahhs over cherry blossoms and inspects the Bill of Rights.

But if I didn't think of Wassaic, I did think of Emily. If she were our daughter, could we have managed such a trip? She would have loved the seemingly endless car ride, but how would she have done in crowds? She couldn't have climbed the steps we did. She would have stumbled on cobblestones and spongy grass.

One night we walked through dense fog and rain and up the steps of the Lincoln Memorial. I looked at the stern, compassionate face of Lincoln and watched other tourists look at him. Suddenly there was a commotion in the crowd and a wave of nervous laughter moved through a group of teenagers. At the base of the enormous carving of Lincoln I saw two young men with bright pink cheeks and dangly earrings. The teenagers had formed a horseshoe around them.

A boy with a red-visored farm hat stepped forward and shoved one of the boys with the earrings in the chest. He staggered back, almost crashing into Mr. Lincoln. It looked like bad trouble. But the teenagers dragged the farm boy back into their group and averted the fight—though they continued to openly stare and point and giggle.

Watching that small vignette of ugliness, it seemed the words "faggot" and "queer" were as scorching as if they'd been spray-painted across Lincoln's statue. When the kids retreated down the steps and disappeared around the tidal basin, I imagined Emily standing in front of that statue, humming a noisy song of fear, with the words "moron" and "spaz" and "retard" graffitied below Mr. Lincoln's sad face.

"What a great day!" Vera said, pulling her fingers through her curls as though to release stored warmth from outside. "Emily's been in the courtyard all afternoon, but I guess it hasn't been enough for her."

Raised flower beds surrounding the concrete courtyard were planted with blooming myrtle, small, intense blue flowers that peeked from the ground cover. But the only play equipment was a red plastic horse on a spring. A few molded chairs had been hauled out. I kicked a deflated ball that lay on the cement, and it rolled reluctantly from flat side to flat side. Emily ignored it.

She led me to the courtyard gate, the exit to the grounds and freedom. I didn't respond. She led me to the Juniper door. She didn't want to go inside; she wanted to pass through the building and out the front door. But it was 4:30, almost time for her supper. I maneuvered her into the ward.

"Okay Emily, off with your jacket," I said briskly. Her arms stiffened as fast as the tin woodsman of Oz in the rain. It's hard to pull a jacket off rigid arms but I managed, and when she realized what had happened Emily started to cry—an anguished cry, not just a hum, but despair. I couldn't stand it. I knew I should think of her as two-and-a-half; I'd wrestled plenty of screaming kids that age out of snowsuits or bathing suits. But I couldn't do it with her because she didn't look two-and-a-half. She looked like a twelve-year-old who should be allowed the freedom to act on a simple choice: I want to stay outside. I want to take a walk. Confronting her prison, it was all I could do not to weep.

6

The next day a spring storm spread four inches of snow on our road; the driveway was barricaded with large branches, raw ends wrenched from vulnerable trees. Although rain melted most of the snow that night, the following morning was miserable, hovering between a mist that could be rain, fog, or sleet.

The purple-suited speech teacher held up the same tired pictures of sun and clouds for her geriatric ladies. "We had a lesson on the seasons because we seem to be a little mixed up about whether it's spring, winter, or summer. But we didn't get very far so we'll do it again tomorrow."

From her seat little Tillie looked up imploringly and kept her sad eyes on me, her head flopped to the side as though there was no neck attached to her spine. "Oh poor me," she sighed.

When classes changed she pulled me into a corner and peered up at me from the level of my belt line. Her tiny body was twisted with scoliosis. She was no bigger than an eight-year-old. Dressed in a little blue cotton dress with a dirndl apron and white knee socks, she looked like a well-tended child. Her hair was gray, and in the center of her crooked teeth gleamed a gold one. I wondered where and when she'd gotten it.

"I'm very upset today." Tillie's cataract-covered eyes filmed with tears. "I want to see my old teacher, Stuart." Stuart was one of the teachers I knew: he taught Agatha, Earl, and Manny in the behavior unit of Butternut. "Please find Stuart and tell him I have to see him. He was so good to me. He used to take me out for the day. Now it's just the same thing over and over. I need to get out and see people. I'm so lonely here. So bored."

"But Tillie," I said soothingly, "I've been watching you. You have lots of friends here." And it was true. I'd seen Tillie comfort a crying woman. I'd seen her sitting sympathetically next to a depressed Emma. If anyone had been able to carve her own niche, it was Tillie.

"I know I have friends, but I want more. I want new ones. I want to meet people, you know what I mean? I want things to be different." She looked up at me pleading.

Emily begged for freedom. Now Tillie thought I could do something about hers.

"Tillie wants to see you," I told Stuart, her old teacher.

He smiled. "Tillie always wants to see me. I just saw her Wednesday. Her team leader called me three times in one week with that message. Then he got smart and started asking Tillie when she last saw me. Tillie's a wonderful gal, but she's a conniver."

"Consider the message delivered. I've done my part," I announced.

"You're off the hook."

"Did you see Stuart?" Tillie asked, her twisted body looking up at me. She sat on the plastic-covered sofa next to the soda machine in Birch, knitting a rectangle from odds and ends of wool. She concentrated on every stitch and grunted each time she completed one.

"I did, and I gave him your message."

"What did he say?"

"He said he'd just seen you on Wednesday."

She smiled with the memory. "That's right. And what else did he say about me?"

"He thinks you're a wonderful person."

Her eyes filled with tears. "Stuart's my friend. I'm knitting this scarf for him. I want to be with him."

"Why Tillie," I said as I gave her small shoulders a squeeze, "You're in love." I realized I had used the word "love" in a world where only childish crushes are appropriate. Now Tillie was on the edge of tears.

I drew back. The responsibility for encouraging love seemed too great. "You have lots of friends," I said again. "Everyone here thinks you're terrific. I certainly do. Stuart's your friend too." I massaged her humped shoulder to comfort her.

"You don't understand."

I did, but I wouldn't let on.

"Stuart's my father now. He used to take us out all the time, to supper and everywhere. All the time. And when my father died, my mommy came and told me, and then I went to see Stuart. Now how do you tell someone that, tell him he is my father?"

I didn't know what to say. Tillie's relationships with men were all experienced at such a distance that I doubted she really understood the difference between lovers and fathers.

"He's married, you know," she continued. "And he has a little baby boy." She looked at me sideways to see if I'd caught her meaning. "When he left and quit taking us out, I felt so hurt and upset."

"Sometimes people have to change jobs, Tillie. They can't help it." Now what was this? Again my need to deflect things, put them back into safety and reality. Let her know that it was a job, something he was paid to do.

"I'm going home for a visit after Mothers' Day. I want to say goodbye to him before I go." She wadded up her knitting and hopped off the couch, suddenly smiling a mischievous grin, her gold tooth glinting like a flash of lightning.

I took a light-meter reading of Rhoda Alexius, lovely in a red-flowered dress, her gray and black streaked hair pulled back to accentuate her Mediterranean features—long nose, solid thick eyebrows, firm chin.

"I'm rotten, that's how I am," she said. "I got lots and lots of troubles and problems. All day I think about them and that's what I'm doing right now. Thinking about my troubles and problems."

"What are they?" I asked, as I adjusted the shutter speed and aperture on the Speed Graphic. She stared straight ahead. "I mean specifically. Name your biggest trouble." I made the correct strobe setting.

"I got to get out of here. I want a house, nice clothes, a family." Her voice was monotone. "I think about that all the time. I never had no luck, not one bit."

As Rhoda paused I thought of my own troubles: I didn't have enough time to do my work; I was anxious about my father's upcoming week-long visit; I needed to raise tuition money for Katrina's new school. These were not desperate problems and didn't require a complete reversal of my life to solve. I played the bellows in and out, bringing Rhoda back into focus.

"I work all day and I got nothing to show for it."

Rhoda spent six mandated "program" hours each weekday in a basement workshop. There she lined plaid paper shopping bags with plastic, to be used by Delta Airlines for the storage and disposal of used food trays. She was paid forty-two cents for lining twenty-five bags. On a bad day Rhoda could do fifty bags; on a good day, seventy-five. That meant her maximum pay was $1.26 per day.

"This place is so awful," she continued. "The food is terrible. I like good food and this is garbage."

I slid the dark slide from the film holder. "What kind of food do you like?" I asked, cocking the shutter.

It worked. Her mouth twitched, then memory lit her eyes. I pressed the cable release and the strobe light burst out. "Stuffed grape leaves. Moussaka. Avgolemono soup. Baklava." Her face crumpled again. "I haven't had those things in years. I'll probably never have them again unless my cousin takes me home. I'm going to call her. She always cheers me up. She's smart. I like talking to her because she's got sense. Now look at the people in this room."

Her hand gestured around the room to clients in their chairs. "I can't talk to these dummies. It drives me crazy to be in here with them. And you know why I'm here? It's not because I don't have sense, it's because my mommy and daddy died, and I don't have luck. Most people got some luck, but I don't have none. I hate Wassaic. I hated it down at Greenville too. When I was there I was with crazy people. One woman in my room was dangerous. Once she held a fork up to my eye and said she was going to put my eye out. I was trembling and crying I was so frightened. That's the kind of people I've been with all my life."

I wanted to cry out: Rhoda! Perhaps if you stop being so negative, if you cheer up, people will respond and you'll have a better time in this world. Then I caught myself and looked around at the confines of her world. Last week her roommate ate shit. Once more I wanted to deflect reality.

"Rhoda, I make a dynamite moussaka. How would you like me to bring you some next time I make it?"

Her eyes flashed greedily. "You'd do that? I'll pay you."

"Nonsense. My treat. And what do you like with it? Salad?"

"Could I have salad with tomatoes? And feta cheese?" The words came distantly through memory.

"That's what you'll have."

"Can you bring good bread, too? The kind with crust? I'll pay you. When are you going to do it? Tomorrow?"

"Not tomorrow," I said quickly. My father was coming next week and would put pressures on my time and kitchen. "Sometime within the next month, okay?"

"Listen. Bring it to my room. If anyone else sees it they'll get jealous. So don't tell anyone, just bring it straight to my room. When will you be back?" Rhoda asked as I packed up my camera. "Tomorrow?"

Emily and I walked. It was a blustery day, billowing clouds with silver underbellies were lying on the horizon. Because of her cerebral palsy she couldn't walk far, but I could tell by the way she put her face directly in the wind that she loved being outdoors. We ambled onto the lawn; she tugged me to a halt. She pushed my arm toward the ground. There among thousands of dandelions was one gone to seed, a wispy gray round puff. I picked it, held it in front of her face, and blew. The puff flew apart and hit her face like dozens of soft tickles. Emily laughed. A few minutes later she spotted another and stopped me.

This was a girl who had trouble sorting shapes in her daytime program. This was the child that couldn't "see" me until her brain turned over several times, like a worn car battery on a winter day. Yet she could find one dandelion gone to seed in a field of yellow.

7

The first of May is my birthday. I've always thought it a magical day to be born. When I was very young I filled May Day baskets with flowers; once I saw girls dancing and braiding satin ribbons around a Maypole, which I appropriated as a birthday tribute. In my family it was traditional to do whatever you wanted on your birthday. I remember on her seventh birthday, my sister ordered me to carry her onto the school bus in my arms, and to her amazement, I did.

And so this May first I did exactly what I wanted—I put on a pair of dirt-encrusted jeans and spent the morning in my garden. I liberated bearded iris from its own tough, fallen foliage, fed roses and delphinium, then pulled dandelions from a small, neglected bed. At last I turned to my herb garden, scraping away dead mint stalks so the new, green leaves could breathe and live.

My father hobbled across the grass, leaning heavily on his cane and testing the ground before he trusted himself to it. He was dressed in red plaid pants for the birthday party Martha was giving for me later. "Do I need to wear a tie?" he asked.

"Heavens no," I said, looking back at my weeding.

He watched me for a while as I worked to free a tiny tarragon that had made it through winter. Suddenly he said, "Doesn't it depress you, going to Wassaic?"

"Sometimes," I said cautiously. I knew this was not the answer he wanted or expected. Until he retired four years ago, my father had been a surgeon; before that, a brilliant medical and college student; before that, a medical prodigy who, at six, knew the Latin name for every bone in the human body.

"Well, I remember the day Sam took me through there, and I want you to know I have never been so depressed in my life."

I too remembered Dad, ashen and quiet the rest of that day.

"When I was chief of the surgical division at the State Hospital in St. Louis, I saw many insane people. But with them I always thought there was hope. A breakthrough could be right around the corner. With the Wassaic people there's not a hope in the world. They will be the way they are for the rest of their lives."

I thought of Emily, but said nothing. I nibbled a green plant with delicate feathers pushing through the ground to see if it was really chervil. My father twisted the tip of his cane into the soft soil of my garden. It was my birthday. I did not want to argue about hopelessness.

A few days later, before my father's flight back to St. Louis, we went to the Terrace Room of the Hartford Airport, a restaurant with pink tablecloths and white linen napkins, that looks out over the runway. My father ordered a dry martini on the rocks with an olive, and I, a glass of white wine. We watched in silence as a pair of army planes, like giant gnats, landed in formation on the runway.

"Well, there are moral issues at Wassaic I'm glad I don't have to face," he said at last, twirling his ice with a swizzle stick.

"Oh?" I hoped my voice sounded neutral.

"I've said it before and I'll say it again, that's the most depressing place I've ever seen. I'm worried about what it could do to Sam. I mean it must do bad things, working in a place like that."

"Dad, Sam loves his work." Those words came out quickly, while I thought of the recommitment Sam had made to his job during the layoff threat this past winter. It had been only a few weeks ago, when the new state budget was approved, that the threat had been removed. The Wassaic newspaper called it "Christmas in April," and so it was. But I'd not told my father about that time and would not mention it now. "He's able to make decisions that better the lives of the clients," I continued.

"First of all, that ludicrous euphemism 'clients.' That's the most inappropriate word I've ever heard. And the things I saw there. Kids that had to have their esophagus vacuumed after every meal just to keep them from choking to death."

"I've never seen such a thing," I said defensively.

"You haven't been to the right building then." He closed that part of our conversation. "However. The moral issue is this: There are circumstances under which we must not permit life to go on."

"These past months at Wassaic have taught me that I have no right to make those kinds of judgments."

"That's absurd," he interrupted.

"Hear me through, Dad. The other day I asked a question: Might a man with a degenerative brain disease, in the hospital for ingesting an entire bed sheet, might it not be a good time for him to die?"

"There. You see? That's a perfectly valid question."

"But it isn't. Because I don't know anything about his family. I don't know how attached they are to him, or if they're ready to let go. I know nothing."

A few weeks ago Gregory's teacher, Sherry, had shown me a photograph taken when he was admitted. It showed quite an ordinary young man with thin blonde hair and wire-rimmed glasses who looked as though he could work for IBM. Now his head was bald, his skin waxen. He required one-on-one care, became manic over food, was assaultive and assaulted, and was possibly dying because he had eaten a sheet. When I was told how ill he was, I thought: perhaps he should die. Maybe this is the time.

Then I asked Sherry if she had ever seen Gregory happy. She told me yes, when his brothers and sisters came to see him. I thought about that, and it made me understand that it was not up to me to think what the proper time for death might be. I couldn't gauge the value of life to his family. It may be that as long as life is treasured by anyone, until all hope is erased and transformed to memory, we should pull for recovery.

"Now you're back into the kind of thing you usually do, avoiding the issue," my father said lifting his finger in warning.

"I'm not avoiding, I just don't know what the standards should be." I looked at this white-haired man who held his finger over me like a cane. I knew I was going to say something provocative, but I was in it and could not stop. "Once you start asking questions about permitting life to go on, you'd have to start evaluating every old person declining in every nursing home."

"Hardly. They've led useful lives. These people haven't."

"Dad, at Easter we had a little girl home for the day with an IQ under thirty. She doesn't speak. She has odd mannerisms. But she loves music and flowers and motion. She brings great pleasure into my life and is showing me things I need to know. Things like endurance and hope. Things like joy from a dandelion gone to seed. I don't even know what useful means anymore."

The waitress put our antipasto on the table, smiling and commenting on the lovely day outside this sealed dining room. We sat grimly silent.

"You're still avoiding the issue," he said as she left, "and it's called euthanasia. But don't you forget, while you're being so non-judgmental, that you've made that decision before. When your mother died you were part of the decision not to take any heroic measures. We all agreed: no life-support systems."

"Yes, but she was in a coma. She was dying," I cried, while I thought, *that's not fair, that's not fair*. After five years of painful illness, I saw her face white against hospital sheets, her head jerking on the pillow, her eyes fixed to the right. Her breathing was hard and sometimes she moaned. I stood in the spot where her eyes stared and said words meant to comfort. Her eyes did not change; the words were to comfort myself.

"There were things that could have been done," he said looking down at his own pale hands, hands that looked as though a layer of pigmentation had been scoured off in the daily scrub that had been his life as a surgeon. "After she'd been in the coma two days we woke her up. She was so awake she called me on the phone, and she and your sister visited. Don't you remember that?"

I hadn't been there. My sister had called me from the hospital. It wasn't a stroke, it was encephalopathy, a metabolic imbalance caused by her useless liver and failing kidneys. And though she "woke up" for one day she was confused, frightened, "child-like," my sister had said.

"Don't you remember?" my father insisted. "I called her doctor. He said sure, they could do this and that, but each time they woke her up it would be for a shorter and shorter time."

I never knew that. I only knew she was dying and my feelings and prayers had turned upside down. If she had to die, let her die quickly.

My father changed the subject; even for him it was unbearable. We ate our lunch, but an agonized stillness surrounded me, as though I were alone in a room of tubes and pumps and dripping bottles. Every small sound became a crash.

In the waiting room I hugged my father goodbye. I retrieved the parking ticket I had forgotten to have the restaurant validate, and going up the airport escalator, I saw my father's broad back hunched over a magazine stand through the glass doors of the gift shop. When I came down again to the waiting room, I saw his back once more, as he hobbled haltingly on his cane toward the gate.

8

Gertrude was in her room, her back to the door. I had the feeling she knew someone was behind her, and who it was; I cleared my throat as I entered. She sat solid from the waist up, while below dangled her useless legs, each foot turned in like the head of a cane. I sat on her bed and we talked, as we had many afternoons. I asked if she felt Wassaic had become better or worse over the years.

"Oh better. Much much better. The people here used to treat you terrible. They were nasty. Very mean. If you didn't want to eat your dinner they put it on the floor and made you eat it like a dog."

"Did that seem . . ."

"What are you bothering me for every day?" Gertrude interrupted.

"I didn't know I was bothering you."

"Every day you come here. What do you want with me?"

"I've been taking pictures of you, and I've enjoyed our talks," I said, groping. "I come here because I like you."

"I want you to know I'm not that sort of woman."

"What sort?"

"The sort that likes to be bothered. I have my own friends. I have one who visits me at Christmas and Easter, and another who's going to take me out to dinner—maybe in July."

"I won't come again if I'm bothering you."

"Thank you."

And that was it. Her dismissal was dignified and clear. I left. I was barely in the hall when my hurt caught up with me, and I felt a throbbing in my throat. I could too well understand the reasons for Gertrude's rejection. Her life had been shaved to the bone, and suddenly there I was with interest and enthusiasm and my camera. She had a friend who visited her twice a year; that was the way she expected the world to behave. She did not trust my interest. She was right to ask what I wanted from her.

I did not know, myself. I had photographs I wanted to make contrasting her dignity and helplessness. I wanted to know about her past to help me understand what I was seeing now. But were these good enough reasons to invade her privacy, stir up uneasy memories?

At last I could cook Rhoda's moussaka on Thursday night and deliver it Friday. I would re-check the menu with her first.

Since Rhoda was not in her ward, I asked two aides who sat smoking and watching TV where she was.

One blew a smoke ring before she answered. "She's in the hospital." She turned back to the soap opera.

"Which hospital?"

"Poughkeepsie."

"What's wrong with her?"

"She's going to have an operation tomorrow." The aide did not take her eyes from TV. "Her hip."

Rhoda had been in pain since she fell and broke her hip. Though a pin had been put in, the hip had failed to heal. The operation could only mean a total hip replacement, the same operation both my parents had had. My mother's hip had disintegrated; although she never walked much after the operation because of other problems, she could sit without pain. My father had had one hip replaced, but needed the very operation Rhoda was to have on his other hip.

I asked where I could get more information on Rhoda. The aides were still engrossed in "General Hospital." A client—the one who had smeared feces the night I met Rhoda—was sitting on top of another client.

"Try the med room," said the aide reluctantly. "They might know something."

"You see, I was going to bring her dinner," I explained to the woman in white, a stethoscope around her neck, who sat at the med-room desk.

"Rhoda is on a 1,200-calorie diet. She's always trying to get sweets and cookies out of everyone. So she got you too."

"No, she wanted something else—a good Greek dinner. She said it's been years since she's had one." The woman

stared down at her paperwork as I talked. "Are you the doctor?"

"No, I'm the head nurse in this building."

"My name's Rebecca Busselle and I'm . . ."

"I know who you are. I've seen you wandering around
and I asked. I'm pretty skeptical of strangers in the building,
especially if they have cameras."

"And you should be," I said. One reason I had chosen to
work with the Speed Graphic was visibility; I wanted people
to be aware of what I was doing. I did not want to make
photographs on the sly. "I admire staff being protective of
clients."

She didn't smile, but the tension left her face and she
crossed her legs. "Rhoda's got another problem you may
not be aware of. She has a thickening of the esophagus,
which makes it hard for her to eat. She chokes easily. Not
only is she on 1,200 calories, but it's pureed."

I had seen pureed diets. No wonder Rhoda wanted moussaka.

"The esophagus is thickened all the way to her stomach.
She had a choking incident only a couple of months ago.
They tried to dislodge it with the Heimlich maneuver, but
it was so far down they couldn't. She turned blue and was
unconscious before they could get it out. She almost died."

Rhoda had warned me to bring the food directly to her
room, saying others would be too jealous if they saw it. I
had planned to inform the staff, but I also planned to bring
the things she asked for. Now I could imagine lettuce leaves
and thick crusts of Italian bread clogging the esophagus.

"Look, I think it's all right for her to have moussaka," the
nurse continued, "but be sure to chop it so fine it's almost
pureed. She needs that sort of gesture, and she could use a
friend. She absolutely hates me because I have to enforce

these dietary things. It's hard to have your full set of teeth, even bad ones like Rhoda's, and have to eat pureed."

I asked what caused the esophagus to thicken.

"We really don't know, but I suspect it could be a side-effect of the massive psychotropic drugs she's taken over the years. She's schizophrenic, you know. Very delusional. Very paranoid. Very assaultive.

"She probably doesn't belong here," the nurse continued, "but it's hard to imagine how her life would have worked out anywhere else. If she'd been in the outside world, she'd be in a psychiatric hospital. She has a great many delusions she can't let go of. Let me give you an example. She's got this idea that her cousin is going to take her home. She's always telling people that. One time her cousin came to visit, brought her ziti or something. They sat at the entrance hall table. When they finished eating, I sat with them. In front of Rhoda, I asked if she was planning to take Rhoda back with her at any time in the future. She said no. She was kind, said she loved her, but firm. From then on I could confront Rhoda with reality when she went into an aggressive state about going with her cousin. And she hates me for it. If she learns you've seen through her acts, she'll hate you too."

Why, I thought, should she have to be grounded in reality? Why should anyone have to face the truth that they've been abandoned by their family forever and will live out life in Wassaic? Why should she have to deal with the fact that two of her unit mates are shit smearers? Why go through the pain of a hip replacement to face the same tormented life again, filled with the demons of schizophrenia?

I said nothing, but the nurse felt my shock, and she seemed to soften. "Frankly, I'm looking for another job. I just can't stand this bureaucracy any longer. I've said that before and here I am, but this time I mean it." She took the stethoscope from her neck as though resigning on the spot.

"The medical staff is a mess. We just guess at things and most of the time we're wrong. I worked in the community for years and I know how good medicine is practiced. This isn't it. There's no coherent medical policy. After all, the director isn't a doctor. He sends down an order to reduce all psychotropic medications. Everything seems okay for a few weeks, then a month later everyone goes off the wall. Or they'll say, don't give medications on weekends. A medication respite, they call it. Can you imagine what that does? And word comes down from Albany that 33 percent of the clients are supposed to be on psychotropics instead of the 46 percent that are on them now. It all has to do with policy, not with what the individual needs.

"I hope to hell Rhoda gets some good care in the community hospital. They may try cutting out her psychotropics when they give her pain medication—then watch out."

9

"Vera, do you think you and I could take the Ward C kids to the Millerton Memorial Day parade? Afterward we could have a cook-out."

"I doubt it," she said. "Think about the food. Wonder Woman's on a sodium-free diet, June's is pureed, and Louisa's is ground."

"I have a food processor," I said defensively, but already I could see my pleasure in the idea slipping away as I imagined reducing hot dogs and hamburgers to mush.

"And I've heard that food service is only going to provide three picnics a year for the kids—Memorial Day, the Fourth of July, and Labor Day. They're going to do it *on the holiday* too, when the professional staff is off. They'll need all the help they can muster in the building. I'll never get off."

How easily that clinched it. Once again I would be giving freedom only to Emily.

That night Sam built a fire and I put chicken on the grill, the first time this season. The smoky smell of barbeque drifted across the lawn, and Katrina came over. I told her about my plan for Emily.

"You're going to bring her out in public in Millerton? People might get the wrong idea, Mom." I knew she was concerned about her new-found popularity, a fragile thing. "It's just my reputation I'm saving."

"If your friends see us you can be perfectly straightforward. Tell them your mother is working at Wassaic this year and this is a kid she's gotten to like a lot. It's the truth."

Max appeared as I turned the chicken. "What's this I hear about Emily?"

"She's coming on Memorial Day for a few hours."

"Coming here again?"

Katrina chimed in, "I told you she'd be back."

"Why does she have to come? I feel weird around her, Mom."

"Then make plans to be elsewhere." My voice was clipped, my words curt. After Easter I thought Max might be changing his attitude about Emily, and now that I saw him still being stubborn, it hardened something in me. "Go to your friend David's house for the afternoon—I don't care."

"Well, do you want me here when Emily's here? Does it make any difference to you?"

I looked at this twelve-year-old child, my youngest, and realized this was not a fair fight. He had to have fears about being displaced, and his "competition" was a speechless, handicapped child I saw every day. Maybe we could talk about it. I put my arms around him, rubbed my cheek on the top of his head. "Max, perhaps you're a little jealous."

He relaxed against me for a second, then slipped a shoulder under my elbow. "That's not it at all." He wiggled out from my hug. "I just want to know if I have to be here."

My hardness returned. "Yes, it does make a difference to me. I'd like you here, not for Emily's sake, but for your own, because I'd like you to overcome your discomfort."

And then the anguish I felt for Emily came out and I did what I had vowed not to do: I lectured Max. I talked about the conditions Emily lived in. I talked about Max's own humanity. I did it all wrong, but I meant every word I said. I told him he had one of the more comfortable lives on earth and a few hours of discomfort around Emily might be a good thing for him. "At any rate your discomfort means little compared to the continual pain of that child."

I heard myself dig in with every word. Until Max quit arguing back. Until Max left.

I was left with the silence of my own thoughts. I adored Max. His place was completely secure in my heart, and he knew it. It seemed impossible that he could really believe the things he'd been saying. Was he deliberately provoking me? It was a scuffle that was getting us nowhere. I pushed one way; he fell, got up, and pushed me harder the other way. It was a contest neither of us needed to undergo.

On Memorial Day I woke panicked over my disorganization. Neither Sam nor I had any cash. I feared there was no gas in the car. I didn't know if the supermarket was open— source of the cash, juice, and soft bread for Emily. "I'm just not going to have her over if we're not equipped to deal with her," I said churlishly.

Sam assured me I had half a tank of gas. He phoned the market and it was open. I ate an orange, then left to fetch Emily. Sam sewed a split in Max's blue pants so he'd be properly dressed to march in the parade.

No one on the shift had been informed that Emily was to leave, so she was dressed in a faded brown shirt and corduroys with too-long pant legs rolled thickly around her ankles. Her hair was uncombed.

No matter. I grabbed a complete change of clothing for her. We were off.

Millerton wasn't crowded. Boiling clouds and high humidity had kept the weekenders away, and mainly local people—relatives of the marchers—lined the two blocks of main street. American flags fluttered in front of each store. As we parked and helped Emily from the car, we saw our old friend Willard—Grange member, staunch supporter of the VFW Hall, active in town politics. He looked at us politely, then nodded and kept walking. Willard had no interest in being seen with anyone who was obviously from Wassaic.

Emily had Sam and me each by our wrists; we heard the drum announce the parade. There were flag bearers in military dress, firemen in uniform, three "officials" in business suits. The high school band marched by led by two dispirited majorettes without batons, but dressed in white satin skirts. "Clap, Emily," Sam said, and she did, two smashes of her hands like cymbals. Next came the ambulance, followed by the firetruck. Emily made a high-pitched noise so close to the sound of a siren it was surely an imitation.

And then came the two dozen members of the junior high school band. Max played trombone in the front row. I was sure he knew where we were, but he stared straight ahead as he passed. Katrina looked mortified, her face red behind her flute. She'd asked us not to be visible to her friends and we were. Many parents of her classmates worked at Wassaic, and many of their grandparents had worked there as well. Most threatening of all, Wassaic was the only future many of her classmates saw. In other places Emily might be only a curiosity; in Millerton she was a symbol.

"Clap, Emily," Sam said as some Legionnaires and a few scouts came by. But when a straggly group of kids on bikes brought up the end, she was ecstatic, making little frog hops and hitting her knuckles together. The parade was over. It had lasted five minutes, the length of Emily's attention span, and she had adored it.

I saw several people I knew and waved. No one came over to us.

We went to the supermarket before we went home, and Emily was eager to get out of the car in the parking lot. She saw that this stop didn't signify the end of a ride, but the beginning of another adventure. Sam told her to push the cart. She did, in a haphazard way, for she was overwhelmed, startled by the automatic doors, distracted by the wheels of other carts, mesmerized by the ceiling. I cautioned her when she vaguely reached for the middle of a stack of pickle jars, and though she looked as if she wanted to topple a pyramid of tuna cans, she didn't. But when we reached the meat counter, she became focused and alert. She'd found the most wondrous thing imaginable. As she trilled two notes between her teeth, her fingers hovered over the shiny plastic-wrapped packages, the shimmering pinks, mauves, maroons. She recoiled from the icy package when Sam told her to pick up some sausage. I was sorry we were buying something dull gray rather than the more alluring red meat.

□　　　□　　　□

I made egg and tuna salad for lunch, soft and chewable. Emily tasted the tuna but would not touch any more. She ate the egg salad then jammed a piece of bread in her mouth.

"Gross," Katrina said. "I can't believe how long it takes her just to chew one bite."

We were eating on the porch. Emily spent four hours a day, five days a week in a basement classroom. Her dayroom had two windows, but she couldn't see out them easily. Now the porch on which she ate was one giant window, and because she was distracted, she ate more clumsily than she did in Ward C.

There was a lull after lunch. I pulled some weeds from the garden; when I looked up, Sam had Katrina's bike out. Emily was sitting on it, and he was pushing her up the driveway, around the yard. I got my camera and found Emily and the bicycle in the viewfinder. She was soberly ecstatic. Her face was set in joyful concentration, her mouth open with wonder, her eyes intense. She gripped the handlebars; her feet stayed on the rotating pedals as though she'd been doing this for years, as though she were bringing up the end of a parade. I focused, amazed.

"Do you think they know that Emily's a cyclist at Wassaic?" Sam called out to me.

Sam had taken responsibility for Emily with such enthusiasm and good humor that I imagined us as grandparents—grandparents of an eighty-pound two-year-old. I remembered his enormous tolerance for our children when they were small, the fun he managed to extract from situations I regarded as trying. We once traveled down the Jong River in Sierra Leone on a rickety launch crowded with people, chickens, and hundred-pound bags of rice. There was no toilet; Katrina was only four. Sam reached out his long arms and cheerfully suspended her over the stern to pee. Both laughed and laughed.

An hour later Katrina stood by the closed car window waving goodbye, but Emily wouldn't look at her. She understood goodbye too well. She knew she was being taken back. I tried to say encouraging things during the ride, but Emily looked stunned and held tight to my forearm. Once she pulled on it and we swerved a little on the road.

If she'd been able to fool herself that this day would not end, it was over when we entered the Wassaic grounds. Grief contorted her face. Up the hill, around the circle, into the parking lot of Juniper Hall.

How, when you've seen a parade and ridden a bicycle, can you return to Ward C?

She croaked three wrenching sounds, then stumbled up the stairs like someone to the gallows. At the door to the ward she threw a body block against me. She pulled me from the door, all her weight against my arm. Her hand slipped, and she fell to the floor. I picked her up. And this time she let herself be pushed into the room.

I heard David's mother's car pull out of the driveway, then the screen door bang. "What's to eat? I'm starved," Max said, throwing his baseball glove on the counter.

"There's some tuna salad from lunch." I opened the refrigerator and the chill matched my voice.

"We played ball with a bunch of kids and David's dad—he throws a wicked slider." He took out the lemonade pitcher and filled a glass.

"Well, *your* dad gave a handicapped little girl her first ride on a bicycle." I began emptying the dishwasher.

"Yeah?" Max said warily.

"It's too bad you weren't here, Max. We missed you."

"Oh yeah? Doesn't sound like it. I don't get it, Mom. You said I could go to David's, and now you're mad because I did."

He was right. I had given him a choice, and because he hadn't made the one I wanted, I was resentful. I was trying to force him to behave as I wanted him to behave, to believe what I wanted him to believe. Intellectually I knew that never worked, but right now there seemed to be a huge gulf between my head and my heart. It seemed that I needed to control things, to have the perfect family. If Max was out of step, what did that say about us all? And mainly—because I believed that, of my three children, Max and I were closest in tempera-ment—what did that say about me?

10

"Doesn't this place smell good?" Ronald asked as I looked through the Dutch door of the behavior room. "It's such a relief. How the building smells is everything."

At last Butternut Learning had moved into its renovated building. Indeed there was no more smell of disinfectant and excrement, only the new smell of paint and tile adhesive. Each classroom was now self-contained. But the behavior room was barely bigger than the one they'd left. And though the plaster was fresh and the paint new, no acoustical tiles had been put around to absorb the sound of Manny's mono-tone yelling, "Sha-bam bam bam!" or Agatha's random ancient screams.

Nor had there been improvements in the learning materials. A plastic bowl of blocks and a few dead, tired toys were on a shelf. There were nine retarded, emotionally ill adults in the room with no way to give physical vent to their illness.

□   □   □

John Doe Number 11—Delmar Tate—sat in his recliner sucking his thumb, then sucking a finger.

"He don't want me to come near him this morning," said Clay, taking pegboards from the cupboard. "He pushed me away first thing, and if he don't want it, I won't have nothing to do with him."

It was time for "Aid to Daily Living" skills—teeth brushing, face washing, hair combing. John Doe unfolded from the recliner and staggered around the room, his arms flailing like a giant swimmer crashing through air. I moved to a more protected spot with my camera. But I knew he had seen me because I caught a gleam in his eye. I lowered my eyes quickly, the way I do with crazies on the New York subway.

John Doe staggered forward; Clay grabbed his arms, pushed him back in the recliner.

Someone screamed from the bathroom. Another resident fell to the floor self-abusively banging his teeth against the vinyl tile.

John Doe had his long legs in the air, gathering momentum to leave the recliner. "Lo lo lo lo lo," he sang as he unsteadily rose, his hands slapping at his path like King Kong, jerky and mechanical and comical, but powerful, frightening. I clutched my camera.

Another scream came from the bathroom. The resident again slammed his teeth on the floor.

Fred Law ran into the room. "There's going to be a fire drill!" The bell went off, Clay grabbed two residents, pushing a third ahead outside the door.

"Hurry everyone, you gonna get burned!" he yelled. "You gonna burn up!"

I was last out the door.

□   □   □

As though to prove that Mondays were difficult, the Butternut Learning team was short of staff. In Sherry's room there was only one aide, but they were managing because Gregory was still in the hospital, his condition unknown, from the bed sheet eating.

"I said, sit down Hazel!" Sherry stood hands on hips, face to face with Hazel, a woman who flicked her gnarled hands all day, and made continual, loud, grunting noises. "The clients don't get as much to eat on weekends," Sherry said to me. "Look how fast I'm going through this box of graham crackers. And I bring in contraband sandwiches for them too. You should see the scene at my house in the morning before work. The kitchen's a wreck—breakfast dishes all over the place. All my kids make their own school lunch, then it's my turn on the assembly line. But it's worth it. These folks are better behaved when their bellies are full."

Hazel advanced again, but Sherry backed her down with a glower. The grunting was so loud it filled the room, a raw, demanding sound. Then Sherry softened. "She's had a hard time. I don't know if this is true, but they say Hazel was found caged in the bottom of a defunct well on the Willowbrook grounds. When she came here she was abusive and assaultive. She played with her feces. She's been on an appalling number of drugs. The animal grunts she makes were once called 'humming.' "

Emily hummed too. If she'd been put in a well, what would she sound like now?

"Be quiet, Hazel," Sherry said between clenched teeth. "Some days her noise can drive you nuts, and some days I can tune it out, like the radio. But Mondays it's apt to drive me crazy." She whirled back to Hazel. "Okay, this is it. Something's got to give, kid, and it isn't going to be me. Shut that noise off." She dangled a graham cracker in front of Hazel. "None of this until you cut it out."

Hazel resumed pacing and grunting, knotting her fingers into strange shapes and holding them in front of her face. I thought of the Steiglitz study of O'Keefe's hands, gentle and powerful. Hazel's hands would show fear, imprisonment, boredom, self-destruction. O'Keefe's hands were arranged; she held her poses and Steiglitz worked slowly, carefully. I photographed Hazel's hands with the strobe as her fingers darted in front of my lens.

I brought my Walkman and earphones for Simon, another Butternut Learning resident, to hear the Bahamian gospel singing I thought would root his soul. I had no basis for this idea. A skinny man who looked West Indian, Simon seemed to be hearing wonderful internal music; he put out his sinewy arms and snapped his fingers to a beat while his head waggled loose on his neck.

"He'll never like that stuff," Sherry said when I told her what I planned to do. "It's not fast enough. Simon is really jiving."

The tape was set to go, the volume adjusted. As I put the phones over his ears, his face was transformed by the same expression that heard his inner music. A few seconds later he gently took off the earphones.

"Do it again," Sherry urged.

I put the earphones on again. Simon's eyes searched my face to see how I was connected to this sound. And again, after a few seconds he took off the phones. Perhaps Sherry was right, it wasn't jazzy enough. I turned the tape over to a syncopated, robust song. I put the phones on Simon. Out went the arms, fingers snapping, teeth grinning at me. This time he listened almost a minute before he took them off.

Why wouldn't he listen longer? Perhaps the sound was too intense; perhaps he didn't even make the connection that earphones carried the music; perhaps the music was wrong for him. Certainly I couldn't have expected Simon to be enthusiastic about music from the Bahamas any more than I could expect him to love a Brahms symphony.

I hadn't thought of my second cousin, Hannah, for a long time. For some years we both lived in the Boston area, I with my first husband and baby in the student quarters of Cambridge, and she with her parents in the patrician elegance of Chestnut Hill.

Now I realize that Hannah was retarded, though I'm sure I never heard that word used. A tall, knobby, gangly woman in her thirties, she was both loose-limbed and tight at the same time. Children affectionately called her "the Jolly Green Giant."

One day her mother called; they had a Wednesday afternoon subscription series for the Boston Symphony, but this week her mother had another engagement. Would I come for lunch, then take Hannah to the symphony? Hannah's limitations, she explained, were especially severe in dealing with money. She'd give me the fare, and I'd pay the cab to Symphony Hall and back to Brookline.

I was delighted. I got a baby sitter and dusted off my high heels. In their elegant, restrained Chestnut Hill home I ate a luncheon of clear soup and crustless cucumber sandwiches, trying hard not to be overwhelmed by Hannah's disjointed talk.

Hannah and I took a silent cab ride into Boston. I was nervous about finding our seats, but Hannah knew just where to go. Thrilled to be in such a venerable auditorium, I felt content looking around at the audience, since I found little to say to Hannah.

The opening piece was sad and Slavic, with a lush, wrenching melody. The Jolly Green Giant slunk lower in her seat. Midway through the piece she covered her eyes with her hands. By the time it finished she was weeping openly, rooting through her purse for tissues.

Next was a Mozart symphony, and with the opening bars Hannah was bouncing on her seat, giggling. I was mortified. Here in this sophisticated audience was an overgrown woman, shaking her head and laughing. My companion. My relative. There was no skipping out at intermission, nothing to do but endure it.

Because the program was long and varied, I saw Hannah go through a full range of responses that afternoon. And at some point I broke through my humiliation. I enjoyed the music. When it ended, Hannah applauded longer and louder than anyone. As well she should have, for she delighted in the concert more than anyone. I'd seen someone stripped of pretension, immersed in music with pure feeling.

The dandelions had gone to seed; the lawn was a tweed of furry gray puff balls. I blew one at Emily and she smiled tolerantly, tugging me on. She walked in a funny way, her toes turned it, giving a little at the knees, but with great determination. She smiled the whole time.

"Here comes the 'Little Kazoo,'" someone said as we passed. I thought that nickname was probably appropriate, the way Jolly Green Giant had fit Hannah.

As we walked the grounds I wondered, had I really felt this strongly about Emily from the beginning, or was it, as a friend used to say, "the time we waste on someone that makes us love them?" I couldn't remember. But I felt so attached to this child in the present, her little demands, her little happinesses. I very much wanted her to leave the institution for a better life, yet last week when Sam told me there had been some delays in getting her new building ready, I rejoiced secretly.

After our walk, back in her room, she plunked in my lap. She'd done this before, but never so steadily or for so long. She was amazingly light, almost as though she were only putting half herself on me. She pulled my arms around her and stared intently at me in her unfocused way. She flicked her fingers at my lips, exploring them. Suddenly I understood. "Do you want a kiss, Emily?"

Immediately she put her cheek forward, and when I kissed it she laughed and stared at me again. I gave her another kiss. And another. It was the easiest thing I had ever done for her.

11

Sherry wasn't a "typical" teacher. There were none. What made her interesting to observe—and what I liked most—was her passion. She was neutral on nothing. Sometimes there was a feigned passivity, a back bowed to authority, but it was only a disguise. Sometimes there was genuine exhaustion, for she was a single parent with three boys. But basically Sherry liked drama and plenty of it.

Today, I didn't see Hazel in Sherry's room—Hazel, with her constant grunts, was obstinate and disruptive. She was also one of Sherry's favorites. I asked where she was.

"Let's see, this must be Monday." Sherry put her hand to her forehead in mock contemplation. "Hazel's at the hairdresser. Monday's her day."

"Come on Sherry, where is she really?"

"You've been here too long, Rebecca. You've lost the capacity to distinguish between sarcasm and truth. Hazel is at the hairdresser. Her hair hadn't been combed in three weeks.

We tried here, but we couldn't get a comb through her frizz, it was so matted. So we called her residence and told them to send over something to relax her hair. Of course, they were incensed because maybe that meant they hadn't been doing their job, but we calmed them down and made a deal. We'd comb her hair five days a week over here, if they'd just take it on the weekends. They were delighted with that arrangement."

Gladys came in dragging Hazel by the wrist. An enormous black woman in her early forties, Gladys wore her hair in two pigtails secured with pink bows, giving her face an incongruously childish look. Everything else about her looked powerful. It was easy to imagine how she might look overwhelming to a client. She stopped dead when she saw me. "What are *you* doing here?" she roared.

"What I'm always doing, Gladys. Taking more pictures."

"Well you better take one of her then." She pushed Hazel in front; her once-matted hair was now glistening. Gladys ran a comb smoothly through it, while Hazel grunted into her hands. "I had to cut out all them snarls."

"Did she like having her hair worked on?" I thought of African women, their heads in each other's laps for hours while fingers parted and braided and pulled.

"Did she like it? *Shit no.* She carried on a storm."

"But I can tell she likes it now," Sherry said. "She's letting me touch her hand, which shows she's not really upset. And look, she's smiling a little! Only three weeks in here and she's learned to smile."

Sherry turned to Gladys. "Okay Gladys, I want to show you something that came while you were gone. But first I'm going to shut the door, because other people don't like to hear you scream."

Sherry had a memo from her building head. Curt and to

the point, it said all professional staff and therapy aides were to be allowed only thirty minutes for lunch. No longer would they be allowed to add on a fifteen-minute coffee break. Unless there was a very special reason to extend the lunch period, this rule would be enforced. The memo was issued because three therapy aides were caught returning seven minutes late from lunch last week.

Gladys read the memo slowly. There was silence in the room; even Hazel had ceased grunting. Glady's pigtails were vibrating by the time she reached the second paragraph. *"Up you ass!"* she screamed, facing the closed door. Her hands were on her hips; her flesh shook. "Who these fuckin' people think they is? The state pay me for a thirty-minute lunch and two fifteen-minute breaks every day. Now if I takes my break at lunch, it's because I needs that time, and that the way it be."

Sherry shrugged. "Gladys, don't get all agitated. Remember our motto." She pointed to a crudely crayoned sign above her desk:

> INSANITY IS HEREDITARY.
> WE GET IT FROM
> OUR KIDS.

Negatives from the Wassaic photographic archives had been crammed in a table top card file and two wooden boxes twice the size of a shoe box. I hoped to find images that would show more of what Wassaic had been like in decades past, when it was the "State School." Age had turned the glassine envelopes tan and brittle, and the ink-scrawled captions were dulled. I pulled out the first negative by its edges, holding it to the window light. "Slugger, 1958"—a dog lay on a flowered rug. "Dotty, 1950"—a portrait of a tightly coif-fured matron with a lace collar. Prize bulls. Weddings. An Amenia High School dance. State photographers had clearly used Wassaic time for their own freelance work.

I stacked the boxes in my car, took the negatives to my studio, and spread them out on my light-table. The dust made me sneeze. And there I found history constructed from formal events. Decoration Day, 1946, with bands and flags. Twenty-five-year employee dinners. Staff awards. "Minstrel Show, 1952"

The few existing negatives of residents showed them well turned out, the boys busy at industrial arts in fully equipped workshops, the girls practicing their skills in the school beauty parlor. One was titled "Retard Fishing Near Employee Pool," and when I held the emulsion close to my eyes, I saw a child who could have been Emily.

Finally, there was a collection of pathology negatives of brains. I looked at them in awe; I held them in my hand. Some brains had been sectioned and lay on trays like cauli-flower slices. Most were whole.

I knew the human brain was the approximate size of a grapefruit; I cranked up the enlarger head until the image on the easel was twice that size. It looked transparent and unreal. I made the exposure; when I developed the print, it came as slick and wet from the fixer as the brain had from the skull.

I remembered pithing a frog in ninth-grade biology, insert-ing a needle to destroy the brain. I thought of the "treatment" for mental illness—lobotomy. I thought of Emily's brain, in-completely formed; Gregory's, deteriorating; my mother's, her electrical impulses weakening as death approached. I thought of my children's, strong and developing.

I looked at the brain print, the rippled cortex dividing into corrugations, organizing into lobes, the cerebellum tight below it. This brain controls everything we are—muscles, breath, memory, intellect, sight—everything.

Summer

1

In one day summer came, steamy and powerful. Flies thrummed and circled the ceiling of Locust Hall, deftly avoiding the wall-mounted blue lights meant to vaporize them. Though Locust—a men's residence—had been renovated like the rest of the campus, it looked shabby. The furniture was only the essentials, curtains were fabric lengths nailed to windows. The halls had super-graphics on the walls—as did all the residential buildings—and had they not been there, Locust would have been without a single adornment except for the bulletin board that held two posters: one for AA and one for a drug rehabilitation center.

"My name's Ken and I'm supposed to show you around," said the aide who slouched toward me. Thick glasses made his eyes look tiny; dandruff snowed on his beard and chest. "I may not be here tomorrow though. It may be I'm getting canned. They want to let me go because of time abuse. I've had a lot of trouble with my knees, been to the doctor a lot, and he told me not to work. I got notes to prove it. But they don't care. They want me out.

"It'll be ten weeks before I can get my unemployment," Ken continued, "and I don't know if I can live ten weeks without a paycheck. Me and my girlfriend are planning to get married." He removed his glasses and the little rat eyes became full, set in a kind and childish face.

"We live a few miles from here in the Beautiful Hills apartments." I knew "Beautiful Hills"; they were shoddy motel units occupied primarily by state workers, often the site of domestic violence. "Before I started working here I was on welfare, and that ain't no fun, I can tell you."

I followed him through the first floor of this mens' unit, dark except for the television sending blinked light and static sounds. The bedrooms had no decorations at all, no bedspreads, nothing on the tables. Nothing.

"They said at personnel maybe I could keep my job if I got a special recommendation from the director. But I ain't gonna kiss no asses. That's not why I'm here. I just want to do my work when I'm not sick, not suck up to bosses."

In the hall I saw Gregory, whom I'd not seen since he had eaten the bed sheet and been hospitalized. His thumb was stuck in his mouth, forefinger hooked over his nose as though he needed a place to hang the weight of his adult hand. His eyes were huge in his head. An aide wearing plastic surgical gloves held him by the arm. "He's soiled himself and he's been playing with his feces," he said disgustedly as he walked Gregory past.

Upstairs, Ken unlocked one door, then another. This was the first locked ward I'd seen—the notorious Ward 13. Ken said it had been locked since a resident got loose and attacked the building supervisor.

In there were men I'd known in Butternut Learning: Jacob, quiet, frightened, muttering in his mysterious Slavic language; Melvin, who had bad days but seemed easily pacified in Sherry's room; Ron, who frightened me, flicking his fingers in his mouth and just missing them as he chomped down with guillotine speed; Earl, from the Behavior Unit, who was a biter and a hepatitis carrier.

"But here's the one to be careful of," Ken said nodding at a cherubic-looking young man who circled me with great curiosity. "He does things to women. Stay away from him."

The young resident circled and stared. I pivoted as he moved, my face tight on his. And I saw his eyes were low, on the camera at my waist. Once he put out his hand to it, and Ken barked at him not to touch.

I asked if he wanted his picture taken. He gave me a big, gummy grin. In my most firm voice I told him where to stand. He pulled his sweatshirt off over his head, turned his face coyly, and grinned again. I made the exposure. He clapped and danced.

"It's a tough place to work," Ken said, as he watched me photograph. "You gotta watch out. But I've worked for the Division of Youth—the prison system. Now there's one place you gotta stay on your toes. Wouldn't want to be high on nothing there."

"Wouldn't want to be high or nothing here," I said, watching the young resident begin again to circle me like a panther.

Ken shot me a pained expression, as though I'd been sent by the administration to test him. "No, man." His voice became high and whined. "But a few beers with dinner, what can that hurt?"

□   □   □

When I developed the negatives from Locust, I found four of the dozen blurred. I put them on my light-table to see if the problem had been the focus, but in each case the entire negative was blurred. That could only have been caused by my not holding the camera steadily. Camera shake. I had tried to deny my fear on the locked ward in Locust, but there it was, unmistakable on the negatives.

"So what are you doing with that camera? Make sure you don't have me in any of those pictures." A young aide licked his finger tips, then slicked back his blond hair to expose early-thinning temples. "No one takes my picture. They tried to take my ID picture twice and both times I moved and blurred it." With his palms he touched the outline of his hair.

Fred Law bounced back in the room from his coffee break. "All right Albert, snap to."

"You still here?" Albert said later when he came back from his lunch break, bread crumbs undisturbed on the front of his shirt. "If you like it so much, why don't you get a job as a therapy aide?"

"I probably should. It would be good for everyone to work as an aide for a while."

"Might be good for everyone but the clients, 'cause the therapy aides aren't good for the patients, most of them. These people would be better off with robots. See this gut on me?"

I couldn't miss it. Albert jiggled a ponderous belly.

"That's how you tell how many years someone has worked here, by the size of his belly. What you're looking at now is a seven-year belly. I've gained fifty pounds since I've worked here, 'cause until two weeks ago I worked evenings. That shift just flicks on TV. That's where they sit until the clients need supper. Then at six they start watching TV again until the shift is over. So that's how you get the gut, just sitting there all those years.

"I've worked every shift. Listen, you want to hear something? I was a grade eleven, supervisor of the evening shift in my building—I won't tell you which one, I might get in trouble. When I became supervisor I wanted people to do things right. None of this TV watching all night. And they were furious. The aides told me they were going to get me out. They didn't want their routine disturbed. When you get a new grade you're on probation for a year. And these guys promised that within one year they'd get me out. They did everything they could. Started taking two- and three-hour dinner breaks. Played cards in the bathroom. I wrote them up for it. But nothing worked. It seemed the more they got themselves in trouble the more they did."

Fred Law interrupted Albert to have him help serve lunch. Stuffing a slice in his mouth, Albert distributed bread distractedly; he wanted to finish his tale.

"So it's ten-and-a-half months into my probation year. One night two aides beat a client black and blue. I mean he had welts all over him, he's a mess. And they say I did it. They go to the building head and say they heard screams from a room and found me beating this client with my belt buckle. It's a complete lie, but it works. I'm fired. And you know, I can't say they didn't warn me fair and square. Said they'd get rid of me before the year was up." He slid his finger from ear to ear, a knife slicing flesh.

"I was in arbitration for eight months before I was cleared. Only then the administration had me. They demoted me from my job because they said even if I didn't do it, as a supervisor I should have known who did and reported them. So that was it."

Fred called him again to help with lunch, and I followed Albert to the table. He spoke over his shoulder as he tied bibs and adjusted plates.

"When they demoted me I was very, very careful to do things just the way I was told. After a few months my supervisor wrote an evaluation saying I was lazy and did only the minimal amount. Now, as a full-fledged grade nine I wasn't supposed to be evaluated at all. So I went to the union, got it taken out of my record. Supposedly taken out. There's probably some trace of it somewhere. And that's the really terrible ending to all this. I'm pretty sure I'm going to be black-balled. I want to get a better job in the system, but I have a feeling they'd just as soon not deal with me at all. I probably don't have a future here.

"But you know what I'm going to do?" He brushed the lunch crumbs from his shirt as though that were the first step. "Go on a diet. Yes I am, in a month. If I get rid of this gut things will be better."

Stuart brought his class of nine outside on a glorious spring day. He walked them a hundred feet from Butternut to a concrete pad, shaded by a corrugated tin roof that had rusted along its furrows.

"Wassaic in the summer," he sighed. "When I worked in the music therapy department six years ago we used to have music all the time. We'd get big amplifiers, wire in our instruments, and go to it. The staff would all be under the trees and the clients would be having seizures in the sun."

As he hung his guitar from his neck and started singing a Beatles song, I looked for a place to sit. One bench had a jagged end, as though chewed by giant teeth. Another bench was in the hot sun. A third bench was empty except for Earl, whom I'd seen a few days ago in the locked unit of

Locust. I sat down three feet from him and reached in my camera bag for a film holder.

Earl pounced. His hand grabbed my forearm. His fingernails sank in. Later, I remembered a flash of madness in his eyes as he leaned over me.

It was a vicious pinch and I reacted instinctively smacking his hand from my arm.

"Did he get you?" Stuart said looking up, still playing the guitar.

I felt humiliated. I had considered myself extremely cautious, my peripheral vision acute enough to keep me from this sort of thing. So I told Stuart it was nothing and moved to the other side of the concrete pad. Then I looked at my arm. Earl had broken the skin; around the wound was an angry red welt and white bumps, like an allergic reaction. And it hurt.

"Fill out an incident report," the nurse said as she washed my arm with Phisohex and put on an antiseptic. She was most casual and so was I. It was nothing. Still, as I left I pointed out again that the skin was broken. "Is Earl by any chance a hepatitis carrier?" I asked, embarrassed by my fear.

The nurse laughed. "You bet he is. But it's got to be blood to blood—his blood to yours—to transmit hep."

2

It was Emma's sixty-second birthday. Last week, in her halting, contracted speech, she told me there was to be a cake in Evergreen Transitional.

The recreation therapist—unshaven, wearing a thin, rumpled T-shirt—said he hadn't seen Emma. "But we're not going to have a party here. I haven't got time for that. We had some cake the other day so we wished her happy birthday then. If she's here at all today she'll be in that room." He gestured to the large holding room where clients waited for lunch.

"Yes, I guess if it's Thursday it must be Emma's birthday," the holding-room aide said. "But she's not here. She's getting her new wheelchair."

The door opened and there was Emma, all smiles, her hair tied back with lavender yarn, her handsome face glowing. She was sitting in her new electric wheelchair. It was a beauty. She glided into the room smooth and free with none of the jerking of the old chair. Before, Emma had to push a control handle—a joy stick, they called it—with her clawed hand; now she could control the movements of the new chair by touching her forehead or temples to air cups mounted inside a ring that circled her head. Furthermore she was able to sit up straight because custom supports had been built into the chair.

The physical therapist sat at the desk doing paperwork. She explained to me the procedure for getting a chair such as this.

"The clients are evaluated for their needs and whether they're bright enough to use one. Then the chair is ordered. Getting it takes ten months to a year. Medicare pays, so that's no big problem. And these things cost." She turned the form so I could see: One wheelchair, $3,285.00. Half the price of a new car for Emma's mobility, her freedom, her life.

I wished Emma happy birthday and placed a package on her tray. I'd struggled over what to get her. She had jewelry, most of which she never wore; she said necklaces gave her a rash. She was on a restricted diet, so no candy. Perfume seemed inappropriate.

She instructed me to open the card first, then the package

wrapped in shiny paper. I opened it slowly to make her anticipation last longer and to reckon with my choice. Why on earth had I bought such a thing? What had I intended her to do with a chintz, quilted cosmetic case? We both looked at the gift bewildered. I picked it up, my voice full of false enthusiasm, but as I opened it I saw a mirror glued inside the flap. There was a reason for the gift after all. I laid it flat on her wheelchair tray. Emma looked down, her face pulled tight by a huge smile, because for the first time she could see the controls of her new chair, like a crown around her head.

Rhoda Alexius was back in Birch Hall after her hip operation. Her face was that of a beautiful young girl who'd aged well, cheeks firm and smooth, chin tight, skin the color of an early summer tan. Only her rotted teeth betrayed her age, each tooth indistinct from the next, a sloping mass in her mouth.

"Remember you said you'd bring me moussaka?" she called as I walked toward her bed.

Sheepishly I promised again to make it.

She said she was out of pain now, though she felt discomfort because she had to lie with a styrofoam wedge between her legs. I could not equate the calm, lucid person who said that with the one the nurse had described as delusional, paranoid, and assaultive.

"Every morning I wake up, brush my teeth, then say my prayers. Every day I pray that God will change my luck."

"Your luck has been changed," I interrupted. "You're out of pain. That will make a difference."

"That's right. No one can stand pain all the time. But I got to get out of here. I can't stand it here with all these dummies. My cousin came to see me yesterday. When I saw her, I started to cry. 'Don't cry,' she said. 'I'm going to take you home soon to live with me.'"

I did not tell her the nurse had said that this was a fantasy; her luck had not changed that much.

"I need bright people I can talk to. I can't talk to any of these people. I'm miserable." She said "miserable" rolling out syllable after syllable, as though it were a word as endless as her pain.

Eight other clients sat in chairs along the walls. They stared quietly into space, except for one old woman who screamed "Troublemaker! Troublemaker!" Three young therapy aides sat at the table, absorbed in a soap opera.

"You've lost weight," I said to Rhoda. "You look well." I searched for any words that would distract her, make her feel more positive. Then I caught myself. Would I do this in a concentration camp, counsel someone to "make the best of it," look on the sunny side? The compliments I was handing out to Rhoda were pacifiers.

"I'm thin because I haven't been eating. You wouldn't eat this mush either." I thought of Rhoda's throat closed down from years of psychotropic drugs; yet her teeth were still in her mouth, her taste buds were intact.

"You know what I want to do? I want to go out to dinner. I want to go to Four Brothers. I went there twice. I had spaghetti there, and I had salad too. It makes my mouth water to think about salad."

Rhoda looked at me. After a silence she said, "I wish you could see me sometime when I'm not miserable. When I was a young girl I was miserable because I had to do so much work. I had to do all the cleaning, mop the stairs, do the laundry—in a tub with a washboard, not a washing machine. I was always tired and miserable. But better days are going to come, I pray for that. My cousin will come for me and I'll go to her house. I'll help her do all the cooking, and I'll help her clean."

Brenda was in her early sixties, corpulent and ungainly. She looked at me and yelled, "I don't want my picture taken. Don't take my picture."

I promised I wouldn't, but that didn't calm her. She screamed obscenities. The other clients became grim. "She's crazy," one said. Another circled his ear with his index finger, then pointed to Brenda.

"The clients hate it when she gets this way," an aide said. "Try not to pay any attention to her. She loves an audience."

I did try, but it was hard because she yelled "cunt" and "bitch" and "fucking" this and that. She screamed at me never to take her picture. I sat with my camera zipped in my bag. She pointed to her groin, bumped her hips and big stomach, waggled her rear.

"This is nothing," the aide said. "She gets into some pretty heavy stuff. One time when some big shots from Albany were here she went on one of these things, and in one second, while no one was looking, she had her dress over her head and was spread-eagled on a table."

The aide took her off to calm down, but when they returned Brenda was still screaming. "You cunt! You whore! That man slapped me!" She whirled around to a man feeding a client. The other clients were calmly eating. After their initial anger, they shut her out. They had to. She screamed "pussy" and "snatch" pointing to herself again.

"It's really amazing about her," said the aide—a sexy woman in tight, tight jeans. "She'll go off like this, and then it's like she comes to. She goes around and apologizes for what she's done to everyone. But somehow I kind of like her. She has spirit, you know? At least she doesn't just sit there."

An ancient-looking woman slumped over her arms, head on the table, the window light slanting across her back. I isolated her for a photograph, but just before I pressed the cable release, she sat up in the chair. Cataracts clouded her eyes; her fingers were clawed with arthritis, her skin was a waxy yellow. Her head fell back in a soundless scream, her mouth a black open cave.

My mother looked like that when she was dying. She lay in a coma, head arched back, mouth gaping. Her skin was parchment, so thin her bones almost pushed through. Her eyes stared out at me though she could not hear her name when I cried it.

"Kathleen, do you want to go to the bathroom?" the teacher shouted, as though to someone in a coma. So the woman was named Kathleen, my sister's name. As she was being wheeled off I asked how old Kathleen was. The teacher didn't know. Maybe sixty-two or sixty-three. A little younger than Mother when she died. Only Kathleen wasn't dying; she was going to continue to live—blind, helpless, able only to scream with her body. Mother pulled out of it by dying.

Clients waited for lunch in the holding room. Brenda sat there, large and calm in a pink dress, pink bags under her eyes. "Don't take my picture," she warned again.

An hour ago she had screamed obscenities as she pointed to her groin; now she was regal in her heaviness and tranquility. I gathered some courage and went over. Like so many of the older, "higher-functioning" women, she was eager to talk about her life to anyone who would listen, and without any preliminaries, she began to tell me her life story.

"I was born in Brooklyn," she said as I pulled up a chair. "My mama and daddy were born in Italy. Mama couldn't speak any English. I always spoke Italian with my mama. But I don't have anyone to talk it to here. *Buon giorno.*

"I'm a Catholic. I used to go to church every day. Now I don't go to church. The priest used to come around, but now he don't do that. I remember all the saints: St. Paolo, St. Giovanni, St. Francesco, all of them.

"My mama had long dark hair." Brenda's hair was short, the institutional cut. "She died when I was little. I remember how she looked when she was laid out. They combed her hair over her shoulders. She wore her best dress, a pink one. I remember how she fit perfect into the box. The priest was there and all the saints too." Brenda's eyes had tears in them, as mine had tears when I saw Kathleen this morning.

"I guess we never stop missing our mothers after they die," I said.

"No, we don't," Brenda said, blinking a tear onto her cheek.

At home Sam and I were busy with gardens and yard work; dinners had become haphazard and late. It was nine o'clock before we sat down on the screen porch, with blue fish, salad, and wine. The evening light was almost gone; a white moon rolled up above the hemlocks.

Sam said he was having the glazed tile in the Juniper wards painted and covered with a fabric wallpaper to make the ward look less institutional. He'd been told by the only parents who regularly came to visit their child that it was unnecessary; the residents couldn't appreciate it and it was only being done for the staff. "We have no idea how much people are taking in," Sam said. "There's no way to measure what profoundly retarded individuals think of their environment."

Again I remembered my mother in a coma, dying. There

was a nurse who always talked to her: "We never know how much someone can hear and understand," she had said. I spent the next day at my mother's bedside, while her life slowly, painfully drained from her, and told her over and over how much I loved her.

3

"I haven't heard anything new about moving to my cousin's house," Rhoda said, looking up at me from her wheelchair. "Maybe it will be soon. I have everything packed downstairs— a trunk, and a box of books. My social worker said, 'I wouldn't start packing yet, Rhoda,' but I've done it anyway.

"Do you know the first time I saw my cousin I didn't recognize her? But why should I have—I hadn't seen her in thirty-two-and-a-half years. That's how long it had been.

"One day a few years ago they put me in the sun room— they call it that 'cause the sun sometimes comes in it. Then they tell me there's someone here who knows me. I look around but I don't see nobody. There's a stout woman there, but I don't know her. 'Rhoda,' she says. 'Don't you even know your own cousin?' The last time I saw her she was nineteen and a little slip of a thing. Now here's this big woman trying to tell me she's my cousin. But then she calls me Rhody, and I know it's true, it's my cousin. After thirty-two-and-a-half years it's her. 'Forget the half year, Rhody,' she says, but I can't."

"These are my sisters," Emma stammered, her mouth and tongue working for the words.

The two women were identical, still twinned as strongly now as they must have been as toddlers in matching sunsuits.

Their suntans were the same shade, their wrinkles carved to the same depth. They unloaded paper bags onto the table, moving with the efficiency and timing of one person.

"I'm Adele. Won't you have some fruit, or some ice tea?" Silver bracelets tinkled on her arm as she reached into one of the sacks.

"And I'm her sister Lenore." She reached behind her neck to retie the halter top of her bright orange dress, then turned to her sister to recheck the knot. "We haven't seen Emma in two, or maybe it's three years. Last year I was too depressed because of my divorce, and the summer before—what were we doing?—oh yes, we were on the Cape."

"I'm glad to see Emma in such good shape," Adele said. She fingered the ends of long dangly earrings, eyes darting to my camera. "Last time I came here she was a mess, slumped over, didn't even know who we were or why we were here. They were giving her some medication and the person in charge said maybe they gave her a double dose by accident, maybe that's why she was so dopey."

"I promise you, I was mad as could be," interrupted Lenore. "I told them I didn't want that happening to my sister. I guess they stopped doing it, because she looks like she half knows what's going on now, don't you Emma?"

Emma nodded happily. I cringed at the words "half knows." Emma took everything in fully.

"And you're not shaking so bad now, are you Emma? That was the Valium, I guess." Emma nodded again.

A red-checked plastic cloth had been spread over the Birch vestibule table, and the door propped open to let the summer breeze in. Emma sat in her wheelchair, her treasured photo album on the tray.

"I don't even have an album myself, I just keep the pictures in an old drawer," Lenore announced. "And look, here's

Emma and she's got herself this lovely album. Isn't it wonderful?"

"Do you have a picture of Mama I can have?" Emma asked.

"I only have one, and I'm not giving it to you."

"Maybe I got one you can have, Em," Adele said hesitantly, flicking her eyes to her sister.

Lenore pulled out a lizard wallet, took out two pictures of children, apologized for the fact that they were old, and passed them around.

"Who are these kids?" Emma asked.

"My grandchildren," Lenore said, sounding wounded.

Emma had never met them. "Are these pictures for me?" she asked.

"No, they're the only ones I have."

Lenore stretched, pulling her wrist above her head and bending to the side. "We're three years older than Emma, you know," she said giving the proud smile of someone in good physical shape who knows it. "We were twenty and she was seventeen when she went away. We just couldn't lift her any more. She was breaking all our backs." Hands on her hips she began making circles with her torso.

"Adele, tell her," Emma said nodding at me. "Tell her. Didn't I almost finish high school?"

"What? You've been drinking, Emma."

"I did, I did, I almost finished. Tell her, Lenore."

"Oh Emma, that's some idea you have." Lenore stopped exercising and laughed. "You never went to school at all and you know it. What are you trying to pull?"

Because she lived in a room with women far more retarded than she, who couldn't speak and soiled themselves, Emma had invented a life before the institution. School was Emma's self-deception, the thing she told herself was true to get her through another day.

Adele joined her sister laughing, head back, curls shaking, earrings bouncing against her neck.

Emma watched the twins, then her palsied mouth twisted to the side, and a low gurgle, something like laughter, came from her, too.

4

I took ten days off from Wassaic. The last few months had been so difficult I needed time to reflect on them. But leaving made me deeply aware of the difference between my position and that of the staff or residents: When I was exhausted I could leave. When they were exhausted, they had to stay and face it.

Instead of walking with Emily at five o'clock I went to tell her I'd be away. Because I wasn't going to take her walking was no reason not to see her, I reassured myself. And indeed she pulled my wrist to go outside with only half strength, not as demanding as usual. I sat, and she plunked on my knee. She sensed something was different, and she seemed to understand when I looked hard into her face and told her that I was going away for ten days, but I would be back. She let me hug her, but when I said goodbye and asked her to wave, she began to drone one low note.

In mid-afternoon half the deck outside the Hackney's kitchen on Martha's Vineyard was in shade, half in brilliant sun. I wanted an hour alone with Lucy Hackney—a lawyer who represented the rights of the handicapped. But her mother was visiting—Mrs. Durr—a lively, outspoken woman of eighty. Also there for the 4th of July weekend was Mrs. Durr's namesake, Lucy's oldest child, Virginia, who was retarded. I'd first known Virginia when she was a little girl in Princeton, where her handicap had presented itself as a sluggishness, a dullness that was of little interest to me in my hyperactive new-mother state. Later she went "away" to school. Now, in her late teens, she was self-sufficient enough to be in a program where she worked and shared an apartment with another girl.

"Make yourself a glass of ice tea," Lucy called as she came out on the deck in her bathing suit. "Virginia and I are going for a quick dip. We'll be back in five minutes."

The screen door banged again, and Virginia came out, also in a suit, tugging at a strap. "This suit's too tight," she said hooking her thumb under the spandex.

"You're right. Go to the Vineyard Dry Goods tomorrow and get a new one," Lucy said.

Not a remarkable mother-daughter exchange, I thought as they walked across the lawn to the beach, except that they'd come through so much to get to this point: Virginia was accepted in the community (as they passed the Yacht Club tennis court I heard people call out greetings); Virginia was able to go to the store alone and make her own choices; Virginia was independent and free. And Lucy was able not only to "cope" with her, but to make Virginia and other handicapped people the core of her work.

"Let's sit in the shade," Mrs. Durr said coming out of the kitchen with her tea. Generously sized, she eased herself into a metal patio chair. Lucy crossed the lawn again, beads of the ocean on her tan legs; a few seconds later Virginia trailed after, still tugging at her bathing suit.

"Let's sit in the sun," Lucy said, slipping a T-shirt over her suit. Virginia left to change into shorts, and I began telling Lucy about Wassaic.

"I've only known one child in my life who was in the shape that most of the people at that institution must be in," Mrs. Durr said when I paused. "He was the son of a dear friend of mine, and I must say a life like his raises grave considerations about the ethics of allowing such a child to live. There's so much talk of pulling the plug now, and having been intimate with this family makes me really wonder."

"Oh mother, how can you begin to talk about who should live or not? There are so many moral and legal considerations. And there are as many individual cases as there are handicapped children."

"The whole family went to pieces because of him," Mrs. Durr continued. "He ruined my friend's life. The child couldn't speak, couldn't dress himself, couldn't do a thing except be destructive—not out of malice, you understand, but because he couldn't help himself. That's just the way he was. His mother tried and tried to get him into institutions, but no place would take him. Finally, when he was twenty, she got him into a place in Tennessee. And quite shortly after he died a horrible death there. He died eating worms. They gave him a pass to go around the grounds, and I guess no one knew it, but he'd learned how to dig worms. It wasn't until after he died that they found out what killed him."

As her grandmother finished this tale, Virginia came out in white shorts and sneakers, and sat on the deck railing. I asked Lucy if she knew anything about an incident that had been in the news, which involved retarded children from a private school near Philadelphia.

"Certainly. It involves the Crestview school. Lots of people in the Princeton program went there—I think your roommate did, didn't she Virginia?"

"Oh yeah. Lots of my friends did." Virginia rolled her eyes to the left as she thought, as though reading off a cue card.

"Yes, it's been very much in the papers recently," Lucy

continued. "There's a dinner theater in Philadelphia—a place to have supper and see some sort of show. It seems the kids from Crestview saved their money and bought tickets to this dinner theater. There was an old movie star and nightclub entertainer doing the show that night. The management had done everything it could to accommodate Crestview—many of the kids were in wheelchairs. They'd placed everyone as close as possible to the front table. Well, the movie star came out, saw these wheelchairs and handicapped kids, and refused to go on with her show until they were removed. Needless to say there's been a big uproar. She was fired and now claims she never did such a thing, although there are hundreds of witnesses."

"Well I never heard of a thing so dreadful," Mrs. Durr said shaking her head.

Virginia shook her head.

"By the way, Virginia," Lucy said, "I stopped by the cerebral palsy camp the other day. Do you know they now have twice as many volunteers as they can accept?" She turned to her mother and me. "Virginia was a volunteer there two summers ago, and she loved it. She knew everyone there by name. And some of these kids are very, very handicapped. It's in getting to know them as individuals, not by labeling groups that we make progress."

Virginia wandered off the deck across the grass. A sprinkler threw a fine spray of water near my feet.

"It's true, Lucy," Mrs. Durr said. "You know I never told you how much it used to bother me to visit Virginia at her school. I'd be upset for days afterwards."

"And it was one of the best," Lucy interrupted.

"Perhaps it was, but still some children there were in pretty bad shape. I'm so relieved that's all over. Why it makes my heart more glad than I can say to see Virginia doing things for herself now."

We all looked towards the young woman walking toward the tennis court, followed by an ancient Labrador retriever.

A few nights later I had supper with an artist friend who is physically handicapped and walks with crutches. As a child she had polio, which had led to other physical problems she was continually fighting.

Over Greek salad I asked about her latest hospitalization. "No complications this time?"

"The only complication was after I got out, going to my nephew's bar mitzvah. It seems my relatives didn't really want a cripple there." Her voice slid to a bitter edge. "It was a big event—lots of blank checks and fancy people— and they really didn't want me seen on crutches. So they stuck me out on the porch, where I couldn't even see the head table. It made me furious."

Later she asked about my Wassaic work. "Isn't it depressing? It certainly depresses me to see people like that. A friend of mine on dialysis went into kidney failure, and she received a kidney transplant from a sister of hers who was mentally retarded. A few months ago my friend got married, and she had this sister in her wedding party. I found it pretty uncomfortable."

She looked at me for confirmation and, when she found none, searched for words. "I mean, this retarded girl was all dressed up in a brocade suit, and the difference between the way she looked and the things that came out of her mouth was amazing. She was screeching in a loud voice all through the service. Her family had to keep trying to hush her up. I just couldn't understand why my friend made her so visible. I mean, she was going to include her because, after all, she had given her a kidney, but I just wondered why she had to make her so public."

Back in Millerton, I went to a dinner party held before a jazz concert. Our host and hostess lived in a fine eighteenth-century house with a triple-sided fireplace and wide, old floorboards. The guests were convivial and well dressed. I wore a long India-print dress and earrings from Paris. A friend was there, one I'd not seen since early winter. In the screened geodesic dome porch, with vines growing up the inside, holding glasses of chilled white wine, we talked. Most people were quiet when I told them about my Wassaic project and asked few questions. Rosina wanted to know everything. She leaned forward and her dark hair fell across her cheek.

"I've lived in this area all my life, and I have two images of Wassaic. In the first I am a little girl, being taken down to New York City to see a play. We stop for the traffic light at Wassaic and I see people inside the buildings, clutching the bars at the windows. That's all. In the second, I am taking my own children to New York to a musical. We wait at the same light. This time there's no one at the windows, but someone is outside on the lawn, hopping up and down. And the hopping is violent, not normal. I can tell it's been going on for a long time and won't stop until long after I've left. I think everyone in the area has strong images of Wassaic."

"Rosina," I said to this woman I liked and admired so much, "that's not Wassaic."

"It's not? Well, what was it?"

"That's Harlem Valley Psychiatric."

"Oh yes, that's right. Where is Wassaic then?"

Gently, not wanting to embarrass her, I described where it is.

"Really? Then I've never seen it. It must be quite invisible."

"Well there she is," Vera said as I stuck my head in the dayroom. Sheets were on the table, and lunch was almost ready. "Two weeks without seeing you's a long time in this place."

Emily sat in her corner staring ahead. She didn't respond to my first hello, but then I saw something catch hold, her face turn up, her eyes become aware as though preparing for seeing, then she was up out of her chair, leading with her body not her eyes. She was on her way to me. I hugged her. She stood still, incredulous that I was back. Her eyes said she had given up on me.

My pocket was full of balloons I'd bought for her on Martha's Vineyard. Each one said "Emily" in white letters. I blew one up, but she still stared at me. I let the air out in her face, and she jumped back a little. She had forgotten this was fun. I tried it again. She smiled. Again, and this time she laughed.

I blew up the red balloon and tied it. Then I blew up a blue balloon. An orange one. A yellow one. I liked the idea that they all had her name on them, though I knew it made no difference to her. But other people would see them and know she was not invisible.

5

Simon's dark profile was silhouetted against the blaze of summer sky as he sat on a broken park bench. I photographed him often, for his expressions flicked across his face like the shimmer of light on black satin. It was for Simon that I had once brought my Walkman, to see if it could be Bahamian spirituals that were going through his inner channel.

One morning a month ago, he'd come to program with patches of hair shaved away in neat rectangles showing ugly cuts that oozed crusted brown blood, slits held together by black sutures. His head bulged with lumps. I was told he'd been beaten by another client who often roamed the halls at night and was known to be aggressive.

This explanation bothered Sherry, who taught Simon every day. She said he was strong. He'd have fought back. It was not like him to just take a beating from another client. And where was the staff? You could bet Simon screamed—yet no one heard him? There was something fishy.

Two weeks later Sherry told me that Simon's mother had come to Wassaic over the weekend and raised hell. The administration had not called her, nor had they sent a telegram; they mailed her a letter a week after the beating. She was furious.

I looked at Simon and thought his face held all his secrets. He couldn't tell us what they were, though he could make music and snap his fingers.

Outside I asked Sherry if she'd heard any more about the beatings.

"You bet. It was a staff person."

A beating that severe could only have been given by someone with great rage and accuracy, and though I agreed with Sherry that there had been "something fishy" about the roving client story, I still could not believe—no, could not comprehend—a staff member doing that.

"Was it a new staff person?" I asked. Had they hired a psychopath by mistake?

"Nope. He had eleven years of state service. They never would have found out a thing about it if Simon's mother hadn't raised a stink, and that's a fact," Sherry said. "They were ready to whitewash the whole affair and hang it on a client.

"The aides had zipped the lip. So they called them into personnel, all seven of them working that part of the building. Told them if they didn't get the truth they were going to fire all seven of them. They meant business. So one of them started to sing. Then they all joined in and it was over. There'd been a witness.

"I think Simon urinated on the floor or something like that. There's no doubt that he can do stuff to make you irritated. I don't know, it was something minor. I saw the guy two days after this all came out, and he said he didn't know why he did it. He couldn't remember. He just lost it, that's all. He took the mop handle and smashed the metal end on Simon's head."

"Is that all there is to it? Will anything else happen?"

"I don't think so, unless they re-open the investigation. The staff person is gone. They let him resign. That means he gets to keep his retirement."

Gregory was sleeping on a floor mat in Butternut Learning; his color was yellow, but his face looked less gaunt. The one-on-one aide watching Gregory was Squire, whose scalp gleamed blue beneath a regrowth of shaved hair. "The main thing that can happen to you here is burn-out," he was saying to Red, another aide. "I've been here ten years, and the only reason that I don't burn out is I raise too much hell!" Squire put back his head and roared with laughter. "I never meant to be here that long, but it's a steady job and the money's getting better, and what the hell? Not much else I could do anyway."

"Well, I don't like my job," Red said. A tattoo peeked out under his T-shirt sleeve, smeared as though it had been partly erased. Later I was told it was his ex-wife's name, which he'd tried to burn off with a cigarette lighter in a drunken rage.

"Then you shouldn't be in it. No, I'm serious. That's the trouble with this place. You got too many people can't stand what they're doing. You see 'em all the time, sitting there staring at TV or goofin' off like us!" Squire roared again. "Now me, I really like what I'm doing because I got seniority. I'm one-on-one with him because I want to be." He jerked his thumb at Gregory, still sleeping on the mat. "I get my pick of jobs, and that's what it's all about. You don't do shit work for years just to stay in the shit."

"Don't tell me I should get another job," Red said trying to control his anger—Squire was bigger. "I got a new wife and she's going to pop a kid any day. And I ain't got much in the way of education. Where else am I going to find work with benefits? And it's not the clients I don't like, it's the way people try to play games with your head, supervisors especially."

"I'll second that," Squire said. He reached under a red flannel shirt and scratched his considerable stomach. "They get you any way they can. Like they write you up for being five minutes late. That kind of shit." He glanced at me, acknowledging for the first time that I was listening to this conversation. "And take Gregory there. I'm one-on-one with him because he'll eat absolutely anything. I have only one responsibility and that's to see he puts nothing I haven't given him in his mouth. If he does, it's my ass. So I'm supposed to be not more than one foot from him at all times. Now a supervisor could come in and see me standin' over here, even though Gregory's sleeping, and write me up for it. But I'll tell you, I ain't layin' down on that mat with him for nothin'!

"I been brought up on a lot of charges, including client abuse. Each time I was acquitted. I was caught sleeping once, and fined a thousand bucks. But I was caught red-handed, and even though it hurt like hell to pay it, I knew I had to. Trouble was the next month I was written up for the same thing, and this time it was a lie."

"What about the client-abuse charges?" Red asked.

"They went to arbitration and were dropped. I was framed and they knew it. I'd slap a client, but I'd never bust a head open with a metal mop end, the way that fellow did last month. I knew him, used to play ball with him, and he's a good guy. Been here longer than I have. But I'll tell you, while I'm sorry he lost his job and all, I think he's better off where he is now. I mean the next time he did something like that he could kill someone."

Squire unlocked the cabinet, and took out a package of chocolate-covered graham crackers. Gregory sat up on his mat.

"You know it's amazing, but you could set a bomb off next to him, and he'd sleep right through it. But crinkle a package of cookies, and he wakes up right away."

"You," Sherry said, putting a finger in the middle of Gregory's chest, "are going nowhere." Her voice rumbled like lava waiting to explode. "You've been nothing but a pain in the neck all morning. Now *sit down!"* She backed him toward a chair and pushed his shoulders.

Gregory landed on the floor. She looked down at him in despair, hands pressed against her head. "And you *know* you aren't supposed to sit where there's no chair!" She helped him up into the chair.

"Oh God, by breakfast I knew it was going to be a bad day today. One of my kids is home with a sore throat, and another only went to school because I forced him to. Now Gregory's on the buck." She took a pack of M&Ms from her desk, ripped it open.

I liked Sherry. I admired her spirit. I knew she cared for the clients, and it was hard to watch her appear otherwise. When it was a bad day, her clients knew it.

Gregory saw the small, dark brown package and lumbered toward her.

"Oh-no-you-don't," she said turning her back. "Do you think you can get away with your behavior and then get rewarded? No way." Sherry passed out M&Ms two at a time, slamming them down in front of each person. She skipped Gregory.

Squire came in, hitching up the tight, black jeans that rode below his belly. On his feet were crusty, frayed running shoes that trailed dirty shoelaces. "Well, at least I won't go blind," he said wiping the remains of a sausage hero from his mouth with his flannel shirttail. "They say if you don't eat you'll go blind, so at least I've put that off for a little while." He wadded up a greasy sandwich paper.

"You heard the grosser than gross jokes? No matter how grim it gets in here we keep our sense of humor, don't we Sherry? Okay, you asked for it. What's grosser than gross? You dreamed you ate a five-pound marshmallow and woke up with your pillow gone."

I looked at Gregory who had eaten his bed sheet. "Enough," I said.

6

Emily sat on my lap staring vacantly ahead. She rubbed the back of her hand along my cheek. I held perfectly still, so as not to miss a moment of this affection.

And suddenly I was terribly, deeply sad, as images of Emily and Max merged. It was Max's thirteenth birthday. He was with cousins on Cape Cod, and I missed him very much. Max was in that wonderful stage between child and adult, when he would still sit on my lap, but carry on a well-reasoned conversation at the same time.

Emily stroked my cheek, the same absent-minded gesture Max might make. From Emily it was everything; I could ask nothing more. Sometimes I did, I asked for a hug, and Emily put her arms around me in a perfunctory way. It meant nothing. But this gentle hand against my cheek was everything. I didn't have to ask Max for hugs—he gave them freely, strong, with his arms tight around me.

Today I missed them both—Max who was on Cape Cod, Emily who was only partly here.

On a magnificent, luminous afternoon, I set up my tripod and wooden 4 × 5 Deardorf under the trees. I wanted to take the time a view camera demands, almost as a way of extending the day. I like the feeling of the brass knobs as they tighten the swings and tilts and send the bellows out over a cogged track. I like being under the black cloth, where the world is narrowed to a small screen; surrounded by darkness, I feel invisible. I like the world seen upside down, just as the eye registers an inverted image until the brain unscrambles it.

Clients from Locust were on the grass after programming.

They'd been marched out in straight military lines, but once they reached the grass they were allowed to relax. A few of them used the swings, pumping wild and high. Seen upside down on ground glass, they arched back and forth like wind-shield wipers.

Robert sat running dirt through his fingers, the sifted soil glinting light as though he were panning for gold. Jacob squatted and muttered in his Slavic language. The deceptively sweet-looking young resident peered into my camera lens and recited a list, fast and intensely: "Bathtub. Front porch. Outside. Chain saw. Bathtub. Puddle."

In the lower corner of the ground glass I saw a figure running my way. As it came closer I recognized Earl. When he filled half the ground glass I saw his hand stretched out, a smear of brown on his shirt, brown oozing between his fingers.

I yanked the black cloth off my head, swooped the tripod and camera to me. I ran. The black cloth wrapped around my leg and I stumbled, but the tripod kept me from falling. I darted behind a tree. Earl would smear the feces on the first one he could reach. His teeth were bared and his eyes swung wildly. An aide pushed a client aside to avoid the shit-filled hand. There was a dance on the grass of pushing and turning; the aide yelled, lunged for Earl, and deftly gripped the arm that swung its fearful deposit.

In a moment it was over, and then I could tremble. It was Earl again, the same one who had grabbed me at Butter-nut, gouging my skin with his fingernails.

"John Doe Number 11 has taken a turn for the worse." Fred Law drank a Coke on the stoop outside Butternut. "He's gone downhill fast. You won't believe it when you see him. He can't even walk now. When he came to Wassaic he was one of the fastest runners on the hill. Now he has to be wheeled over to the program and then positioned on the mat. Most of the day he sleeps."

I couldn't imagine John Doe—Delmar Tate—any way but ranging around the room, arms swimming through air.

"They've put him on Librium, even though the Butternut psychologist has found out that Librium is definitely contra-indicated for anyone with organic brain syndrome, which is what John has. Yet he's on double the dose for any normal person, and John surely isn't *that*. There's only one term for it: chemical straightjacket."

Delmar was on a floor mat covered with a sheet, his hands crossed on his chest as though he were a corpse. "I'd rather a hundred times over have him the way he was than have him this way. It's pitiful. He can't even make his duck noise any more," Fred Law said, though I knew the constant noise drove them all nuts. "They're taking him to Poughkeepsie for a CAT scan later in the week. I guess we'll know more then about the brain disease. But I think it's the Librium, I really do."

Clay, who had worked with Delmar for years, sat down wearily, stretching out his legs and making circles with his feet to relieve the long hours of standing. "I think there be a bunch of clients going downhill now because of this pro-gramming. There be too much pressure on them. That's what's happening to Delmar."

Two very different points of view: One, that Delmar had been drugged into a zombie state, and two, that he'd been helped into it by an over-structured, demanding routine. Could both be right?

A few days later Fred Law told me John Doe Number 11 was in the hospital. "Last Sunday night he had one of his hypothermia attacks. Some staff person gave him a hot water bottle—very well meaning, I'm sure, but it burned the hell out of his stomach. He had filled it with boiling water and put it right on John's stomach without wrapping it in a towel. He has second-degree blisters. Skinny as he is it must have been very painful. Now it doesn't take much common sense to know you should wrap a hot water bottle up. It wasn't or dered on his chart either, and you're not supposed to do that without orders. There's going to be an investigation about it."

It was another example of the problem of being a therapy aide. A helpless person is in your hands, you try to make the best possible decisions, yet according to the rules you are supposed to make none. This was one of the questions on the therapy-aide exam: "You find a client dangling from the ceiling by a rope. a) You cut him down; b) you get your supervisor."

7

"I'm miserable," Rhoda said. "I want to get out of here. I want to have a home and money and a life of my own. I got so many problems. I got a bad hip, I got an ear infection, I got diabetes, I got gall stones."

I didn't tell her she had a throat that was closing up, too.

"And look, my hands shake. They never used to do that before. I guess it's from smoking. I'm going to buy a carton of Marlboros, then I'm going to stop smoking."

I didn't tell her that her trembles were probably from medication.

"You know what I want? I want to go home with you for Christmas. Can I do that? Will you take me?"

The Birch supervisor told me that Rhoda had recently assaulted clients and been verbally abusive to the staff. "If you ask me," he said, "—and I got no paper on the wall to back this up—Rhoda is more crazy than she is retarded. I mean she goes in and out.

"The other night was just terrible, the way she treated everyone. She wanted to call her cousin, but we wouldn't let her. Told her she'd have to calm down first. The next night she wanted to call her cousin again and started getting upset, and this time we let her do it. When she got off the phone, she was fine. Well, I guess she just has her bad nights. Face it, everyone has their bad nights or they wouldn't be here. They'd be in their own homes."

Tillie was back from a month-long visit with her family. She sat knitting on the dayroom couch, which, even with three cushions missing, gave off a urine stink.

"I've been in the hospital on the outside, did you know that?" Tillie's little face was squinched up, her eyes full of tears. "It was awful. They put needles in my arms and needles in my fingers." She jabbed at her thumb with a knitting needle. "Oh, I was so frightened. I couldn't breathe. Do you know what I'm saying?" Her voice sounded desperate, and she made occasional little gasps with her mouth.

"I could hear my heart pounding and pounding, and I couldn't do nothing about it. Oh, I was so frightened. And I scared the life out of my mother too. I was supposed to stay with her, and then I couldn't breathe. It was terrible." She was crying, this tiny, little old lady whose mother must be ancient. "Now my mother's never going to have me back, I gave her such a scare. I'm going to be here for the rest of my days. I was supposed to help my mother and instead I couldn't breathe. It's all my fault." A big tear rolled down her cheek, her mouth opened just a little and made the gasping noise, like a fish desperate for oxygen. "I've broken my mother's heart, and I've broken my own too."

"Tillie's a grandstander," the Birch supervisor said. "Give her an audience and watch her go. She really carries on, especially after a visit to her family. We have trouble with her for weeks. She's always on a crying jag of one kind or another. A few days ago we thought she was having a cardiac incident, so we took her to Sharon Hospital. The EKG showed that wasn't the case, however. She's just got angina. And this morning she hyperventilated, but that was from anxiety, nothing else.

"Still, it was no coincidence that she developed heart symptoms at her mother's the day she was supposed to come back to Wassaic. This kind of thing happens all the time. Maybe I shouldn't say this, but there are some families that bring the clients back a wreck. Tillie's mother must be really, really old. That's where the trouble usually is, when there's a real old mother. So, be around a while, then you won't take it so seriously."

The music room had an out-of-tune piano, with rhythm instruments stored on top. There was nothing else in the room. Elaine, the music teacher, opened a folder of sheet music and told Emma to choose a song. "Take Me Out to the Ball Game," Emma said immediately.

They sang together, Emma's voice almost inaudible but on tune, "Buy me some peanuts and crackerjack . . ."

When she finished she said, "My mother used to sing that when she was working. One day I asked if I could sing with her, and she said yes. So I did. I sang the whole thing. 'You got a lovely voice,' she said to me." Emma was quiet. "Do you know sometimes I see my mother? I really see her. She's standing behind my wheelchair."

"And is she saying anything to you?" I asked.

"Yes. She's saying, 'You got a lovely voice.' "

"Elaine is leaving," Emma said a few days later. "She's leaving a week from yesterday. She's going to take a job somewhere else." Her face was slack with despair, the twitching and trembling stilled. She and Elaine had three music sessions a week together, and they took walks, Elaine pushing Emma's chair.

"I've never made a friend in my life that didn't leave me. I got to get out of here, I got to. This is no way to live."

A woman walked by, on this fine, clear summer day. She wore high heels, walked briskly swinging her bare arms. We watched her pass in silence. "Do you know what I would do if I could walk like that? I'd wait until night, I'd go to the second-story window and jump out and run away from here. I wouldn't care where I went."

She pulled up from her slumped position and looked me full in the face. "If you were me, if you were in my position, would you want to be here?"

"No Emma, I wouldn't." God, no. Not for a second, your position makes me rage and weep and wonder how I ever could have been born so lucky. To be here physically helpless, often in pain, completely dependent and at the mercy of others, yet sane and aware—there could be nothing worse.

"I don't understand why my relatives won't put me in a home some place near them, on Cape Cod, where I could see them more often. It would be nice there, and I would be happy."

"Well, Emma," I began lamely, "maybe it costs a great deal of money to be on Cape Cod. Maybe they can't afford it." This occurred to me as a real possibility, but it lay in front of Emma limply, an excuse. "I'm sure your family loves you."

Emma's face broke into pieces. Tears showered from her eyes, splashing on the wheelchair tray. "If my family loved me I wouldn't be here."

As Emily and I started down the sidewalk, her social worker called to me, waving a piece of paper. "I've got something here that might interest you." He read a letter saying Emily's community residence had run into problems putting in the septic system. The residence would not be ready until late fall. That was bad news for Emily, but secretly good news for me.

Emily and I walked arm and arm, our skin adhering like sticky playing cards; I tried to explain things to her. It might seem like a long time before she moved, but it really wasn't. She was going to a home where people would take her for walks and play with her. She'd eat good food. Her grandmother would be near by—she'd see her much more often. And sometimes I'd come too.

Emily hummed serenely as we walked. Perhaps she understood.

I'd brought two balloons in my pocket. When we were under the big maple, sitting on a bench, I pulled one out. She twisted back and forth, humming on one tone, the waiting hum. Her hum moved to a higher pitch as the long hot-dog balloon began to take shape. When I tied it she waved it in the air, then put it on the ground. It popped.

She picked up both halves of the balloon and put them to my mouth. Then she made blowing noises, puffs of air. It was a put-on. She really didn't expect the balloon to revive, but it was worth a try.

□   □   □

The new Birch doctor smoked a cigarette on the hospital steps while he waited for a meeting to start. He had a curious way of half-smiling while he talked, his voice so light and tentative it belied the importance of what was said. "Rhoda Alexius had an episode of not breathing and turning blue. She's in Poughkeepsie Hospital now, and she's scheduled for a CAT scan on Friday. I'm afraid it isn't just something simple like a blood-sugar problem."

"Could it have to do with the thickening in her throat?" I asked.

"No, it looks more like something in the brain."

"Do you think her throat problem has been brought about by all the medication she's taken over the years?"

"Heavens no."

The Birch supervisor was in the medication room catching up on paperwork and gave me more information. "Rhoda fell out of bed and was found unconscious on Sunday night. But I think something had been going on for quite a few days, starting on Wednesday. She'd become very aggressive toward the clients, so much so that I had to move her to a different ward just to give them some peace and quiet. And she was bad-mouthing the staff, generally making life terrible for everyone."

I had seen Rhoda on Wednesday, and though she wasn't happy, she didn't seem aggressive and wasn't rude while I was there. She said she'd been told she might go to a community residence soon.

"No way," the supervisor said. "Her behavior's way too bad. I talked to her about it, told her the only way she was going to get out of here was to shape up. But she couldn't hear any of it, she was so far gone."

So far gone they fed her thorazine day after day without keeping close track of her emotional and physical state. So far gone she was now in the hospital.

A few days later the doctor sat in the cubicle of Birch which doubled as a storage room and his office, cigarette in one hand and a soda can in the other. I asked about Rhoda.

"Actually, she's back now. They think they've found the problem. It seems to have been hypotension caused by her thorazine. She's off all medication now. And she seems quite proud of it. We're going to try her this way. If she flares up, we'll get the psychiatrist to prescribe something that won't have side effects for her."

Upstairs Rhoda lay on the bed. "I want to get out of here. I can't stand it here with these people."

I put my hands on her shoulders, looked hard in her eyes. "Rhoda, if you want to get out you're going to have to get along with the other people here."

Her temper rose. "I don't do nothing with them. They're crazy! They're always trying to fight with me."

I kept my hand steady on her shoulder, made her eyes look back to mine. "That may be so, but when that starts to happen, you've got to get away. Go be by yourself then. That is the quickest way out of here."

She was looking directly at me now; she believed me. "That's what I'll do," she said.

It was Gertrude Healy's eighty-third birthday. She had spent seventy-six years in an institution for the retarded.

I shopped for a present and found a cloth rose sealed into a brandy glass—the kind of knickknack so popular in Birch Hall. Gertrude's room was bare. I bought a large, cheerful birthday card, and had the rose put in a box with a yellow ribbon.

Gertrude was alone in her room. She wore a sleeveless gingham dress, her little curved legs dangling below it, but her cheeks had color, and her eyes sparkled. "How did you know it is my birthday?" she asked. "Did I tell you? I didn't mean for you to buy me anything."

"I wanted to," I assured her. "Someday I want to be as old as you are."

"But you should be careful with your money. You shouldn't just spend it on anything."

I opened the box for her.

"What kind of flower is it?" she asked.

I wondered when she had last seen a rose. "Does it need water? Will it die?"

I explained it was sealed in the glass, and would still look pretty in winter.

"I like it," she said at last. "Let me give you a tip for bringing it to me."

"No Gertrude. You don't pay someone for a birthday present. It's my pleasure to give it to you."

"Are you sure? You don't want money for it? No? Well thank you very much. And come and see me again some time, okay?"

8

Emily waited by her grandmother on the steps of Juniper Hall, hand around her wrist, a quiet, settled expression on her face. This was not a foster grandma paid to love her, it was her real grandmother.

Mrs. Benedict held on to the railing, peering anxiously toward the parking lot. Her face had Emily's delicate bone structure and, behind round glasses, Emily's eyes, smudged with age. Fine wrinkles puckered her lips, as though her mouth had been gathered and drawn by a string. Her pewter-colored hair was pulled back from her head in a no-nonsense way, and two large hairpins secured a figure-of-eight knot at her nape. Standing in front of the cement building in a blue print dress with a lace collar, she looked as though she'd been hand-tinted in a black-and-white photograph from the thirties.

It was two days before Emily's thirteenth birthday, and Mrs. Benedict had driven down to celebrate with her grand-daughter. "I'm afraid I'm one of those old ladies no one wants to get behind when they're driving in a hurry," she said ruefully when we met. "I don't usually make this drive alone because I don't see so well any more, so I make up for it by taking my time."

Emily had hovered between us in her dayroom looking back and forth with bewilderment and indecision: Here was the woman she'd seen infrequently but consistently over her thirteen years, and here was the woman she'd seen almost daily for the past few months. It seemed as though her affection couldn't embrace us both, and she would have to choose between us—at least whose wrist to grab. It was no contest. She lunged for Mrs. Benedict.

Emily had been dressed in a ruffled shirt and baggy corduroy pants. Mrs. Benedict asked if she could be changed into a skirt.

"No luck. The only one she has comes up above her knees now. This girl's growing like a weed," Vera said.

"Well then, I know what to give her for her birthday," Mrs. Benedict said, her lips setting more firmly.

With Mrs. Benedict's vision and Emily's safety in mind, I had offered to drive them shopping, and now they were ready for our outing; I gave my horn a little toot to announce my presence. Looking at them on the Juniper steps, they seemed such a unit that I suddenly felt alone. I needed my own children. Or maybe I needed my own grandmother, who had died many years ago.

"I don't want you to feel like the chauffeur," Mrs. Benedict said, leaning forward. In the rearview mirror I saw Emily next to her grandmother; she wasn't twisting or humming, she sat quietly, her mouth shaped into a smile, steady with powerful joy. "Emily really does love to ride in the car. Years ago that's all we used to do. I'd pick her up, we'd drive around, and she'd wind up that "Pop! Goes the Weasel" music box, or get that hum of hers going. Then she'd be happy for hours.

"As a matter of fact the car was a savior when Emily was a baby, too. Those days were something else." Her voice became scratchy, as though memory could wear her out. "She'd scream and scream—not a healthy cry, but a continual wail, like a cat, high and thin and grating. I knew she couldn't help it, I knew she couldn't stop, but every moment she wasn't sleeping she was crying. At night Sue—my daughter—and I'd try to calm her, but nothing worked. Not walking her, not singing, nothing. I had a Chrysler wagon that was on its last legs, and when Sue couldn't stand it any more, she put her in the car. We never knew whether it would start. Sue would be half-asleep herself, but if she could get the car going, she'd drive around for hours. I'd go to bed but I couldn't sleep, I was so nervous."

"Let me tuck her shirt into those pants," Mrs. Benedict said as we got out of the car. She fiddled with Emily's waist, then straightened slowly, pressing one hand on her lower back as she rose.

We had settled on a pizza lunch before we shopped, "a

birthday bite," Mrs. Benedict called it. Emily sat down on the padded leatherette seat, but didn't seem to know what I meant when I told her to slide into the booth. I gave her bottom a little push; she moved sideways. I started to sit next to her, but she made a whimper, and reached out her arms to her grandmother. If we'd been alone, I'd have been the one she would've reached for.

"There's so much I don't understand about her," Mrs. Benedict sighed as she moved next to Emily. "My own child was so normal, at least when she was a little girl. Later on she had troubles, but still, they weren't the same as these troubles." She touched Emily's head, her palm smoothing down her temple and cheek as though she were both petting her and pushing her away.

"I was forty-two when Sue was born. We didn't have a lot of money, but my husband provided as best he could, and that was good enough. I'd always wanted a baby, and Sue was the answer to my prayers. But you know something?" Mrs. Lawrence looked down at her hands twisting each other, her thumbs pushing waves of loose skin toward her knuckles. "Having a baby at forty-two isn't that easy."

She had been my age when she'd had Sue. I tried to imagine myself with a new baby and could not.

"Sue was an adorable baby, but she had a temper. And she turned into a feisty little girl. I'm sorry to say I had a hard time keeping up with her. Just getting her home to supper and homework every night took more energy than I had in me. By the time she was in high school it was the sixties, and you know what they were like. Maybe she didn't smoke marijuana or take psychedelic drugs—I can't imagine where she could have gotten them in our little town—but I know she drank whiskey and was out every night of the week. My husband and I tried threats, punishments, everything. She was always a step ahead of us." She clenched her fist and the wrinkles disappeared, stretched out over her big, arthritic knuckles. "I was bitterly disappointed that my only daughter had turned out like that. I know somehow, it must have been my fault.

"She graduated at the bottom of her class, though we paid to get her tested and she had plenty of ability. She just didn't care. And graduation night she left home. She didn't want to go to college. I knew there'd be no keeping her in our house, but still, I couldn't believe it when I found the note under the front door. It said she was part of the 'love generation,' and she dotted every letter 'i' with a heart, and signed her name by drawing flowers. Oh God, that letter. My husband cried, I remember that. I was heartbroken, but I have to admit there was some other kind of feeling mixed in there. She'd been too much for me. I was exhausted."

A waitress brought glasses and our drinks. Emily grabbed a soda can and took three gulps from the keyhole, first pulling out the straw and throwing it down in a gesture that seemed to say she knew what a straw was for, but she couldn't possibly use it. As orange soda dribbled down her shirt, her grandmother mopped it up with a napkin. We ordered pizza. "Do you really think Emily can eat pizza, what with all that stringy cheese?" Mrs. Benedict asked.

"Oh yes," I said. "We'll cut it up in little bites." I couldn't help the small, smug thrill that I knew more about her eating patterns than her grandmother.

Mrs. Benedict continued. "Without Sue at home I had a real life of my own for the next two years. I played cards with a bunch of gals twice a week, and I spent time at my piano. I'd never call myself a fine musician, but I sight read well, and I'm the organist for our church. Now I had some real time to practice, and that's what I did. Sue sent a postcard from San Francisco, and one from Arizona. That's all we heard. And then my husband passed away, and that was a horrible blow. He was only in his mid-sixties. I was alone. I didn't even know where Sue was to tell her about her father's death.

"She came home a year later, pregnant with Emily. She wouldn't talk about the father. I was just beginning to get used to life without my husband, and even though I was frightened of the problems she'd bring, I couldn't turn her away: She had no one. For the first time in her life, she was really asking for help. And I found I looked forward to having a grandchild, I really did. It was going to be a new way to start over with a family. I wanted to hear a child call me Nana, or Granny, or any of those names." She bit her cheek, and her face flattened as though she'd become paralyzed on one side.

"Sue was in labor for seventy-two hours. Whether that caused Emily's retardation, or whether it was the life Sue'd been living in Arizona, or something from this unknown father, I don't know. All I know is my granddaughter had troubles from the moment she was born. She screamed all the time. She wouldn't suck properly. The nurses tried to tell Sue that lots of babies have trouble getting their digestive systems and nervous systems going at the same time, but it looked bad to me.

"At home it got worse. Emily would nurse for a couple of minutes, fall asleep for a couple of minutes, then start crying that same pathetic wail. When she was quiet she was a perfect beauty, with dark eyes just like Sue's when she was a baby. But week by week the nightmare came down on us. She'd lie in her crib without moving her position. She never tried to hold her head up. I kept remembering Sue kicking at the world when she was a baby, and into everything when she was a toddler. The contrast between my daughter and granddaughter was too much to bear."

The contrast between Emily and my children was also too much to bear. As Mrs. Benedict had complained about Sue, so I had complained about my children's excess of activity: Max at three months in an infant seat grabbing the cat's tail; Katrina, a fiendish crawler at six months; Wynne, relentlessly tottering up and down the cement library steps at one year.

"My own life had drained away. I'd given up card games with my friends. I never touched my piano. I *knew* something was very wrong with Emily, but couldn't admit it, not even to Sue. We were at it again all the time. She took offense at every suggestion I made. When she came in the living room I'd turn on television so we wouldn't have to talk. I just wanted moments where I didn't feel the pain; I didn't care about being happy.

"Emily finally rolled over, she finally learned to sit up, but she did these things much later than other children. And she was so awkward."

How easily those developmental milestones had passed with my own children. I'd never worried about any of them; nor had I felt any special gratitude for not having to worry.

"Her only sound was her crying. We had her tested and her hearing was fine. When she was three I used to try to get her to babble—or even make the humming noise she does now—by putting her hand on my piano. I'd read something in the *Reader's Digest* about how deaf children respond to vibrations, and a corner of my mind held out for her to be deaf rather than dumb. Emily would leave her hand on the piano a few seconds, and then it would just drift off. She was bored with the world. The only things that could excite her were flashing lights or something spinning around, even bike wheels and car tires.

"Sue would take Emily to doctors, and I'd wait for the bad news, because I knew it was coming. And it came in layers, small bits at a time. She had cerebral palsy, but they didn't know how bad. She had some brain damage, but they didn't know how much. Finally, two specialists said what I already knew: Emily was severely retarded. And they said flatly that it was a condition that would never get better. They said we should apply for 'residential treatment.' I remember someone said, 'A place where she can be with her own kind.' "

"But I wanted Emily to stay at home with us. Hard as it was, I wanted it to be the three of us. I couldn't imagine abandoning that little creature. But Sue wasn't having it that way. She was tough as could be. Stone. She told me I might be an old woman now, but she wasn't. She had a life to begin again and taking care of Emily was going to make her into a caretaker. She was going back to Arizona. She wanted Emily in an institution."

Mrs. Benedict fed Emily the pizza, bite by bite, cutting the triangle piece, popping each little morsel in her mouth. While she ate, Emily never stopped smiling. Sometimes she giggled a sound of pure delight. Her grandmother's words had no meaning for her.

"I said I'd take care of Emily myself if she was going off. I thought that I could be the kind of mother I'd never been to Sue. Finally I begged her to let Emily stay with me. And that wasn't easy. Before she went away, when she'd been a teenager, I *told* her what to do. I made the rules, even if she broke them. But everything had turned upside down since then.

"Sue took off again for the West, and I tried to take care of Emily on my own." Mrs. Benedict paused, drawing a deep breath that rasped in her throat. "And in six months I was as exhausted as I'd ever been in my life. I'd developed arthritis in my back, and it put me in terrible pain. The burdens were just too much. Emily had a brace on her leg, and she was too heavy to carry. If I were a young woman perhaps I could have done it, but I couldn't, it almost broke me." Mrs. Benedict's voice broke, tears wavered in her eyes. "With our doctor's help, I filed papers to get her placed.

"But it was a terrible time to try to get her in anywhere. All the state and private agencies had waiting lists because of the overflow from Willowbrook. It took another long year of trying to cope alone. I talked to the social worker every month or so, but all she said was her hands were tied. Then in the winter of '75, I fell on the ice and broke my leg. That was it. The state had to take Emily on a temporary basis while I was in the hospital, and then they worked it out to make it permanent. It took me a long time to get back on my feet, and all that time I missed Emily so much, and I felt so bad about what had happened. I couldn't even visit her for a year. It seemed like it was one thing to fail as a mother to Sue, and another to wash my hands of my only granddaughter."

Grandmother and granddaughter walked in front of me into the department store, both limping slightly, almost the same height. Mrs. Benedict guided Emily through the foyer, jammed with video games, and gumball machines that spit out jawbreakers, or tiny tattoos, or a bracelet and ring for a quarter.

"Oh my goodness," Mrs. Benedict sighed as she gazed around the vast warehouse of a store. "I don't know where to start." Emily ignored the displays of bright plastic earrings, and paid no attention as we wandered through hangers of leotards and rows of shimmery tights. She hung on to her grandmother and scuffed her feet on the shiny white linoleum floor, the same kind they have in her dayroom. When I took her arm to steer her through "full-figure ladies apparel," she shrugged me off.

"I don't know why she clings to me so," Mrs. Benedict said apologetically. "I've often wondered if she thinks I'm her real mother."

I recalled being mistaken for Emily's mother, and the conflicting feelings that had raised.

"Sue's only been to Wassaic once, several years after Emily was admitted. And I'm afraid that visit wasn't much of a success. She went back out West the next day, and she hasn't been here since. Oh yes, she calls now and then to ask about Emily." Mrs. Benedict could not keep the bitterness from her voice.

Emily had frozen in front of a bin of furry bedroom slippers that had little Mickey Mouse faces mounted on them, with crossed felt eyes and pointed snouts at the toes. "I think we could add these to her birthday present, don't you?" Mrs. Benedict asked, as she sifted through for a pair in Emily's size.

I had wanted to buy the slippers for Emily myself.

"Now where's the sales girl? I'd like to find a couple of skirts, and maybe a new sweater." We located the girls' department, and at last, a skirt the right size for Emily. There were only the tiny, locked cubicles for dressing rooms, so Mrs. Benedict held the skirt up to Emily and declared it a proper fit. "Let's pay for these things and leave this place," she said. The flat fluorescent lighting made her face pale, and she seemed to have shrunk with fatigue.

And then, on the way to the cashier, Emily let go of her grandmother and began to lurch down the aisle, her hum winding up to a manic squeal. Other shoppers, who'd tactfully ignored her, now stopped to stare at this child suddenly out of control. Her eyes were on the ceiling, her arms pointed straight up. And there, ahead of us in the sports department, suspended by yellow hooks, hanging above rowing machines and bar bells and weight benches, was a row of bicycles. The back wheels were anchored to the acoustical panels, the front wheels dripped down, with silver handle bars as tantalizing as tinsel on a Christmas tree.

She pawed her grandmother's arm, then she looked at me, as though she dimly remembered that I'd been somehow connected to bicycles. She began to wail her high, cat-like, baby sound. Her noises got louder, the noises of a desperate infant, but I couldn't scoop up this girl who came almost to my shoulder and carry her out of the store. I had to do something. I gave a little jump, and spun the wheel of the nearest bike, and it whirled, so I spun the next one, and the next, all of them turning, spokes blurred, wheel reflectors circling into crimson streaks, down the row, while Emily became quiet, and stared, and at last, began to hum.

Louisa was twirling around the dayroom, her chin and mouth masked by her turtleneck. "Isn't there any way they can calm her down?" Mrs. Benedict asked. "Well, maybe she can entertain Emily. Maybe this time she really won't cry when I leave.

"Show Vera what we bought for your birthday," she said, laying the crinkly plastic bags on the table. She collapsed onto a chair. Vera told Emily to sit down, and Emily sat, quietly humming while we talked, gazing at Mrs. Benedict's profile. Slowly, as though pulled by a string, her hand came up and touched Mrs. Benedict's head. She began to smile. Her fingers slid down to the figure-of-eight knot at her grand-mother's neck, and by the time they tangled in the hairpins that held it together, she was grinning. Long, pewter hair tumbled down her grandmother's back.

"Oh Emily, you're up to your old tricks," Mrs. Benedict cried.

Emily laughed and laughed, as though something completely unexpected had fallen from the sky.

I let go of all the small jealous feelings that were nagging me, for I saw how clear and direct her bond of love was to her grandmother. I could feel it, mingled with the adoration I'd felt for my own grandmother, my mother's mother, the person who had always loved me, no matter what.

9

At twilight Jennifer and I stood in a doorway between a friend's kitchen and screen porch, where a small breeze cooled us. Outside was a well-tended rose garden; in the kitchen, other friends made pesto from fresh basil and washed blueberries for our supper.

"I want to tell you about the Christmas party where I met Adam and what he did for me," I said. Jennifer's son was fourteen, autistic, and probably dying. Adam, the first born. I had only seen Jennifer once since, at a time we could not talk; I wanted her to have every scrap of meaning from Adam's life.

The party had been two days before Christmas. There was buffet food and wine, and after dinner we were to sing Christmas carols, accompanied on guitar by our host. The guests included several people I cared deeply about. But it wasn't an easy night for me; only hours before I'd heard that a book I'd written had been rejected by a publisher I respected—a cruel early Christmas present. I was full of self-pity and on the edge of tears.

The party was well underway when the doorbell rang with late arrivals: Jennifer walked in, each of her healthy twin daughters holding one of her hands. There were kisses and greetings from the many that knew them, then a lull. A minute later Adam appeared, well bundled against cold, carried in his step-father's arms. Our host followed with a folding wheel-chair.

"I'd just received word that my Wassaic proposal had been funded," I told Jennifer, "but that's not what was on my mind that night. I could only think about my disappointment."

When I saw Adam I didn't know what to make of him. Angular and dark haired, his head lolled, and he made strange noises. His arms and body jerked in odd ways. I could not look at him closely. I was afraid of his visible, physical misery and preferred my own, psychic and less substantial.

After dinner we gathered in the living room, where Adam had remained the whole time. There was a hearty blaze in the fireplace and evergreen ropes hung above the mantle-piece. Children snuggled in laps or settled at our feet, eager to sing. "Oh come all ye faithful," we roared, primed with food and Christmas spirit, "joyful and triumphant." But it seemed a bit ironic to me. Despite the love of friends and family, I couldn't describe myself in those terms that night.

Above the singing I heard Adam screeching, and when I looked over to his wheelchair I saw him smiling, his head wagging to the music. At first Jennifer tried to quiet his noisy delight, holding him and putting his head on her shoulder. But Christmas music and a party were too exciting for Adam. He joined in every song and made eerie high whistles between each one. No one minded.

"I began to understand that Adam, with his happiness that night, was forcing me out of my self-centered pain, back into Christmas," I told Jennifer. "There was something about his presence in that room that made things whole—for all of us, I think."

Jennifer smiled. "He has that effect on people. He's never spoken—that's part of his autism. And he's had a lot of other problems. A year ago—just a week after we'd moved here, leaving Adam in Illinois until we could find a new place for him—I got a call from his school saying that he'd fallen and broken his nose. That seemed odd to me, because he was always well coordinated. I got in touch with his long-time pediatrician, who looked at him and told me he thought—he didn't know, but he thought—that Adam had muscular dystrophy.

"I immediately left my new house, left the twins, and went to Illinois where he was put in a hospital for tests. It was a nightmare week. The doctors said it was probable that I was the carrier and possible my daughters might have the disease too. On top of the guilt I already felt for Adam's handicaps, there was now this. I was brought up in a Calvinist-Lutheran household. It seemed like justice, like punishment for my sins. No matter how much my adult, intellectual self tried to rationalize it, that was always there.

"The dreadful week crawled by while Adam had CAT scans and bone scans, while he had blood tests and I had blood tests, while he had muscle biopsies and I had muscle biopsies. At ten o'clock one night a doctor stopped me in the hall and announced that they'd discovered a genetic defect in Adam. He had a virulent form of muscular dystrophy and would live not more than two years. I was the carrier, I was responsible. But my daughters were okay—this form could only be passed from mother to son.

"Think how lucky I am." Jennifer's voice honed the words with grateful irony. "If they had been boys I'd now have

three sons in wheelchairs. I was trying to get pregnant again—
we wanted a large family. I went to doctors at Yale. They
thought there was no problem. Just have an amniocentesis
and they'd take all the boys. They couldn't understand when
I cried and cried."

We moved into the kitchen for our meal. We knew we'd
only have a few more minutes to talk.

"Adam had lived at home for thirteen years. And now
he's finally in a school we're really pleased with—after a
great deal of searching. It costs a fortune—over $50,000 a
year. We don't pay all that, but someone does."

It cost the state over $60,000 a year to keep Emily at Wassaic.

"The ratio of staff to residents is one to one, and I think
he's doing very well there. I visit as often as I can, but sometimes it's just too hard. Last night I couldn't bear to go. Can
you imagine how I feel? There are parents who visit every
day, and of course there are those who never go. Most of
them are single parents though—oh yes, that's the first thing
that happens. The men bolt.

"Last week I got a letter from Adam's teacher. She writes
me every two weeks to let me know how he's doing. In
this letter she told me something I already knew—Adam
just loves men. There are mainly women on the staff, and
he loves men. They use a reward system there—behavior
modification—so whenever Adam does something well, they
now reward him by getting the janitor to come up and play
with him for ten minutes."

"Look at my baby, isn't he something else?" A Juniper night
supervisor showed me an 8 × 10 color picture of a teenage
boy with dimples like Max's, and a shy smile that displayed
a full set of braces.

"That's my youngest son—I call him my baby when he's

not around. But he's really very special. He's handicapped."
The supervisor lit a cigarette and jauntily pushed smoke from
the side of her mouth, directing it up with her lower lip.
"When he was a year-and-a-half-old, they told me to put him
in an institution. Told me he was profoundly retarded. Now
look at this picture. He's graduating from Hinton High next
year. Yup. I told them to go fuck themselves when they told
me to put him away and look where he is now. Quite a
picture, isn't it?" She took the photograph from my hand,
brushed imaginary dust from her desk, and settled the photograph firmly.

"He was sixteen months old before he could sit up. And
he didn't walk until he was four-and-a-half. He has CP, and
this is the first year he can walk up steps without holding
on to the railing or crawling upstairs. I'm so proud of him
I could bust.

"I knew he was smart long before anyone else did. I'd
put some colored beads in front of him and tell him to
pick out the yellow one. He couldn't sit up, and it might
take him twenty minutes to get that trembling hand over to
the right one, but by God he'd pick it out every time. And
from then on he's done it by himself.

"He handles all his school problems—it's more important
for him than most people to forge out his identity. The school's
called me a couple of times, and I've told them I don't want
to hear it. If they've got a problem, they have to talk to
him. He does have a temper, but he's needed something to
help him out. Kids tease him. So when the school called
me and said he'd called some girl a bitch and I should talk
to him about his mouth, I refused. When he got home, it
was like I thought, the kids had been teasing him. 'I hope
you used worse words than bitch, honey, and I hope you
used more of them. Those stupid kids need it.' "

□ □ □

Since much of the professional staff was on vacation, Emily's teacher had twelve kids for the summer. She created a contained unit by blocking off part of the recreation room with wardrobes. "I'm doing the best I can, though I'm afraid it's at the level of just hoping no one gets hurt.

"But Emily is doing very well. Today she did nuts and bolts." She picked up a yellow plastic child's toy. "I asked if she could do it—and she put her fingers on the nut and unscrewed it until it came off. Then she put it back on and handed it to me when it was finished. She's terrific at that."

I thought of Emily examining my camera and pressing the red button that set off my strobe. I remembered the determined way she kept her feet on the bike pedals as Sam wheeled her down the driveway. Oh Emily, if someone had worked lovingly with you, if someone had refused to accept your profoundly retarded diagnosis, would you be in school now? Would you be learning to use a camera instead of screwing plastic nuts and bolts together? Would you speak and maybe be a slow learner and still walk with your little limp and now and then hum to yourself, but would someone have taken your graduation picture, put it on their desk, and shown it off to anyone who walked in?

Autumn

1

I felt suspended, a way station between the arrivals and departures of my children. First Wynne, who'd been vacationing in Europe, flew back from Paris bringing fresh, crusty loaves of bread. Then Katrina and Max returned from their vacations. Everyone had dentist appointments, everyone needed new school clothes.

There were continual negotiations. Max called my studio while I developed film: Could he spend the night at David's? No. Why? Because we hadn't had dinner together in six weeks. Would I get him some sneakers? Yes, I'd meet him at the clothing store in forty-five minutes. No, that's too early. Why? He wanted to play baseball. But I thought he didn't have shoes. He borrowed Katrina's but they hurt his feet. Wasn't there any chance he could spend the night at David's? No. None?

One hot day Max reluctantly put away summer and began eighth grade. Then Katrina left for her first year away at school, and I missed her with the fresh pain of a bleeding cut. Three days later Wynne packed up his car, kissed me goodbye, and drove to his last year of college in Chicago.

Emily wasn't to be settled in her new home so easily; the news was frustrating. Work on the septic system had not yet been approved, which meant amending the original contract in the budget department in Albany. Even if all went smoothly, that would take a month. Then four separate contracts—electrical, heating, plumbing, and general—would have to go out for bid. Those take a month. Next, the choice of contractors has to go to Albany for approval. That takes forty-five days. Then they can begin renovations, which should take three months. The house couldn't be finished before January or February.

How could Emily bear another winter locked in Wassaic?

I scheduled days in my studio and darkroom. I developed dozens of 4 × 5 negatives, hung them to dry from clothespins strung on wire. I printed contact sheets, four negatives at a time, soothing myself with Brahms quartets. I dated and numbered the contact prints, then picked out a few to enlarge. Suddenly Emily was there in my studio holding her music box; Tillie—looking elfin; the young Locust resident who "did things to women."

An artist friend came by and asked to see my work. I was nervous about showing it. I knew how I felt about the pictures, but would others see them the same way?

"Oh," he said tilting Jacob under the light so he wouldn't catch glare from the bulb, "this reminds me of my grandfather. They don't look alike, but there's something about his posture."

And while gazing long and hard at Tillie standing by the

soda machine he said, "I have a friend who has a retarded child—have I told you about her?"

He didn't talk about composition or balance or tonal qualities. He didn't speak of aesthetics. He spoke personally, as though the photographs meant something to him.

I spent a day in New York City, buying photography supplies and going to galleries. While I was there, I stopped by to see a friend in the offices of Aperture, publisher of beautiful, glossy-paged photographic books. By the light from a high, arched, Victorian window, a designer worked on the cover of a book of nineteenth-century British photographs. While I waited for my friend, I watched her slice out type with a mat knife, then meticulously center the letters on her paste-up. We talked for a few minutes about color choices for the jacket she was designing, then she asked what I was working on.

I told her I was photographing at a large institution for the developmentally disabled near Millerton.

"The one where they package our books? What's the name of it? Yes, that's the one where they shrinkwrap our books."

The contrast was overpowering: lavishly printed books of turn-of-the-century photographs from India, China, and Tibet, books rich with the world vision of such masters as Paul Strand, books by contemporary humanists like Robert Adams—all passed through Wassaic along with boxes to be assembled for Bergdorf Goodman and plastic-lined trash bags for Delta Airlines. I tried to tell myself it was no more ironic than the factory worker who assembles a tiny part of a custom limousine for William Buckley; yet somehow it was. This was my field. These were books I would read. And the leap from the office in Manhattan with marble fireplaces and rococo ceilings to the bleak workshops at Wassaic where for a few cents a day the "brighter" clients like Rhoda did light factory work was very large indeed.

"I did something at school today," Max said at supper, as he set a chicken drumstick on his plate and licked his fingers. "I defended Wassaic."

Sam and I both looked up.

"Yup. You want to hear what happened?"

"Most certainly," Sam said, striving for a neutral tone.

"Well, Mr. Winslow, our science teacher started talking about the State School. I raised my hand and said, 'It's not called the State School any more, Mr. Winslow.' He got all sarcastic and said, 'Oh pardon me, Max, I mean the Developmental Center.' "

"A lot of people . . ."

"Now wait," Max continued. "There's more. The reason he was even talking about the place was because he was saying it's such a waste of money to have lights on there all night. He was going on and on about the cost of electricity and the State School wasting the taxpayers' money."

"Mr. Winslow's a jerk," Katrina said.

"So I risked my life and raised my hand again." Leaning his elbow on the table, Max picked up his drumstick, held it straight up, and waved it. "He tried to ignore me, but I kept it up there. So when he finally called on me I said, 'Mr. Winslow, if our school ran twenty-four hours a day and teachers had to come to work at midnight, we'd have lights on too.' "

And Max took a big, satisfied bite of the drumstick.

I walked Emily to my favorite grove of trees. When we sat she began to frisk me, poking at my ribs, spearing my pockets. I tickled her. I wanted to give her a balloon later, not on demand. When she did get it, she would insist I blow it up, then let the air leak out. I wanted a few minutes to make some notes. To distract her I threw her ball, but she shook her head and wouldn't go after it. She poked at me, searching for the balloon, while I got out my notebook.

The feeling of her pulling on me took me back to Washington Square with Katrina and Max at ages two and one. They were pestering me to do something repetitive and boring—catch them at the end of the slide, or help them pack a bucket with sand, or stand underneath them while they climbed on a jungle gym. I was trying to read a book; this should be my play hour too. I suggested things they could do for themselves. They weren't buying. I offered to read to them aloud from my book. They weren't buying. Finally I gave in, and, anger barely contained, I did whatever boring thing they demanded.

I tried again to distract Emily, printing her name in big letters in my notebook. "Now you write, or draw something Emily." The pen dangled from her fingers as she trailed it over the paper. In a few seconds she handed me the pen and began to poke at my pocket.

2

Rhoda lay on her bed in a housedress and heavy black shoes, her face to the wall. I called her name softly.

Reluctantly she turned over. Her murky eyes took time to settle on me. "I wish I was never born." Those were her first words. "My ear hurts. The pain is so bad I can't sleep. And I can't stand living with these people, they're all crazy. I never had any luck. If I had luck I'd have money—that's what I want."

"What would you do with it?"

"Spend it." Her words were thick.

"What would you spend it on?"

"Pants, shoes, underclothes."

"Did you go to your workshop program today?"

"No. I didn't feel good, my ear hurts. Why should I go to program?"

"Because that's where you make money."

"Not enough. I'm so miserable I could die."

"Rhoda's deeply depressed," the doctor said. "I've given her an anti-depressant, Elavil, but it takes three weeks to take hold. And you have to remember that she's off the massive amounts of thorazine she'd been taking. If she doesn't level out soon though, I'm going to call the psychiatrist to see if he has anything that could help. She also has this psychosomatic ear problem. There was an infection, but it's cleared up now. I've prescribed ear drops—just to make her feel better—but she refuses them. She's a very difficult woman."

Emma made her way down the Birch corridor, driving her wheelchair with her halo. "Hey," she called to an aide watching a soap opera, "I'm going outside."

"Going outside where?"

"Just right in front. I won't go no place, I promise." A conspiratorial smile took over her face as she turned to me. "They're worried because last Friday I left this place."

"She sure did," the aide interrupted. "She ran away. Didn't tell anyone she was going. Caused a hell of a stink. The worst was that she had to cross the road twice, right where all that traffic merges. Scared us all pretty bad, I'll tell you. There were incident reports to make even though nothing happened to her. She better not do that again."

"I guess I showed those bitches something," Emma said. Her head wobbled and she struggled for words, but there was a new sense of freedom about her. "I wanted to see my old social worker in Maple Hall and I did. I couldn't talk to the one I have now, and I want help getting out of here. So I went to see her. Now they're trying to say I didn't tell anyone, but I did. I said, 'I'm going to Maple,' and I went."

I glanced at the aides engrossed in their soaps.

"And now they say I ran away. Look at me. I'm crippled. How the hell could I run away?"

But that's what she did all right; even though she never left the grounds, even though it was only for a half hour. She exercised her own determination and will.

"They're not going to fuck around with me any more."

"May I ask you one favor before this meeting starts?" The nurse from Juniper put her notes on the conference table and slid into a chair facing me. "I know you mean well, but please, please don't bring Emily any more balloons. They bust, and the kids could easily choke to death on little pieces of rubber stuck in their throats. It's too dangerous on the ward to have something like that around."

Blood rushed hot to my face. I had no idea I was placing children in a hazardous situation.

"Maybe in a well-supervised home she could have one, but not here—there are too many times the kids are alone on the ward."

She was right, but I felt resentful, unjustly accused of teaching a baby to light matches. It was an uncomfortable way to begin this meeting.

Today was Emily's annual case review, held during the month of her birthday. The Juniper supervisor was on vacation and so was Emily's teacher. It was Vera's day off. Mrs. Benedict wasn't attending. The nurse, a physical therapy aide, the recreation therapist, Emily's social worker, and I were scattered around the conference table. By legal rights Emily should have been there, but if she had been, she would have just been pulling on my arm to go walking.

"Do we all know who Emily Benedict is?" the social worker asked, opening the meeting.

The door to the conference room was open for ventilation; from the hall echoed the clamor of kids being taken to program, laundry being collected, floors mopped.

First the nurse presented her notes on Emily's physical health. She described her general appearance as "very slender," reporting that Emily had gained no weight in the past months. "We're doing everything we can about this. We give her double portions, and we don't rush her through meals. But we want her to gain weight through sound nutrition, not by eating sweets." She looked over at me, and I read in her glance the suspicion that the balloon culprit might also be supplying her with clandestine goodies. I was innocent.

The recreation therapist said she couldn't hear a thing because of the racket in the hall and would the nurse mind repeating all that.

"What's with her humming all the time?" the physical therapy aide asked. "Does anyone know why she's always doing that?" The social worker suggested she did that to wall herself off from people. I agreed, but added that it sometimes seemed a form of communication.

"If there's no more in the sensory-motor area, let's move on to the cognitive," the social worker said.

Oh, let's just talk about Emily, I thought.

Each presentation began by listing her strengths, then her needs in positive terms. A few days ago I overheard a supervisor tell a teacher she could no longer use the word "attends," as in "he attends class regularly." It had to be more active. "Participates," she suggested. Now Emily's social worker told us she has "receptive language vocabulary"—meaning she can understand though she can't speak; "good auditory tracking"—meaning she knows my voice the instant I enter the building.

"Last year one of Emily's goals was to get through a couple of hours without her music box, and she's learned to do this. She used to cry if she didn't have it with her. Socially, she loves games. She loves to have the bowling pins brought out, and she loves playing ball. Her attention span is between fifteen and twenty minutes. And her real strength is putting together nuts and bolts."

"And what's this thing she's got about bicycles?" the physical therapist asked. "She goes nuts whenever she sees one. We had a tricycle in the PT room that we had to hide whenever she came in. She'd just stand there and stare at it."

"Let's move on to her emotional skills," her social worker said. "She adjusts well to her environment. She has likes and dislikes. She has moods."

"What? She dislikes rooms?" shrieked the recreation therapist as a janitor's bucket crashed against the conference room door.

"I know she gets very upset after she's been out and is returned," her social worker continued. "She gets quite aggressive and will throw things with all her strength. I don't know how we can train her to get over that."

"Perhaps we have to accept that she's angry and hurt. She's letting her feelings out the only way she can," I said. I had planned to say little, but here I was in the middle of Emily's heartache. "What we're not facing is this: Compared to being in the outside world, Emily *hates* it here. She doesn't want to come back. She cries. One time she pulled my arm so hard to keep from returning to the dayroom she fell. It's a wrenching experience to bring her back."

"It's true," the nurse said leaning forward, looking at each of us intensely. "It's true for so many of the kids. I took Donna with my family to Mystic Seaport. On the way home, when we entered the grounds, when she knew where she was, her entire face changed. My daughter noticed it—said her face was becoming stone. But you see Emily's one of the lucky ones—she's getting out. I wish more than anything we could get a placement for Donna."

The social worker was eager to speak. "Last week we took the kids on a drive—a really long drive. They had a great time. When we got back Louisa sat at the table and cried. I told her we'd do it again tomorrow and she stopped."

We sat silenced by the truth. Through all the talk of cognitive skills and receptive language vocabulary we'd reached the bottom. The children—the clients—have bleak, repetitive lives. The staff can barely tolerate the institution, and they're able to go home every night, paid for their work. They try their best, but they can't succeed because the clients are here against their will. The staff can't face such systemic failure on a daily basis; they are as well meaning as I am with the balloons I bring. Yet a speechless child, aged thirteen, cannot be trained out of showing her rage and despair. Another child, spastic, in a wheelchair, shows by her stony face that she doesn't want to leave the love and warmth of a family and return to her ward. A third child, who spins on her toes, giggles to herself, and gashes her body with her nails in the shower, weeps after an outing in a van.

3

"I would hardly say it's been an easy first week," said the new supervisor in Butternut Learning, looking up from a lunch of potato chips and vegetable salad. "There have been a host of problems already—a pinworm epidemic among the clients, and worse, one of the teachers has come down with hepatitis, type A. That's got the staff really nervous. Type A can only be passed blood to blood, mouth to mouth, or through intimate contact. There's no way to prove he got it here, and none of his clients are especially virulent carriers, but he has gotten scratched, and I suppose someone could have drooled on his wound. So we're offering free blood tests to anyone who's been around the clients a lot—and that means you."

Earl's hand had clawed my arm lightning fast, blood had oozed through my skin.

"Of course by the time the tests come back in, you'll know if you have hepatitis." Delicately she bit a potato chip in half. "You'll have turned yellow."

"My goodness you have small veins," said Hilda, the nurse. "The needle's bigger than any vein I can bring up." The velcro tourniquet was tight around my upper arm; she rubbed at my elbow bend with a cotton wad. "I'm going to have to go in after it now. If I wait much longer your arm will get numb." I sat in a metal chair, my arm steadied on her desk. Next to it were two dark red vials, labeled, dated. She peered into my face. "You don't faint, do you?" I assured her the African years had cured any fear of needles.

"That's good," said Fred Law, coming into the med room,

" 'cause Hilda brings needles from home. She likes using the dirty old blunt ones."

I looked away as Hilda approached. "You're going to feel a prick—it may hurt." I stared at the sign on the med-room door. "Now the pressure you'll feel is the vial filling with blood." It read *Medication Room* at the top, and *Hilda* at the bottom. "Now you'll feel the alcohol sting as I withdraw the needle." In the middle of the sign, in red crayon, someone had written *"Hot Lips."*

"I never felt a thing," I said.

"Fill in this form." She handed me a small yellow paper.

"When will I get the results?"

"Five weeks."

"You mean five days?"

"No, five weeks."

The new supervisor was right. If I had hepatitis, I would be yellow by then.

Sherry looked helplessly at the notebooks spread on the main table of her room. "Have you heard? The administration in its holy wisdom has decided to change clients and programs. This building is getting sixty new clients—and losing sixty we've been working with. There are going to be all these transfers and there's got to be some order to these records. The paperwork is awesome. I'm supposed to do what I can't get done here at home, but I'll be damned if I can do that, *plus* help my guys with homework, *plus* catch up on the housework, *plus* try to develop some kind of social life."

She pushed away the notebooks and leaned back in her chair. Hazel began to make grunting noises in the corner. "She's the one I'm most concerned about with this move. Hazel has really made quite an adjustment here. The new program is going to be mighty hard for her. In fact it's going to be mighty hard for all of us."

I asked what would happen to Gregory.

"He stays with us. But right now he's back on the ward with two broken fingers. He slipped in the shower. Come to think of it, a lot of people have been slipping in the shower in that building lately. That supposedly happened last Friday night. They brought him in here Monday, his hand all black and blue and puffy. We looked at it and called the doctor. Finally at five o'clock that evening they put those two fingers in a metal splint. So that's where Gregory is."

September continued to be hot, but Squire never took off his flannel shirt, his belly distending it like a red cape waved for a bull. In charge of the room, he heaved his feet on Sherry's desk and wiggled his big, yellow toenail through the hole in his sneakers.

I asked if he wasn't hot in his flannel shirt.

"Shit, I just shave my head in the summer and call it quits. I can't be bothered to be hot or cold. When it gets winter I've got some plastic bags I can tie around my shoes. You think I'm kidding? I take life as it comes. I've been sleeping in my pick-up all summer. I got a sister who would take me in, but shit, why bother to drive back to her place? I figured I could sleep in the truck just as well. I get drunk and just crawl in and stay wherever I am. I take a shower and shave in the building when I get to work. I got homes in parking lots all around here."

Squire stretched again. "Time to feed the animals. And we got a whole new bunch of them since you been here last."

The enormous switch had taken place. Only two of Sherry's clients were the same, the rest were new.

"Now that animal in that there cage is driving everyone crazy." Squire pointed to a corner that had been partitioned off by standing floor mats on end. Through a crack I saw a helmeted head moving restlessly.

I asked what he'd done to be caged.

"Everything. Won't stay in his chair, escapes from the room, throws himself on the floor and knocks himself unconscious. He's a real pain in the ass." I looked again through the crack; a lion paced back and forth, desperate and ready.

"You can't keep him locked up like this all the time."

"Can't I? He'll stay right here until he learns he can't behave the way he's been doing. And he'll learn. I promise that."

Hazel was gone; her grunting and hand wringing gone. She had been found in a well—in a cage—at Willowbrook; now Squire had also put a client in isolation, in a cage.

I asked him where Gregory was, for he was to remain with Sherry's group.

"You haven't heard about him?"

"Last I heard he'd slipped in the shower and broken his fingers."

Squire snorted. "He's got worse problems now. Monday I come in at six. I'm tripping Gregory, and I notice a spot of blood on his undershorts. So I pull them down to have a look. There's a huge gash about two inches long on his penis. And behind that is a big, huge black and blue mark. I check the records and there's no incident report, nothing. Everyone says things were just fine. But here's this big gash on his penis—so big it needs stitches, only they can't sew it up because after six hours it's considered infected."

"There are three possibilities how that could have happened—a heavy shoe or a piece of glass or a knife. I go with the shoe idea because of the huge bruise. It must of taken some whomp with a hard toe to cut him like that. No way a client could have done it. It must have really bled, a cut like that being where it is. There was only a small spot of blood on his sheet. Everyone knows it was staff. Someone's trying to cover up. Two guys have been put on administrative leave. Anyone who got a little carried away like that should have the sense to fill out an incident report. Make up some story, anything. That way you got a better chance than just hoping no one ever notices."

Walking through another program building I passed a black man being pushed in a wheelchair. I glanced, then stopped. Because I didn't expect him in this building I almost didn't recognize him.

"Isn't that Delmar Tate?" I asked.

"No," a small blonde teacher said, "his name is John Doe Number 11. He's been transferred to my class because they didn't want to bus him across the campus anymore. They said they were worried about hypothermia. I think he's getting ready to walk again—he took a few steps in the bathroom the other day. When I saw how tall he is, I knew there was no way I could handle him. Luckily I won't have to for long because I'm being transferred to another building."

I asked if they had ascertained whether his medication had been causing his problems.

"I don't know. In fact I don't know much of anything about him."

He had come to Wassaic without a past. As his teacher, Fred Law had developed an empathy for him. For a short while Elaine had been able to follow his rhythms and cadence with music. Clay had been with him for years and called him "my son." Now he was with a teacher who knew nothing about him and once again, he was without a past.

4

Martha had been pregnant again since July, but after last winter's miscarriage she had not announced it. "If I lose the baby this time, that's it. No more trying. I'm going to get the damned thing sewed up," she told me.

Now she had passed the twelve-week point for most miscarriages. "I went to a doctor yesterday and the most amazing thing happened. The doctor put this gizmo on my stomach and I could actually hear the baby's heart beating! I could hear it! That made me realize there is really someone in there. Somehow it made me feel not so much alone. But I made an appointment for the amniocentesis on the first of November. I'm scared, but I made it."

"We had a baby boy last week," Stuart said, "seven weeks early. It's been quite a time." He massaged his temples with his palms, pressing in slow, hard circles. "The baby's birth weight was three-and-a-half pounds. The doctor told us he'd be one of the biggest in the nursery—some of them weigh only a pound. He's in the medical center in Albany, where they have the best staff and best equipment to deal with neonatal problems." Stuart pulled his arms over his head and cracked his knuckles as he yawned.

"My wife thought her water broke—the doctor hospitalized her and gave her steroids to develop the baby's lung expansion. You don't have to have worked here long to know that's one of the things you need to worry about: there's got to be enough oxygen getting to the brain. When it became clear after a couple of days that they were going to have to deliver him, we were told what the chances were.

"I was right there in the operating room—told them I

just wanted to hear him cry properly when he came out. And he did—a good loud cry. He was on oxygen for a couple of hours, then on his own. As soon as I could I tested his reflexes and rotated his joints. Everything seems to be okay.

"But we have to reckon with what the consequences will be if it's not. We have to have faith that he would have a role in life if he's not perfect."

He did not say the words "brain damage," the same way he did not call the baby by name.

"Yesterday for the first time we took pictures of him in the hospital. I'm optimistic, but I'm not trying to pin any great hopes on the future. It's been a hard time, and it's not over yet."

Stuart's words rolled through me: *"We have to have faith that he would have a role in life if he's not perfect."*

Mr. and Mrs. Mitchell were regular visitors to Juniper Hall, coming at least once a week from New York City, and frequently taking their son Glenn, a teenager who required total care, home for visits. The supervisor had told me they were the most vocal and watchful parents in the building.

Mr. Mitchell sat slumped in a chair. His wife was tall enough that she had to bend as she stood by the crib-bed that held Glenn, who slept, stroking his bare leg. They were aware of everyone passing in the hall in front of the large dormitory window.

"So you're still snapping pictures?" Mr. Mitchell called. He did not change positions in the chair, as though he expected no answer. "You're like whats-his-name . . . Steichen. Everyone's heard of him. He was a very famous man."

Mrs. Mitchell continued to rub Glenn's leg. There was a silence, as though it were her turn. When she spoke, her voice was suspicious. "So what is it you're planning to do with these pictures anyway?"

I had told them about the project before, and I explained again.

"I still don't see the purpose in all this," Mrs. Mitchell said.

"I hope the photographs will be exhibited. Handicapped people have been hidden too long. I want to make visible what people have been afraid to see. I want to make people take responsibility."

"Did you see 'Best Boy'?" Mrs. Mitchell interrupted. "Now there was a film. Everyone around us had puddles after that one. But look at these people you're photographing. Compared to them, 'Best Boy' looks terrific, really handsome." Their own son lay reed thin, angular, pimpled and dark on the crib-bed.

"There are a lot of people who are photogenic and a lot who aren't. It's easy to respond to the cute ones. They're the ones who get all the attention. And by the way, the cute ones are the ones who get the best care too. That's a fact. It's hard not to be resentful if your child isn't one of those."

I told her I was working hard on learning not to visually discriminate. I thought her eyes began to soften. "Perhaps one day when Glenn is awake," I said, "you'll let me do some photographs of the three of you."

"You can do pictures of Glenn and me," Mr. Mitchell said, coming to life.

"Not me," Mrs. Mitchell snapped, her hardness returning. "I'm not going to be publicly displayed with Glenn. I'll have no part of it."

5

Emma's wheelchair was in the repair shop—the chair that had made her so happy on her birthday, the chair she had waited a year for, the chair that cost half the price of an automobile. "The fucking thing just went crazy the other day," she stuttered in her halting, difficult voice. "It started going around in circles." Without her wheelchair there was no way to "run away," show her independence. But she could cuss.

"Where the hell have you been?" yelled Tillie. Her hands were on her tiny hips, her head cocked to the side.

"Tillie, please, I'm sorry," I began.

"Sorry is fine but I've been here all alone. I waited and waited for you all lonesome and you didn't come for such a long time." Her twisted little body led me to the dayroom, and she hopped onto the couch, tucking her legs sideways. "I thought maybe you had quit or something. Every day I waited for you." She shook her head sorrowfully, her cloudy eyes intent on my face.

I apologized. "Tillie, I've had work to do." My voice sounded strange not because I lied, but because I choked on the consequences of not seeing her for a few weeks. For Tillie, every person who dropped out, even temporarily, was another promise broken. In several months the photographs would be finished and I would drop out for good.

"Well, you should let people know where you are. And remember, it gets very lonesome here. There's no one to talk to." She leaned forward. "Now I have something to tell you. My mother's going to take me out of here. She's going to find me a place to live near her when she moves to Arizona.

And that's the truth!" Tillie grinned a wide smile, her gold tooth thrusting happily from her mouth.

"That's wonderful, Tillie. Who told you this good news?" I tried to keep suspicion from my voice. How many people had been told they were being moved out because a relative could not bear a client's despair?

"My mother did. She wasn't the one who signed the papers for me to come in here. It was my aunt. She was the one who signed the papers. My mother had nothing to do with it. She would never do something like that. She's the one who bought me my gold tooth."

Tillie fingered a chain with an enameled butterfly. "Stuart gave this to me a few days ago. He's the one I'm really going to miss in Arizona," she said wistfully—as though she'd already departed.

Rhoda stood in front of her closet dressed in a faded house-dress much too big for her, belted at the waist. Her gray hair was braided down her neck, but wisps stuck out wildly as though she'd just gotten out of bed.

"Don't you like my jacket?" She took a light blue parka from the closet. "If I had money I'd buy lots of pretty clothes. I love to have nice clothes." She moved quickly around the room. There was no wheelchair, no sign of a walker, only a tripod-based cane to prove the complete success of her hip replacement. She pointed to the two stuffed animals on her bed.

"My cousin gave me that bear. And the poodle's mine, too. Have you ever seen a live poodle? My cousin had two of them at her house. She had a little red jacket for them when it was cold, and she put little booties on them!" Her mouth twitched crookedly up into a laugh, as though it were something she had not tried much. "I used to see all kinds of things when I lived in Red Hook. I went to the world fair. I went to the carnival. I could buy a slice of pizza. I love pizza."

"Rhoda, are they giving you Elavil?" This was certainly not the depressed woman I had seen lying on her bed last month.

"I don't like to take medicine. They don't give it to Dora, and she's crazy as a bed bug. They don't give it to crazy Josephine. Just me. I don't like that."

An aide bustled in the room and hovered around. Rhoda waited until she was out of earshot.

"She's always looking at me. Watch her, all the time she'll stare at me. It makes me feel funny. She's nuts. I wish they'd get rid of her."

The aide circled closer and eyed us both. "The best time of your life is when your kids are little," she cackled. I looked around to see if she was addressing someone behind us, but it seemed she was talking to Rhoda and me. "My sons used to get up in the morning and go out with their fishing poles. They'd come home with these little trout and I'd cook them for breakfast. They used to catch frogs too. Frogs' legs are $10.00 a pound. One of my sons lives in California and I'm going to visit him next month. I'd better get me a new bathing suit."

A few days later there was a big, brand new, pea-green E-Z Boy lounge chair taking up a third of Rhoda's room. She stood by the closet examining two large boxes of clothing.

"Here are the shoes I bought you," said an aide holding up brown leather lace-up shoes. "They're your size. And here are the slippers." She held up one baby-blue fleece-trimmed bedroom slipper. "I told you you'd like my taste."

The aide glanced at me. "It's her money all right."

Rhoda was overwhelmed, looking from one box to another. She held up dresses, blouses, skirts.

"Now they have to go be marked with your name before you can put them away, but first sign this receipt so they know you've received them."

"Did you see my chair?" Rhoda asked. "I bought it with my own money. It cost $244 and it can fold all the way out, like a bed."

"Come on, Rhoda. Sign. Here. Your name."

The first receipt was from a nearby furniture store—the E-Z Boy lounge chair was $450, not $244. And the clothes were over $450 also—all bought at one small dress store in Dover Plains. It was too much trouble for most staff to bother taking clients to shop, and I'd been told local shops make it worthwhile for staff to spend clients' money.

Rhoda signed.

She tried on the new shoes; they fit perfectly. "My mother left me a thousand dollars when she died, and they finally let me have it. I didn't want her to die, but she did. I always say you lose your best friend when your mother dies. These shoes are nice, huh?"

Rhoda caressed the shoes, tried on the bedroom slippers. She asked if she could try on the clothes. Always in her depression she'd talked about wanting money and nice things; now combined with the Elavil, they seemed to be making her happy.

"I never had no good luck, but now maybe I will. I'll knock on wood." She rapped her knuckles on the plastic seat. "Hey, that's not wood!"—then she laughed as she reached over to knock on the wood end table.

It was the first time I'd seen Rhoda really laugh.

The next time I saw Rhoda she was watching TV in her pea-green E-Z Boy chair, and she greeted me with a smile. Rhoda, whose depression was severe, who complained incessantly of ear troubles, who wanted to die—that Rhoda smiled at me and offered me her chair. "I'm happy. You know why? 'Cause I'm going to a group home, that's why. I'll be near my people. My cousin wants me to live with her but she doesn't have money. Now I'm going to get away from these dummies. And they fixed my hip good—I can walk again and it don't hurt. I got new dresses and pants just like I wanted—you want to see them again?"

I followed Rhoda from the dayroom to her bedroom, and admired the clothes she brought from the closet one by one. I knew the change in Rhoda had been brought about by drugs as well as circumstance, but the combination of the two had changed her completely.

The mainstream of Freudian psychoanalytic thinking maintains that it is not external situations that produce neurosis, but how the spirit adapts to them. An extension of this theory would hold that Rhoda's anger, suspicion, and "inappropriate behavior" were not caused by being institutionalized with profoundly retarded roommates—isolated from potential growth and normal life—but rather were caused by her own maladaptation to those circumstances. The healthy person would accept and work within those limitations, even when they are severe.

There are, however, psychoanalysts who reject that point of view, and believe that the key to behavior is rooted in biographical reality. Rhoda's response to her altered situation seemed a proof of that thinking. Her yearnings and fantasies were for a home, some money, some clothes. It may be that she has a psychosis too deep and long lasting to respond permanently to small changes, but it was obvious that as soon as one of her desires began to be realized, she seemed, for the moment, better.

I asked the Evergreen social worker about Rhoda's community placement.

"Rhoda was number one on a list for a vacancy in a behavioral house, but another client, whose parents are friends of a state senator, seems to have first priority. She's taking huge amounts of medication now, and she seems to be doing pretty well. I'm hoping a vacancy will show up. It's true I've told her she's going, but it won't be tomorrow."

"And Tillie? Is she really going to Arizona?"

"No way."

6

"Emily's at loose ends today," Vera said. "Her teacher's out sick, and there's nothing for her to do. I'm going off duty now, so I've put Emily down in Loretta's ward."

Loretta. The bitter, angry aide.

"Don't look at me like that. Loretta's all right, in her own way. She shoots off her mouth a lot, but you know what? She says what a lot of people are thinking and don't dare say. She talks big, but she shows up every day."

Loretta moved alone through a ward crowded with wheelchairs. Emily stood when she saw me, but didn't move toward me, her expression was stunned and vacant.

"Welcome to Ward D for Damned, Allen Funt. You've come for your pretty one, huh?" She picked up a pamper and wheeled a client off.

"I'm going to take Emily to the movie in the gym," I said, my voice steely.

"Oh yes," she called over her shoulder, "that's a very good idea. She'll understand every word of it, of course. Maybe it will be a foreign film with subtitles, and she can read them to you."

The movie had already started when we arrived. The gym is a large, multi-functional room used for dances, events like the Passover Seder, and as an auditorium. Perhaps a hundred clients and twenty aides faced the screen, which had been erected below the basketball net. The film being shown was "Jodi," the story of a young girl whose back had been broken in a diving accident and how she overcame her handicaps.

Emily pulled back on my wrist, afraid of the loud noise that rolled off the tile walls. I eased her into the room and shut the door so that light from the hall wouldn't disturb the screening.

I need not have bothered. The room was not dark at all. Curtains had been drawn over the tall windows, but the curtains were in shreds. One at the back had a huge square hole in it. All were torn, none blocked the light. We found a chair, and watched washed-out colors move across the screen. The entire movie was shadowy, except for the few scenes that had been shot in brilliant sunlight. In front of us, clients squirmed in their seats.

And the noise we had heard when we entered didn't change much either. At first I thought it was just the volume, but then I realized the film and sound track were out of synch—the dialogue sounded as if it were being gargled. The music seemed played under water. We could neither see nor hear the movie.

I saw Rhoda, her head turned from the screen, staring at a window framed by glare. Emma had her head down on her wheelchair tray. Tillie was restlessly popping up in her seat. Emily had begun to hum an anxious, growly note.

When I recognized someone from the recreation department, which had sponsored the event, I asked what was going on. Could the film be fixed?

"It's the print of the movie," he said. "Maybe the next reel will be better."

I had heard the bell that signaled a reel change and knew we were already in the next reel.

"Oh well," an aide next to me said. "At least the kids don't care. It's all the same to them."

As we sat outside at dusk Sam told me about a conference on autism Wassaic had sponsored. "The keynote address was given by a man who said he'd almost single-handedly battled the so-called 'experts' led by Bettelheim, who say that autism is produced by a problem in the family, poor infant mothering. He talked about the use of vitamin therapy. He has an autistic son who was in terrible shape to begin with, but now at age twenty-two, is living in an apartment and attending a workshop. His father's avowed goal is to make him completely normal. He's used vitamin B-6 on his son and done a number of controlled experiments on other clients. It seems that of sixteen clients he has worked with, twelve of them responded very well to B-6."

Emily exhibited autistic behavior, yet I'd never heard of vitamin therapy being used on her.

"As the man said, it can't do any harm. The worst that can happen is you're out eight dollars for the vitamins."

The next morning, waiting for Max in the orthodontist's office, I read an article about an autistic man, legally blind, with a diagnosis of severe to profound retardation and an IQ of thirty, who is now an artist in Scotland, selling his paintings. He never spoke until he was eleven. Nor was he ever in an institution. His improvement was attributed to vitamin therapy.

I had argued with my father in the spring about hopelessness and euthanasia. At that time I had so few facts and examples to support my feeling that we could not make proclamations on who should live and why. But since then I'd heard about a girl diagnosed to be profoundly retarded who was now graduating from high school; I'd looked at a blotched baby having little seizures and found him beautiful; I'd heard and read about new hope through vitamins.

At home I called Mrs. Benedict—I couldn't help myself—and told her about the vitamin B-6.

"Well, I have friends who are interested in that sort of thing." Her voice was open and receptive. "I probably ought to look into it."

"I had my amniocentesis today," Martha told me on the phone. "It was a remarkable and quite scary experience. First of all the genetic counseling—you have no idea how many things can go wrong until you've been through that. And then there are the statistics on Down's syndrome. At age thirty the percentage is one in a thousand. I'm almost forty. The chances then are one in a hundred. That's significant.

"I finally gathered the courage to ask about abortion if the amniocentesis has bad results. I found out that abortion in the second trimester is no small thing. It would be a nightmare to go through; it's a real delivery by then. And there are the moral issues to deal with—how can we kill life just because it's less than perfect? But they reassured me that of the hundreds of women who go through the clinic, they only see about one negative result a month.

"We went into another room for the amniocentesis, but first I had the ultrasound. They rubbed some sort of sticky magnetic jelly on my stomach, then put on something that looked like an iron and moved it around. Seeing the baby on the screen was a thrill, but odd—sort of like looking through a fish-eye lens—one part swam into focus, then another part. I was overcome by how tiny it is. I thought it would be the size of my cat, at least! There was a sea-horse-shaped spine and little blips for limbs. I could see the teeny heart beating. They made a polaroid of the screen, but it doesn't look like much, just a gray blob.

"The amniocentesis itself didn't hurt, but it was terrifying having that needle stuck into me and not being sure where it was going and what it might hit on the way. When we came out there was a waiting room full of nervous forty-year-old women. The whole procedure had only taken about half an hour and I told them not to worry—it was a cinch. Now comes the hard part—waiting another month for the results. I'll be in maternity clothes by then."

7

"I've had it with this place," Stuart said, his voice unnaturally quiet. "Things are at a new all-time low. I don't see how I can stick it out." Stuart held a man's scabby, red forearm to keep him from biting himself, but sometimes his head swung under the table, teeth clicking. Everyone else in the room was quiet, rocking and staring in front of empty tables. Stuart looked up at me with brown sad eyes, while the resident dipped down for another taste of his arm.

"Monday they came in here and took away all our program materials."

I didn't understand.

"I mean the team leader came in with a plastic garbage

bag and ordered me to throw away any object that could be put in the mouth. I thought it was a joke at first. But she meant it. Seems someone in the girls' school choked on a puzzle part or something, so now they've taken everything away. For the safety of the clients, they say."

I looked around the room. The shelves were bare, the tables were bare.

"We just spent all our materials money on new puzzles and pegboards and toys. This is just a ruse. The administration has been dying to get rid of all the toys. They want 'age appropriate' things."

"What have they given you to replace what they took away?"

"Nothing. They told us to concentrate on aid-to-daily-living skills. That means toothbrushing and hair combing. But look around. These clients don't care how much their hair is combed. And as to the toothbrushing, that's absurd. You can't spend two or three hours brushing teeth. *That's* not appropriate. Can you imagine the congestion in the bathrooms? So they tell us to bring basins of water into the classrooms. Talk about inappropriate. You don't brush your teeth in your living room at home, and I'm not going to do it in the classroom."

Arthur, a blind client, ran his hands frantically over the table in front of him. His fingers touched nothing. He began to scream.

Stuart took a piece of paper from his cabinet, shouting over Arthur's noise, "I guess we'll color turkeys for Thanksgiving today. I can't imagine what else to do." He put the paper before Arthur, and the instant his fingers felt it, his screaming stopped. "Okay, I'll get a crayon and you can draw. Okay?"

"Okay," said Arthur.

"He's blind, but he likes to draw?"

"I don't know if he likes it, but he's got to have something to do. There aren't any crayons in this drawer. Oh shit. I wasn't here yesterday. Do you think . . . that's it. They came around and took all the crayons too. Now there's zero in this room."

Arthur screamed again.

"I'll explain it to you," Sherry said, "though what you see is pretty much what there is." Her room was bare.

"First of all, I don't want you to think they made this decision arbitrarily, without giving us a replacement for what they've taken away. No indeed. We have new toothbrushes and best of all, toothbrush holders. That's the new skill to be mastered—the brush in the holder. Anyway, the supervisor was sent around with these bags to collect the materials Monday. She was as upset as the teachers, but there's nothing she can do about it. It's the directive. Came right down from the top. Now we've got the new toothbrushes. That's one of the really good things to swallow. In fact there's lots of bathroom stuff to eat—toilet paper, toothpaste. Gregory has no trouble at all with a towel.

"The whole thing's so absurd. Part of me thinks it will all blow over—it's got to. After all, when the administrators get their daily charts with blank activity lines, they'll figure out something's wrong. We're doing the same kind of custodial care we did ten years ago, only in smaller rooms. But meanwhile it's client abuse for clients whose only pleasure is pegboards and puzzles."

I rushed to Juniper, jumped the gate, ran down the stairs to the basement. If they'd taken the toys from Emily's classroom I'd drop my impartial observer's role and lead a rebellion. I'd had enough: garbled movies in a bright room; no staff able to walk with her; an angry, sarcastic aide substituting when ward duty doubled up. Now this.

Noise came from her teacher's room, but I couldn't tell what the sounds were. Using all my restraint, I quietly turned the doorknob. The teacher was there, and she had a wooden bowling alley set up on a table with plastic pins at one end. Wonder Woman had pushed the ball and most of the pins had been knocked over. Around the room were toys, puzzles, games, and a record player with stacks of records. Wonder Woman stood with her head back laughing. Emily twisted and clapped.

"No, the answer is no. We don't have our program materials back. And the teachers are as upset about it today as they were last week," the Butternut supervisor said. She sat in her office doodling, her head leaning against her fist. "And I'm as upset about it as they are. It's the program coordinator's personal feelings about pegboards and toys that's gotten mixed up with health issues. But there is another side that's got to be looked at." She stabbed at her doodle with the pencil. "There *has* been abuse of pegboards. Some clients have had one put in front of them and that's it for the day. Nothing else.

"Still, I know things can get done in the classroom with very little. When one of the teachers was out with hepatitis, I helped take over his group. He had no supplies—almost nothing in his room. So we improvised—played ball with the clients; worked on gross motor skills and bad habits that needed correcting. There are lots of ways to fill a day."

"But," I interrupted, "aren't you then making the teachers custodians? Aren't you putting them into the role of angry, frustrated mothers who merely yell at their children's faults all day?"

"It's a fine line all right," she sighed. "And it's the real philosophical flaw with this programming. We go over and over their defects, trying to correct them. By doing that we don't focus on what they can do right, and we lose a sense of the residents as whole people."

That was it: the emphasis was on defects rather than assets. The teachers were under constant pressure to make corrections and adjustments in human beings; there was neither time nor encouragement for valuing the client as a complete person.

"Marylou, get your feet on that floor," Sherry yelled.

Fred Law appeared in Sherry's doorway, jangling his pocket change as he waited for attention. "Ahem. I just had a talk with one of our bosses." She whirled around. "It seems they're going to let us have some of our materials back. Everything can be returned except for pegboards, stacking rings, and marbles."

"Hallelujah! How did that happen?"

He leaned against the doorframe, arms folded. "I demanded an appointment with the program coordinator, and I got it. No one else has tried to talk to her. These people are all sheep and that's the way the state likes it. Nice and orderly, do your job and go home. Don't start braying."

From the corner came the sound of fabric ripping. "All right Marylou. You know better than that," Sherry barked. "Now everyone is going to get a cookie but you. Watch, I'm going to pass them out." She unwrapped a cellophane pack of graham crackers and distributed one to each client.

Fred continued without pause. "I made all my points, and she tried to make a few of her own. The coordinator claims she never said we had to give up anything that could be put in the mouth. She's concerned with the appropriateness of the materials themselves. If a client chokes on something and dies, she wants to be able to justify it. It should be a toothpaste cap rather than a toy."

There was more ripping; half a dozen buttons popped on the table. "All right, Marylou, this is it. I can't even have a two-minute conversation without having you act up. This time I want you to smell the cookie first." Sherry held one under her nose. Marylou stood there like stone, her arms crossed over her torn blouse.

"I mean, the administration at last discovered that some clients put things in their mouths. So they're using that as an excuse to force their own program materials. Look at this." From a shelf Fred pulled down a board covered in red plaid flannel with two shirt pockets stapled on. "What on earth are you supposed to do with this all day? Put money or handkerchiefs in the pockets? Come on. These clients aren't going to be handling money in the real world. The most they can get out of this absurd board is to get cut by loose staples.

"I asked the coordinator where we were going to get new things for the clients to do. She told me we could bring in things from home. I told her I'm not being paid to bring things from home. They are supposed to be supplying materials. That's the responsibility of the institution. She said we must have money in the program to buy new materials. I reminded her this is the middle of the year. We spent our money at the beginning of the year on materials which are now in garbage bags."

Marylou had been easing closer to the door, and now she made a dash down the hall.

"Okay, everyone up. Let's all go to the bathroom with Marylou." Sherry said in a weary voice. "If we're lucky we'll make it before she gets it all over the walls." She shook her head and chuckled. "Once I was looking into some graduate courses, and someone said, 'What's the trouble, Sherry? You tired of cleaning shit all day?' 'Oh no,' I said. 'I just want to learn more about it.' "

8

The Juniper physical-therapy room had twisted black and orange streamers tenting the ceiling, stacks of cornstalks in the corners, white sheets covering the walls, pumpkins, ghosts, skeletons, and witches everywhere. The room was packed with wheelchairs, the most severely handicapped children. As the band—two guitars and a piano—assembled at the head of the room, the children gazed silently inward. The staff donned wigs and funny plastic faces.

"The first song will be "The Twelve Days of Halloween," the guitarist announced. "On the first day of Halloween my true love sent to me, a bat in a dead hollow tree."

One of the children began to cry. "Please Dickie," an aide said. "Just a minute, sweetie. This is supposed to be a good time. Hold on." The crying stopped.

"On the second day of Halloween my true love sent to me, two flying witches and a . . ."

The Butternut supervisor, in a pointed black witch hat, sat with two other judges in the foyer with pads and pencils. The building secretary had autumn leaves scotch-taped to her yellow sweater and brown skirt. I wore a rubber mask of two gnarled hands holding up a camera, and hung around my neck a blue and yellow plastic camera that squeaked and shot out a silly face when the shutter was pressed.

The clients were paraded out group by group. The first, in wheelchairs, were draped with sheets, their faces painted white, like a secret society I had once photographed in Africa.

We clapped and cheered. Another group was dressed as angels and devils. We laughed. Another group was in drag; Fred wore a leather jacket and skirt, with round rope toys hung over his ears for earrings and a sign pinned on his back, "Wassaic's finest—$50." Dan wore a peach dress and make-up, "Cheryl Tiegs in the year 2000." Melvin, who ate cigarette butts, came wrapped in a sheet with a red cylinder on his head.

I made photographs, my rubber mask squashed against my face. All the teachers presented their groups except Sherry.

"I think it's a form of client abuse," she told me when the festivities were over, and we were alone in her room. "I know the people I have now, and they're anti-social. There's no way I'm going to get a costume on Henry—he won't keep his regular clothes on. Ben shrieks if you touch him. They're confused by the noise and the crowds. They don't want to be dressed queerly and paraded in front of the staff. After all, that's who we're really doing this for. How many of the clients looked as though they were into it? Not many."

And that was true. Most seemed bewildered: An Indian kept tearing off her headband, and an angel was asleep in her wheelchair. Melvin-as-cigarette seemed happiest, hopping up and down and smiling. A few other clients seemed to enjoy it, but most were passive and disinterested. At the Juniper party there had been elaborate decorations, Halloween songs, and forty wheelchair clients oblivious to it all. Yet we had no idea how much was getting through. If there were only a few clients identified as capable of really enjoying the event, shouldn't it still be held for everyone, on the chance one or two more might be getting more from it than we know?

In Africa, ten years ago, as I developed film I would agitate my developing tank every thirty seconds with my right hand, while my left hand turned the pages of the only photography book I'd brought with me—the work of Diane Arbus. Night after night I looked at those images of people outside my world; hermaphroditic, head-to-toe tatooed, nudists, a giant. The last few pages showed untitled work Arbus had made at a large New Jersey institution for the retarded, shortly before she took her own life. Their placement at the end of the book gave them cumulative power after the "freaks" that came before.

I'd often thought of Arbus as I photographed at Wassaic, and how far I wanted my images to be from the ones she had made. While she worshiped realism, she created fantasy. The people she photographed, ("retardates," Patricia Bosworth called them in *Diane Arbus, a Biography*), were isolated from their nightmare world on a grassy lawn. "She was fascinated by their 'extreme innocence'. . . In front of her cameras they behaved like bizarre, overgrown kids. . . . Their complete absorption in what they were doing—whether it was trying on funny hats or pulling at each other's hair—delighted and moved her," Bosworth wrote.

In one Arbus image someone is draped in a sheet with a death-head mask; in another, a costumed and masked group, holding hands, staggers under a mysterious sky. Arbus had photographed residents in funny hats, or doing somersaults on a lawn, or masked on Halloween, protected from reality, closer to how we wanted to see them than how they were.

9

"You want to have a tantrum? Okay, go have yourself a good one," Sherry yelled, nose to nose with Gregory.

Gregory's face—gaunt three months ago and fat now—balled up. His mouth opened into an *O* and the sound that came out was of an adult squalling like an infant. A six-foot tall, completely bald man wailed and stamped his feet.

"I'll give you a drink of juice, Gregory, but not until you sit down. *Now sit!* Oh this is too much today, it really is. He's not only twenty pounds heavier, he's spoiled rotten after a month in the building."

Gregory stole an open can of juice and drank it down. Sherry grabbed his arm and steered him—roughly—to a chair. *"Now stay there and I mean it."* He sat and put his thumb in his mouth. Sherry stared at him. "Starting Monday we'll get rid of that habit too."

I asked why. It seemed to me that after all Gregory had been through recently—broken fingers, cut penis—he could at least be allowed the comfort of his thumb.

"There's a good reason," Sherry said. She knelt next to him and pulled his thumb from his mouth with the gentleness and protection she must give her own young children. "See that poor thumb? It's all red and raw now."

Gregory's hair was slicked back in greasy streaks, the cream giving off a sweetish smell. "Shamuna Sissy Sasa," he said, looking earnestly at Sherry.

"I don't know, where does Sissy Sasa live?"

"Shamun," Gregory muttered, and pressed close to her as she dished out chocolate pudding.

"Gregory, sit down and I'll give you pudding. Sit *down.*" She turned to me. "That's the main thing I get out of his talking—his brothers and sisters. You have to remember he had a full life until his late teens. There's a lot of memory there. Now I hate to say it—because it usually means a backslide—but I think Gregory's made real progress. He's a lot easier than he used to be and a lot happier too."

Gregory stared at her, his arms folded across his chest like an entombed Egyptian.

"Give Rebecca the big-city smile," Sherry cajoled him. Gregory stared, not moving. "You gotta see this. Please, Gregory, let's have the big-city smile." And Gregory's mouth turned up at the corners in a Dracula-like grimace, something in the category of a smile.

A week later Sherry's arm was in a sling. "Gregory's handiwork." She nodded at the six-foot man who stood in mummy position, hands tucked in opposite armpits. "He wanted to see 'Sissy Sasa' a little too much—pulled on my arm too hard and this is the result. The shoulder isn't dislocated—I'm wearing this sling for protection and because the damn thing hurts. Also, it has its advantages at home. The boys are actually doing the dishes for a change."

"Sissy Sasa? Sissy Sasa?" whined Gregory.

"She's gone in the blue car, Gregory," Sherry said.

She turned to me. "I've something to show you. There really is a Sissy Sasa. Gregory's building charge took it upon herself to write her, and here's the letter she got back." She picked up a thick, blue sheet of paper, with a letterhead of dark purple; the words were small and cramped, slanted slightly backhand, as though reluctant to come onto the page.

Dear Miss Dunham,

Your letter was quite a surprise, and though it makes me feel guilty to know my brother speaks of me constantly, I am grateful to have news of him. My other siblings are close enough to visit now and then, but I rarely leave the West Coast. I suppose it's often true that those we see the least we think of the most. Since your interest in Gregory's well being seems most genuine, I thought I would tell you who 'Sissy Sasa' is, as well as a few personal and emotional details to help you understand Gregory, and what he means to me.

I was six years old when he was born and, having four older brothers and sisters, I was both relieved to relinquish my position as the youngest and slightly jealous of my new competition. He was a sweet and lovely baby, and seemed completely normal. But around the time babies usually sit up and begin to explore the world, we knew something was wrong. My mother took him from doctor to doctor. It wasn't until I was grown that I learned the truth about his birth. He'd been born after a long and difficult labor, with his umbilical cord wrapped tightly around his neck. His brain had been cut off from his supply of oxygen.

None of his behavior was abnormal enough to keep him from living at home with us. We all loved him and were touched by his extreme gentleness. I remember that he kept a little gray rabbit in his room, and took total responsibility for it, even feeding it with an eyedropper when it got sick. He attended a special school. Despite his problems he learned to read, and for a while showed a gift for math, being able to memorize multiplication tables and add long columns of numbers with remarkable speed.

Then at age sixteen his problems caught up with him, or he had some sort of breakdown, I don't know which. It broke all our hearts to see him enter a mental hospital. We stood by helplessly as he deteriorated. His coordination went first, and then his speech. The part of him that remained—and seems to still remain—is his memory. If only he could regain his speech he could release the frustration he surely feels.

I suppose it's been a decade since I've seen him, but I remember our last visit very clearly. It was a gorgeous spring day, the sort of day that makes even a state institution seem bearable. Gregory and I sat on a bench beneath a willow tree, and in his halting speech he told me what was in his heart. He knew where he was, he knew what had happened to him. He couldn't help his outbursts. He missed the family deeply. And he said, with great dignity and emotion, that the greatest sorrow of his life was that he could no longer play with numbers. After all he'd been through, my poor, sick brother still wanted to be a mathematician.

I've had a fulfilled life and a successful career. I've not lived in obsession or fear or physical pain. It is hard for me to conceive of my brother's life now, and sometimes it's hard for me to believe we were born of the same parents. But a part of my childish heart is always with him, and when I pray, I pray for him to experience peace. I hope everyone at Wassaic cares for him as much as you seem to, and that his days are passing with tranquility. Please tell him that his 'Sissy Sasa' loves him. Thank you for writing to me.

"Pretty amazing letter, huh?" Sherry asked, and we both stared at Gregory. But I didn't answer. Twenty years and the birth of two more children had blunted my grief of losing a child, but this letter made that time fresh and sharp with a new edge that cut me deeply.

When I was twenty-three and Wynne a toddler, I became pregnant with my second child—a planned and much desired pregnancy, though perhaps for the wrong reasons. I was bored, I needed more challenges, needed to become competent and successful in an area of my own while my first husband was excelling in his studies at law school. With one young child already, it didn't seem that I had any possibilities besides mothering, so I decided to do that job as well and as completely as I could. At night, after Wynne was in bed, I climbed the stairs with my big belly and lay under his crib listening to him babble. How I adored his joy in new language, and how I cherished the reality of my body preparing to reproduce again.

One Friday evening, two weeks before my due date, I went to the theater and during the first act of Chekhov's *The Cherry Orchard,* a play that interested me greatly, realized I had not felt the baby kick for some time. Or perhaps I just imagined I'd not felt the baby kick. I didn't know which was true. I tried to concentrate on the rest of the play, but it seemed my brain had a direct line to my body and nothing else counted. I was determined to will movement in my belly. Nothing happened. Afraid I was making too much of it, I told no one. That night I barely slept, and the next day began my vigil again, waiting for the sign I assured myself would come that all was well with my baby. Sometimes I felt tiny rumblings, but I could not be sure they were not gas. Yet I knew this: no big fists, elbows, or feet were thumping inside me.

I endured Sunday. Monday I went to my doctor. He listened intently with his fetal stethoscope, my belly mountainous on his table. At last he told me the baby was dead. And it could be weeks, he warned, before the body expelled the fetus.

I was spared that anguish. Two days later I went into hard, active, pointless labor. Before delivery I asked for an anesthetic. I woke strapped to a cot in the recovery room, and when I was back in my hospital room, the doctor came to tell me my child had been a boy. He had strangled in utero. The cord had been tightly wrapped around his neck.

When I went home, my husband had dismantled the antique brass crib I had restored and polished for the baby. My world became flat, I wept every day, and ignored the advice of friends who urged me to become pregnant again immediately.

And now for the first time, reading Gregory's sister's letter, I saw that there could have been another possibility: The cord is tight around the baby's neck, his oxygen diminished enough to slow his kicks, but not enough for death. I bear him with concern, but with thanksgiving as well. I take him home to the antique crib I have restored and polished, with brass knobs that slide up and down the rails, meant to amuse him, attract his attention when he begins to follow light and motion. But at three months he pays no attention to the click of metal falling on metal, he doesn't seem to care how the knobs twirl and spin. At five months I notice he does not move much in his crib, and by six months he's made no move to sit up. I do not know if I am imagining his lethargy, or if my fear is real. I call his doctor and the tests begin.

For Gregory that nightmare had been a reality; those minutes or hours without oxygen somehow took him from being a child who learned multiplication tables to a man who needed "one-on-one" supervision all his waking hours, who ate towels and had been hospitalized near death, who had his penis cut in a mysterious, unsolved way, whose few intelligible words focused on Sissy Sasa.

The letter I had read was about Gregory, but it could have been about the baby I had planned to name Christopher.

Christmas

1

Though Emily pulled at my arm to go outside, first I stopped by her social worker's office to see if there was any news about her community residence.

"As a matter of fact," he said, "I got a call about Emily this morning. It sounds good—though I'm warning you, I've heard good things before, then seen a lot of delays. But they're saying the house is coming right along, and she'll be moving within a month."

January. That meant Christmas at Wassaic.

The wind blew cold; it was early winter. Emily's coat was tattered at the seams, and too thin. Soon her grandmother would see her in this coat. She wouldn't wear gloves, so her hands were red, cold, her fingers tight against each other. I covered her hand with mine but she shook it off. As we crossed the grounds, the wind tore at us from behind, parting my hair to my neck; my silk scarf flapped in my face like a loose sail. I touched Emily's icy hands again. She was laughing. She loved cold wind, front, back, side.

Tillie was the one who put the question to me. As I squatted talking to her, the way one does with small children, she put her hands in mine and squeezed them, signaling that what she had to say was important.

"I want something. I want something very badly. Please, please take me to your house this Christmas."

All the affection I felt for the old women in this building, mixed with the guilt of knowing that soon after Christmas my time at Wassaic would be up and I would leave them, made me say yes. Without hesitation I said we would have a party. We would have it on Christmas Eve.

I asked the building supervisor about procedure to take four old ladies—Emma, Gertrude, Tillie, and Rhoda—to my house for a Christmas party in two weeks.

"It's not going to be as easy as you think. First of all, I've only got one person in my building trained to drive the van—and you do need special training. Second, electric wheelchairs won't even fit in the van. Then you've got to get all the old ladies checked over by the physician before they go. And get the papers signed by the section heads."

Next I asked the social worker if she saw any problem getting permission to take the women out for four hours.

"Only Tillie. Her mother was here Saturday and there was a real set-to because she wants Tillie moved to a higher functioning group. Called them all dummies. Tillie *was* in a higher group, but they moved her out because she was pesky. They were afraid for her safety because she annoyed people so much."

A few hours ago, Tillie told me that indeed she had upset

her mother Saturday, both of them had cried. But Tillie said it was because she asked to be moved out of Wassaic. She said she told her mother, "I've been here since the place opened. Do you think I want to be here the rest of my life?"

"I'm going to try to straighten it all out tomorrow on the phone with her mother," the social worker said. "I'm told she's difficult to talk to because she's eighty-seven and very deaf. But I'm going to try, and I'll ask permission for Tillie to go to your party at the same time."

"Tillie's the one I've promised to take; she's been asking to come to my house since July. I don't want to cause trouble, but if her mother says no, would it be possible for Tillie to go without her permission?" The truth was if her mother would not "let" her go, I did want to make trouble. Tillie said she'd told her mother she was a grown girl now, who wanted to lead her own life. That had made her mother cry.

"Probably. Don't forget though, Tillie's got a heart condition and we just want to cover you and ourselves."

At home, as I started supper, I showed Sam the letter I'd written to the assistant director asking permission for our proposed outing. I asked for use of the van, but said our house was wheelchair accessible, and with three able-bodied children, we shouldn't need any staff.

Max, who could not bear to be left out of any detail, looked over Sam's shoulder.

"Whoa! Wait a minute," Max said. "You say *three* able-bodied children? Make that two. If you're having four retarded ladies over here, I don't want to be home."

"Max, I thought you'd been making some progress on that front."

"I've been trying, but you know I feel weird around retarded people."

"These women aren't even retarded."

"Not retarded like Emily's not retarded?"

"Their experience hasn't been the same as ours. They've lived their lives in a huge institution—a place we put people when we don't want to have to deal with them. Two of them are crippled. One is tiny and has a gold tooth. Another one has been on medication so long her throat is closing up. But they're just people."

I love this child so much. Somehow, in this one area his sympathies had scrambled, like a radio signal coming in clear and strong that suddenly turns to static. I looked directly into his face, preparing the next things I would say. I wanted him to change his ideas. I wanted him to start thinking differently. And he looked just as directly into my face. He seemed to be telling me he was doing the best he could, that as much as I would like it different, this was new and bewildering territory for him.

I had to back off, allow him to have his feelings and be grateful he would tell me what they were. I said nothing. I'd said too much already.

Dream: It is a cold, windy winter day, and I am sitting at the edge of a pond which has just begun to freeze. I look across the pond and see Emily standing on the other side. To my horror, I see her put a foot on the thin ice and begin walking across the water. I stand and call to her to go back but she does not hear me. I realize I have no shoes on, but I have no choice; I have to rescue her. I jump over the unfrozen water at the pond edge and start barefoot over the ice, so thin I feel the crusty surface sink with each step and see the green water displaced as the ice sinks down.

Sometimes there are cracks in the surface and I leap to ice blocks. At last I reach Emily, grab her, and start back—but our combined weight is too much and the ice gives. We sink into the bitter cold water. I pull her up and to shore. Then she turns into a tiny baby. I hold her naked in my arms and desperately try to remember the remedy for hypothermia.

2

It had been pouring rain for three days; the ground was muddier than in March; flood warnings were posted for the Housatonic; at the foot of the hill the Ten Mile River raged below Wassaic. The radio said if this were snow it would be three feet deep. Snow is beautiful, and this nasty rain was not. On the hill, the stucco buildings had dark half-moon stains, like under-arm perspiration, where the drain spouts emptied along the walls. Twelve days before Christmas Wassaic looked drenched, grim.

There were no Christmas decorations in Butternut except for a few snowflake cutouts on Sherry's door. "We're not supposed to have Christmas parties in the centers," she said. "The wisdom of the administration has it that there are only to be parties in the residential buildings, and those are only to be held on the twenty-third. But that's okay. We're scheduling a party for the clients anyway. We're calling it a 'Seasonal Awareness Session.' "

Squire was back from his three-week vacation; the buttons of his red flannel shirt were strained in their holes over his newly expanded belly. I asked if he had enjoyed his time off.

"God yes. I had my annual bloodbath. Killed four deer

and my buddy got six. Killed 'em road hunting—that way you don't have to get out of your car. It's illegal but what the hell—that's how we did it. Drank a little beer, too. Guess it shows, huh?" He looked down and snorted a deep breath as he pulled in his stomach.

"And to show you what a good time I had, I never gave one thought to this place. Didn't even come in to pick up my paycheck."

Big determined snowflakes were finally falling and Stuart had planned an outing for his behavior group—a pancake lunch in the lodge at Cherry Valley Park, the rustic building I'd seen in the old slides of Wassaic. "We're going to do it if we have to hire dog sleds," Stuart said.

Though the make-up of his group had been scrambled, it still included Earl-the-biter, Agatha with her well-aimed shoe, and Manny yelling, "Sha–bam bam bam!" It was not an easy group.

"It's taken a lot of work to get to the point where we can have an outing like this," Stuart said, unloading groceries in the kitchen—government-issued butter, dozens of eggs, a giant can of blueberries, boxes of link sausage. There were garbage bags, a sack of plastic spoons and forks, sheets, towels, and changes of clothing.

I knew how hard Stuart worked, but I couldn't imagine that this party could be much of success except for the staff. In Butternut, a meal consisted of smearing, mashing, swiping, hurling.

On a paper plate he'd written calculations for increasing his pancake recipe seven times. "I make these for supper at home now and then. Once we had a friend over and she said she only wanted one pancake, she was on a diet." He separated an egg, jiggling the yolk in the cracked shell. "So

I only made her one—a huge one."

A client took my hand and pulled me toward the kitchen. The griddle was heated and buttered, and sausages were browning in the oven. It would be a while before lunch, but there were tantalizing signs it was on the way.

As the kitchen smells became more intense, Ronald, the aide, spread white sheets over three long tables pushed together in the dining room; he added a plastic sleigh and reindeer for a centerpiece. He looked at it critically, went outside, and came back with pine boughs "There," he said, arranging them by the sleigh.

"Ready!" Stuart yelled from the kitchen. The clients were seated with such decorum there should have been place cards, and wine goblets rather than cartons of milk. Plates of blueberry pancakes, soaked in maple syrup, were brought in. I thought of the smells that accompanied the dog-food-looking plates in Juniper, and the daily scenes in Butternut with food thrown across the room. Here Manny, Agatha, all the clients, ate voraciously and sedately.

"They say these people don't care what they eat," Ronald said. "Well I guess that's debatable. Take Earl. I never saw him eat so well. He always gets double portions in the building, but then he steals food and gets into trouble. Tries to eat people. Today you can see he's had enough and feels good."

I looked around the room and saw that everyone felt good. Is this, I wondered, what a community residence feels like? Is this the way clients will adapt when food doesn't come from a central kitchen in steam trays, when a table has been specially prepared? Is this what Emily will know? Doesn't every client have a right to such a life?

Like Stuart's friend who came to supper, I too was on a diet. I had vowed not to have any pancakes, but to eat my meager salad later. In the Cherry Valley Lodge, at a Christmas brunch for severely and profoundly retarded clients, I ate three good-sized pancakes and two sausages with a pleasure I'd not had in a long time.

A week later, Christmas decorations began to appear at Wassaic. From a distance it seemed that big garbage bags had been strewn on the lawn, but as I drove closer I saw it was the plastic crèche, blown over in the gusty wind. The Wise Men, Mary, Joseph, and the manger were all lying on their sides, sturdy flat bottoms displayed to the road. I parked my car at Juniper and heard "Hark! The Herald Angels Sing" blaring from the chapel loudspeaker, filling the parking lot and wrapping around the building.

The Ward C kids were in the dayroom—Louisa twirling, Vincent propelling himself on his board, Wonder Woman reaching out for me. "We gonna be a good gi-wl so Sanna's gonna come," Carrie drawled, vigorously nodding her head.

"Where's Emily?" I asked Vera.

"Emily's gone to Herman's Santa Land in Poughkeepsie with her teacher. This is the third expedition they've tried to get off there and the first one that's succeeded. Snowed every other time."

I looked around the dayroom at the Christmas decorations—silver ropes hung above the three-quarter partitions; a small, plastic tree was on top of an empty bookcase. There was a faded cutout Santa pinned high on the wall, and three red paper stockings with Wonder Woman, Carrie, and June's names lettered on the white turn-over top.

"The kids can really tell there's something going on," Vera said. "They know these decorations mean something. That's why we've hung them all so high—they're always reaching up for them."

That's what Christmas meant in this room, something silver, glittery, and twinkling, too far up to reach.

3

When all the permissions had been properly prepared and signed, it was time to invite my Monday night dinner guests.

"I'm glad to see you," Gertrude said as I came into her room. I hadn't known how she would greet me. There was something about her that made my heart swoop when she turned her attention to me. Her physical projection of regality—her round body alert in the wheelchair—made me sit and take a breath.

I told her I'd planned a tree-trimming party at my house on Christmas Eve; I told her who was coming. But as I asked her to join us, her face tensed and her eyes turned dull.

"Thank you, but I don't want to come," she said. "I have sores on my buttocks and I have to have treatments for them." She looked around the room as though cornered. "But I don't want to hurt your feelings."

"You're not doing that," I said, "but wouldn't it be good to get out for a little while?"

"I don't know. What time do you want me to go?"

"For supper, just after program."

"Maybe if it was daytime," she said. "But I can't go at night. What time would we get back?" Her forehead wrinkled with doubt; I assured her she didn't have to make up her mind now. She could come at the last minute. "Talk to Emma," I said, concealing my disappointment. I reminded myself

that Gertrude is eighty-three years old; she's been institutionalized since she was six; why shouldn't she feel nervous
going to a stranger's house at night?

"The social worker asked if I want to go, but I said I'll wait
'til the lady asks me herself," Emma said. She sagged down
in her wheelchair, hands humped on her tray, her head
twisting back and forth as she smiled. The arithmetic workbooks she always carried were spread on her bed. "I don't
know if I want to go." There was a pause. "Who else is
coming?"

"Tillie, Rhoda . . ."

"She's a pain. I don't want her to come."

"You can get along with her for a few hours, Emma."

"How would we get there?"

I told her Sam would drive the van.

"Do you have stairs there?"

"You don't have to use them. Everything's on one floor,
the bathroom, everything."

"Okay. I want to come then."

"I'm glad. And what would you especially like for supper?"

"Coffee," she said. "And little cookies."

"I need to talk to you. Now. It's very important," Tillie threw
down her knitting, grabbed my hand, and hopped up on
her bed. "Tell me just what it's going to be like at your
house. Is your little girl going to be there?"

My little girl, I explained, is taller than I am. My sons will
be there too. The dog won't hurt her, though it's almost as
large as she is.

She absorbed this information with a big grin, her gold
tooth sticking out at me as though smiling on its own. "I'll
tell you what I want to eat. I can't have candy or nothing

like that. But I love meatballs. You know, with red sauce? And macaroni. And diabetic ice cream for dessert. And soda. And are you going to, you know . . . well, are you going to give us presents?"

Rhoda lay face down on her bed, her hand twitching and trembling on the covers. I whispered her name and she started awake. "My ear is paining me terrible. They looked at it and there's nothing they can do," she said. "But I want to go to your house. I'm so happy you're taking me. I'm going to put on one of my nice new dresses. And I asked the social worker to get out some money for me. I always like to have money when I leave here."

The fears of this woman and mine were not so far apart. While I looked forward to this event, I was also quite anxious about it. There was a great deal to do: A tree must be cut down and set up, the lights tested, and the ornaments arranged for easy access. I would have to cook meatballs for Tillie, the long promised moussaka for Rhoda—and I worried about her choking. I must check to see if Emma can feed herself and drink coffee without a straw.

Clearly, their visit was not going to be what I'd fantasized, a care-free few hours. For these handicapped women it was peppered with doubts, and for me there was the anxiety of responsibility.

Sam and I Christmas-shopped in Pittsfield. Strings of lights festooned main street, and each lamp post wore a wreath. We bought shoes for Katrina, shirts for Wynne and Max. In an art supply store I found pens that write silver outlined in purple. Sam looked for a poster for his secretary's wall. But much as I love the decorations of the season, no matter how enthusiastic I am when I begin shopping, it does not take me long to become tired, depressed by the over-abundance of goods, concerned about my dwindling funds.

In a small shop I looked over choices for the Wassaic women. Nothing seemed right. At last I spied three bright cloth-covered boxes filled with pretty stationary. Just the thing for Tillie and Gertrude, if she came, for they either wrote letters themselves or had someone write for them. Then Sam found a mirror that Rhoda might like. That left Emma.

Increasingly grumpy, I looked over shelves of tiresome goods, the same stuff we'd seen in every store. And then I found a thin chrome pedestal with a figure that balanced like a tightrope walker, swaying and righting itself. I had to choose between a soccer player, tennis player, bowler, or golfer. I bought the bowler, the only one I thought Emma might be able to identify. And a hand puppet for Emily, a rabbit with huge floppy ears. Then I paid the bill and fled.

"It's such a busy time of year," Mrs. Benedict said on the phone. "We just finished our library book fair, and now tonight's our carol sing at church. I'm playing organ for that, like I do every year. And to tell the truth, I'm still trying to decide what to do about Emily. I'd like to bring her home for Christmas, but it takes the better part of a day to drive over there. And she's demanding. I need all my strength to have her for a visit. But she hasn't been here the past two years, and, well, it's a lonely day for both of us."

Smoke hung along the Harlem Valley at treetop height, like a fat, puffy white snake. Though it was cold, the soggy earth smelled ready to waken rather than sleep. In March, Martha would have her baby. The amniocentesis report had come. She was expecting a healthy baby, a boy.

4

"The way some people around here treat Christmas is pretty amazing," Emily's social worker said. He sat at his desk, glasses pushed up on his forehead as though he had two pairs of eyes, one above the other. "Let me shut the door and tell you this one.

"Last Sunday I was here catching up on paperwork when the head of the volunteer department came in with a middle-aged couple, followed by the Wassaic photographer—the one who does I.D. shots and stuff for the newsletter. The volunteer director announced that this couple was donating seventy Christmas presents to Wassaic clients. They were carrying a small shopping bag; it looked pretty unlikely that there could be seventy gifts in it, but okay, who knows?

"We went into one ward and they started distributing the presents. Each one was a tiny vial of perfume, the kind you get free as samples. What is this? I thought. Here the photographer had been dragged from his home on a Sunday, all these elaborate pictures were being arranged, and it was all over the most inappropriate gift imaginable. After distributing forty of these things they ran out. Well, they wanted to make a big deal of presenting them to some of the Ward C girls, so they had to take a few away from the clients they'd already given them to. We all went to Ward C. Carrie got one, and Junie, and they gave one to Vincent, who was off his skateboard sitting in a chair.

"Vincent held this little vial up to the light, looked at it, and took the cork out of the top. Then he drank it. I had to leave the room I was laughing so hard. The med room said there wasn't enough of anything in it to hurt him, though there might have been enough alcohol to give him a little buzz. Merry Christmas, Vincent!"

Santa came to Butternut Learning, a big pillow belted beneath his red shirt, expensive cordovans peeking out under his red flannel trousers. He made a last upward adjustment of his pillow, picked up a string of sleigh bells, and bounced down the hall past the waiting room decorated with a construction paper fireplace. He was accompanied by elves— Sherry, in a red dress with a roll of fluffy white cotton draped over her shoulders, and Bernie, with a Christmas carol book spread flat on his hands.

"We keep hearing you jingling in the halls and yelling 'Ho ho ho,'" Fred Law said. "About time you got here. Look everyone, it's Santa Claus."

"Meh-heh-heh-rry Christmas!" boomed Santa. "I've brought something for all you good boys and girls!" He dipped into his plastic bag to hand out individually wrapped cookies.

"Cookies?" I asked Sherry as I trailed behind, strobe battery pack on, dark slide out ready for a photograph.

"The gifts they gave out from volunteer services were inappropriate. We rejected them all. We figured cookies were what the clients wanted the most."

A resident lying on a mat, turned her head and smiled. Santa rested his pack on her mat. "Meh-heh-heh-rry Christmas! Have you been good this year?" The woman, who could not walk, could not even sit, smiled up at him. "You want to touch my beard?" Her smile beamed wider, a stream of saliva started down her jaw. Slowly her hand came up and she touched the tip of his beard.

"Now let's see what we've got in Santa's sack. Earl, this present has your name on it." Earl bared his teeth at the strange man with a cotton beard and an unknown voice.

"Ho ho ho! Merry Christmas, Agatha!" Agatha methodically shredded the paper from her cookies. Manny ate the paper.

"I've cooked meatballs and spaghetti as a Christmas treat for my clients and my aides—we'll have it in my room at noon," Sherry said.

"I made some venison, too, if you want to try it," Squire added, looking up from his mopping. Squire's "bloodbath" deer, shot from the car window. "Supposed to be meatballs, but I guess I cooked them too long and now it's just meat sauce. Still it's not bad."

"Here's what we're going to do," Sherry said as the steam cart came to her door with the clients' lunch. "We're going to give them a small portion of their regular lunch so they'll taste the spaghetti. If they have it first, they'll just wolf it down."

When the clients had finished eating Sherry nodded toward the spaghetti bowl. "Help yourself, Rebecca. This second batch isn't cut into tiny pieces and it's cooked firmer." The supervisor joined us; we took styrofoam plates Sherry had brought.

"Don't forget the venison sauce," Squire said.

The venison was delicious. Sherry's meatballs were superb. Since there were no knives, we smeared butter on Italian bread with the back of plastic forks.

"It's not even here and already it's been quite a Christmas," the supervisor said. "One of the best gifts came an hour ago. Our Santa was one of the top-level administrators. The gift was that he had to deal with the clients directly for once, and I think he actually learned something. You know what he said when he left? 'It could get pretty discouraging being a Santa every year. There are so many clients you just can't get a response out of.' "

"One day a year and he finds it discouraging," Sherry said softly. "He should try being a teacher."

The Juniper Christmas party was held in the basement recreation room, where a good-sized plastic tree leaned next to the paper fireplace, and silver ropes criss-crossed the ceiling. The physical therapy interns blended eggnog, while aides put plates of iced cookies on a side table.

"Here comes Allen Funt again," Loretta sneered, sidling up to me. "What do you think about all this, huh?"

I felt the same rush of despair I experienced almost a year ago at the Valentine party, overwhelming questions about who this was for, all these hours of work decorating the party room, baking delicate cookies, ordering an ice-cream cake in the shape of a Christmas tree. And then the answers came in: Dwight, his hydrocephalic head propped against the side of his wheelchair; Vincent on his skate board; Wonder Woman waddling and making strange, happy low noises; Emily.

"Merry Christmas! Merry Christmas!" thundered a Santa who needed no padding to fill his suit. "I've got presents for everyone!"

"Got one for me Santa?" an aide called out. "I really want a new job."

"Merry Christmas!"

"Me-wy Cwistmas," Carrie echoed.

"Merry Christmas!"

The loud voice set Emily off into a twangy, frightened hum. She'd been guided to her seat, passing right by without spotting me. I wanted to run over to her, tell her it's all right, it's all fun—but it was almost time for a new life for Emily, one beginning with transitions full of frightening moments like this. Her face looked flushed, her eyes blank.

Santa settled his pack under the tree next to the cardboard fireplace. "Too bad there isn't any whiskey in that eggnog," he said looking around under white cotton eyebrows. "All the store Santas I know are half tipsy."

Since most of the kids were in wheelchairs, Santa took presents to them. The few who could walk were brought to Santa and helped onto his lap. Wonder Woman got a knitted hat which made her look like a fat elf. "Are you coming to see me?" asked Dwight, his present on his lap. Vincent tried on a pair of gloves, carefully fitting in each finger.

But Emily would not get out of her chair to go to Santa. When her teacher tried to pull her up, she stiffened, legs straight. At last Vera came over and Emily allowed herself to be led to Santa; rigidly she endured the lap.

She stumbled back to her chair. Vera knelt and helped her open her package. It was a stuffed crocodile, a lurid green color with a greedy pink mouth. Emily didn't laugh when I nuzzled her cheek with it. Now that she'd found me she only wanted to get out. I told her ice-cream cake was coming. She didn't care and wouldn't eat it when I served her. She only wanted to stay next to me, that was all. She even did what she would not do on our walks—she groped for my hand and held it, her slender fingers firm on mine.

"Emily, I've brought you a present." It was Christmas Eve morning. Emily stood when she heard my voice, rushed toward me with such purpose and faith: Surely I was here to give her the only Christmas present she wanted. Freedom. But alas, I only had a package. She shook her head.

"Emily," I implored, "this is for you." I placed the package next to her on the table. She pushed it away. She pulled at my wrist, her signal that she wanted to go out. "We can't go now, but I've brought you a present." I picked it up from the table, placed it in her hands. Her fingers touched the package as though it were hot, or dirty, something repugnant. She stared into my eyes.

"Open it," I said. She didn't look down, but her fingers obediently picked away at the paper like chicken talons scratching in sand. She lost interest and put the package on the table.

I tore off part of the paper and placed her fingers on the soft rabbit inside it. She looked down while I pulled off the rest of the wrapping, and when she saw the floppy ears and touched the furry body, she smiled at last.

Vera smiled too, but seemed withdrawn and a little melancholy. I asked what her Christmas plans were.

"I'll be working. There are too many staff with families that really need the day off, so I volunteered. It's not the greatest way to spend the day, but what the hell. Me and these kids will make out okay. But do you know if Emily's grandmother is coming for her? If she is I haven't been told about it."

I told her that when I had talked to Mrs. Benedict she hadn't decided whether to bring Emily home or not.

Emily tugged on my arm to go for a walk, go in the car, go anywhere. But I had to leave. I heard my own falsely cheerful voice wish Vera Merry Christmas. Emily—blank and stunned—groped for a chair when Vera told her to sit. And when I told her to wave goodbye, her hand rose from her lap, fluttered for a second at her waist, and fell back.

Handel's *Messiah* was on the radio, its gorgeous melodies and radiant chorales filling the house. In the kitchen I prepared for the old ladies' party. The eggplant was sliced, draining in the colander; peppers, onions and garlic were chopped.

Loaves of French bread cooled on the counter. Meatballs had been spiced, rolled, and were ready for the frying pan when the phone rang.

"Rebecca? It's Helen Benedict. I thought you'd like to know that Emily's on her way home for Christmas. My nephew volunteered to drive her here, so we're all set. He also cut us a nice, big tree from the property, and it's all decorated in the parlor. He and his wife are going to come by while Emily's here and it should be a nice time for all of us."

I couldn't make a fuss about it, couldn't tell her how happy I was that she was having her granddaughter for Christmas, but my heart swelled as large and full as the chords from the *Messiah*.

5

"I want to come, I really do!" smiled Gertrude, her eighty-three-year-old face open, suddenly unlined and young. "What time are we going? It's a lovely day."

The sun of that unexpected enthusiasm warmed and cheered me. Max had been at David's all day; I didn't know if he would show up tonight or not. And I had driven to Wassaic fresh from an argument with Katrina that had left me close to tears; I wanted everything in the house well organized—the table set, the rug taken up so wheelchairs could move around, the food ready, a wreath for the door. That's where it had broken down. Katrina said she didn't want to make a wreath; angrily I cut pine boughs and stuck them in the metal ring. And when I had asked her to wrap the women's gifts, she said, "Can't we do without the wrapping paper, Mom? They won't notice." I feared—though I couldn't quite bring the fear to the surface—that this party had indeed been more than my children could deal with, that once again I'd imposed my will on my family.

I made a last check with the med room. Yes, all the release permissions had been signed. No, there were no special diets, though no one was to have sugar. We once again discussed Rhoda's choking.

"Just tell her if she chokes it's curtains," the nurse advised. "Tell her no one's trained to save her and she won't see Christmas."

I met Sam for a van driving lesson. The only thing to learn, we were assured, was the operation of the hydraulic lift system. "There's one little problem with it," our teacher said. "Sometimes the lift gets stuck with the wheelchairs on it."

"What do we do then?" Sam asked.

Our teacher shrugged.

Four o'clock. All four women were in the reception hall. Tillie wore a red velvet skirt that stuck out like poinsettia leaves. "This party was all my idea," she announced smugly to the group. "You should all thank me." Emma wore a pink pants suit and a grin so large it almost turned her inside out. Rhoda was bundled in a new down coat—sensibly, for it had turned bitter cold. Gertrude's knit wool cap was pulled over her ears and almost over her eyes.

Sam drove up with the van, and we began loading the first wheelchair. I'd watched it done dozens of times, but when I tried to maneuver the first set of wheels in the locks I obviously didn't know the technique for wrestling them in place. These handicapped people were indeed in the hands of amateurs. A labored, grinding sound came from the hydraulic lift, then a catch as it started smoothly up with Emma on it. "Strap me in," Rhoda said from one of the side-facing seats. "Once I fell over going around a corner." I did as she asked.

We were off. "I used to get car sick," Rhoda announced.

"I love long drives," Gertrude countered. "I wish this one was longer than twenty minutes."

"Look!" Rhoda pointed at a pine tree strung with lights. Unable to say more she mutely lifted a hand at every Christmas decoration.

"Look at the moon, it's full," Tillie said, and we all turned to see the moon risen low in twilight, hanging thin and white, almost as if a cloud had made a perfect circle.

Katrina and Wynne were reading in front of the fireplace when I burst in the door. "We're here! Give us a hand!" The house was very warm; they'd followed my instructions to set the thermostat to seventy-five degrees. Their books slammed shut; they rushed to the door, and I knew the bad feelings of a few hours ago were gone.

As the lift ground up and down, Max materialized. He stood by the van watching with fascination, his love of mechanical wonders overcoming his apprehension.

The wheelchairs bumped over the rough flagstones and bricks to the porch door, over the sill, into warmth. I took off Emma's jacket and caught a strong whiff of Wassaic, that medicinal, antiseptic, slightly rotted smell that lingered in every hall and room, so incongruous in this house which smelled of wood and smoke and spices and something faintly summertime.

"Tillie's freezing, Mom." Katrina dragged the rocker, containing a tiny Tillie shivering like a shorn poodle in snow, closer to the fire and rubbed Tillie's hands between her own, while I brought wool shawls from the closet. From the glazed look in Tillie's eyes I saw what had chilled her was the hugeness of this experience. I tried to imagine the size of these new people from her three-foot vantage point— the men over six feet, even the youngest child far taller than she. Our black Labrador snuffled everyone, her wagging tail almost in Tillie's eyes. But Katrina knelt next to Tillie, draping shawls around her, telling her not to be afraid. Shyly Tillie began to smile.

From the semicircle of chairs and wheelchairs around the fireplace I heard snatches of conversation as I lit the oven and put water on to boil. Emma asked Max what grade he was in, her voice clearer than I'd ever heard it at Wassaic. Hesitantly he told her eighth. "I used to go to school. I learned to read and write and almost went to high school," she said. From the corner of my eye I saw Katrina lean forward, fascinated; only yesterday she'd asked me if these women could talk.

Quietly Sam asked Gertrude if she wouldn't like to decorate the tree.

"Oh, I can't do that."

"Sure you can. Look, I'll wheel you over here and you can hang tinsel on."

Soon Gertrude was fitting new hangers into glass ornaments, and alternating fistfuls of tinsel with decorations. Tillie hung up a silver snowflake that belonged to my mother. "This would look great around my neck," she said.

"Whose is this?" Rhoda asked, picking up Max's baseball from the counter. "I like to watch baseball on TV." She tossed it a few inches up and down. "It makes me think about when I was a kid. I used to play stick ball with the boys in my neighborhood before I got put away." She gave the ball another flip.

"You can keep it if you want," Max said.

In between putting the moussaka in the oven and stirring

the meatballs, I made instant Polaroid photographs of each woman. We all watched them turn from white, to sulphur green, to flesh. Emma's hands were raised, twisted back against her forearms, a tragic frame for her shining face. "Isn't this a good picture?" she asked. "I'm going to send it to my twin sisters."

Tillie poked around the house first, and then everyone scattered in different directions. Rhoda shuffled over to the stove where I was melting butter for the French bread. "I've been looking at everything," she said. "I hope you don't think I'm too nosey."

Sam was taken by Gertrude's courtly, dignified qualities and personally escorted her around the house. In the dining room she saw the two life-size mannequins in Victorian dress that stand by the windows.

"What's going on?" she asked. "Are those real people?" Gertrude brought the reality of seventy-seven years in an institution to our house.

"Come here," Emma called, "I want to tell you something. I like your son." She nodded her head at Wynne. "He's handsome. Watch out for him or he'll be gone."

Tillie came over to the stove from her adventures around the house. "Nice set-up you got here," she announced.

Tillie sat closest to the woodstove at the dining-room table, set with candles and a striped table cloth, napkins in rings. Rhoda sat next to her, with Gertrude at the end. Emma's wheelchair was on the other side, with a chair placed discreetly next to her from which I would feed her. Sam and the kids drew up chairs. Meatballs and spaghetti were in a white porcelain bowl, moussaka in an earthenware casserole.

"Aren't you going to eat with us?" Rhoda asked. This was painful; it was the one part of the party that seemed artificial, too close to what happened daily at Wassaic. The clients eat, the staff watches. I explained that there were ten of us and the dining-room table wouldn't hold that many. But the truth, which I felt Rhoda sensed, was that even if it had been large enough we would elect to eat later, closer to our usual dinner time, relaxed with the day behind us.

Rhoda began eating fast and I reminded her to slow down. When had I first promised her moussaka? In June? I tore off a piece of bread and stuck it in Emma's clawed hand; she pulled off hunks with her strong canines, smiling. "It's so good to be out of that jail house," she said.

"What kind of music is that?" Tillie asked. Music-box carols tinkled from the stereo. "Don't you have any polkas?"

"Where's the country and western Christmas record, Dad?" Max asked.

"Put that one on. I love country and western," Emma said.

The new record came on; Max and Wynne went into the living room to dance—"I'm teaching him to box step," Wynne called in to us. Emma giggled. We sang the refrain of our favorite family song—"Christmas ain't Christmas, dear, without you"—abandoned, bellowing the lyrics.

"I heard a new song today," Wynne said, beginning to clear the table when the song was over. "It's called "Randolph the Redneck Reindeer." Everyone roared.

Without saying anything, Rhoda helped clear the plates. "Do you want me to do the dishes?" she asked. This woman three months ago could talk about nothing but her desperate unhappiness; seeing her in our home, I understood her pain more than ever. If ever there was anyone who yearned for family life, it was Rhoda.

Tillie's feet hung halfway down the chair legs to the floor, and she held her unopened present on her lap. Beside her the fire leapt crackling up the chimney, and the light played on her cheek. She looked around the room, her eyes grayed with cataracts, her speech slowed by a big supper. "I've never been so happy before."

I craned my neck to see the moon from the van window; it had climbed high, was smaller, and wore that hazy red halo that meant snow. All wheelchairs were safely locked in place, seat belts on everyone. Max helped with the loading, hitching a ride up and down the hydraulic platform every chance he had. The guests had said "thank you" a dozen times over, shaking hands with everyone. On her way out the door Rhoda passed the onion basket in the kitchen and asked for one. "I like onions. I haven't had one in a long time." She tucked it in her coat pocket, where it bulged next to Max's baseball.

Everyone was quiet as we headed down Route 22; Rhoda silently lifted her hand to point at lighted trees. Tillie dozed. I could not help but think of what they were going back to. Tillie will probably die in Wassaic. No one wants an old lady with a curved back and a heart problem, even if she does have a gold tooth. Gertrude will be eighty-four this year; she too will die in Wassaic. Emma may be moved to a total-care nursing home, though her chances for happiness there are not much greater than they are at the institution. Rhoda is slated to be assigned to a home for behavior problems. How she will fare there—not in the genteel life she covets, but among difficult, assaultive clients—determines her future.

"Back to the fool house," Tillie sighed as we turned in the Wassaic drive.

"Mom, those ladies don't seem retarded," Katrina said. We ate the small amount of leftover moussaka and warmed-up spaghetti too soft for our *al dente* taste. Sam and I had glasses of wine; the way we slumped in our chairs showed our fatigue. "I'd say the quiet one—Rhoda—and the real old one—Gertrude—aren't retarded at all. And I bet Emma isn't either—she just can't talk because of her physical problems."

All year I'd told the kids there were normal women incarcerated in Wassaic. But the concept was so monstrous that they had not understood. Wassaic was for dummies, for retards, or, shifted into more compassionate language, for unfortunate people like Emily with limited mentality.

"And Mom," Katrina continued, "Tillie is—well Tillie's just great. I absolutely loved her. I think you should ask Tillie to come visit us for a couple of weeks."

I looked around the table at my family—their bodies blessedly healthy, their hearts open. I felt I should make a small speech. "Thanks for being so nice to four old ladies," I began.

"Oh stop, Mom," Max interrupted. "It wasn't very hard, you know. They're just people."

6

Mrs. Benedict's white clapboard farmhouse was surrounded on two sides by a verandah; last night's storm had outlined the railing with snow and settled a fluffy cushion on the slatted porch swing. I kicked the steps to knock snow from my boots before I rapped on the door—a handsome one of unpainted oak, weathered a golden-gray. The walkway had been shoveled from the road, but now two new inches covered old footprints; I was the only person who'd been in or out today. And I'd come to take Emily out of this house, to put her back in Wassaic.

"Leave those wet boots by the door or we'll have puddles

all over the floor," Mrs. Benedict instructed as I stepped into her house. I sat in the easy chair she told me to take, my feet on a needlepoint-covered footstool. I wiggled my toes beneath heavy wool socks.

"Put that afghan around your legs if you're cold," she called from the kitchen. I saw a crocheted blanket folded neatly over the arm of the sofa. Emily sat on the rug humming softly, and flopping her head from shoulder to shoulder like a metronome.

"You were nice to drive all this way to pick her up," Mrs. Benedict said. On the tray she carried from the kitchen were two thick white cups with faded gold edges, a flowered china tea pot, a plate of oatmeal cookies. "Emily and I've had a lovely time. Today we made cookies—you stirred the batter, didn't you dear?" she called.

Emily looked up, steadied her head for a second, then let it fall sideways.

"I've lived alone for so many years that I now and then find myself saying something aloud when there's not a soul here. Having Emily gives me someone to talk to, even if she can't say anything." With the back of her hand she pushed a small stack of magazines aside as she set the tray on a table.

I looked around the living room—the "parlor," Mrs. Benedict called it—and wondered how Emily had managed in this house. How had she not tipped over the old-fashioned iron floor lamps that stood behind each chair? How had she managed not to break the oak-framed glass end table? How had she not burned herself on the large woodstove that stood in front of the fireplace?

As though my questions were spoken in every glance, Mrs. Benedict began to answer them. "I never leave anything on the table unless I'm there to guard it, and I don't plug in the lamps until evening, in case there should be an accident. I don't know where I learned these things. No one ever taught me. No one ever prepared me for life with a handicapped child."

She poured a stream of amber tea, and passed the cup without looking at me. "Well, that's not quite true. There is one small part of my childhood which you could call preparation. Now it makes me feel ashamed and confused to remember it. I've lived around here all my life; I grew up in an apartment above the tobacco store in town. And I had a very close friend when I was a little girl. Her name was Patsy. Patsy Boggs. Her father ran the drugstore. Before I was old enough to go to school we played together almost every day, and we liked playing house. She was quiet, and kind of meek, so in our game I was the lady of the house and she did the cleaning. I thought she *wanted* to clean, she liked it. It wasn't until I started going to school that I found out Patsy was retarded. The word they used was mongoloid. At the time I was six, she was thirty-five. And that was her role in her own family—cleaning and scrubbing."

She held her tea cup near her mouth, and blew gently into it over her lower lip. "Patsy moved away and I forgot about her. So that was it, that was the only retarded person I knew until Emily. And when I had to put her in Wassaic, it was thinking about Patsy Boggs that kept me from going crazy. I kept remembering that phrase someone used, 'A place where they can be with their own kind.' It comforted me. Being in Wassaic would save Emily from being a thirty-five-year-old, playing house with a six-year-old, scrubbing and cleaning."

Mrs. Benedict got up as she always did, slowly, hand on her lower back as she straightened. She walked over to the old spinet piano next to the Christmas tree. "This piano came from the apartment I grew up in. Patsy Boggs used to dust it, and wipe down the keys with a damp cloth. Now it entertains Emily. She may have ignored it when she was little, but now she wants to play all the time, and not just pound, mind you, but strike one note at a time." Emily watched her grandmother's every move, and when she saw the keyboard lid raised, she too went to the piano. She put one stiff finger on a key and pressed a note.

"Here, I thought you'd like to see a picture of Sue," Mrs. Benedict said. She took a tarnished silver frame from the piano top, and handed it to me.

It was the kind of photograph I might have taken. A young woman dressed in jeans lies on her side in a field, propped on one elbow, chin in her hand. She is on a mountain, and the background rolls on forever, in tones of darkening gray. She looks into the camera with determination; her eyes are clear and unafraid. Lips together, half her mouth twists into a smile, while the other half remains straight, as though she's both giving and holding back at the same time.

Mrs. Benedict watched as I examined the photograph, then put it back on the piano. My feelings were complex: Sue looked as though she could be a friend, yet she had deserted her daughter, a child I'd grown to love. I felt pain for the events that had made her unable to care for Emily, yet I also felt resentment that she was alone, unencumbered, somewhere on a mountain top.

Because I didn't want to say what I felt, I was quiet for a few seconds. "I was once mistaken for her at Wassaic," I finally said. I looked at the picture again. "But she's much younger than I."

"She called Christmas Eve," Mrs. Benedict said, as though to soften any hard feelings of mine. "I held the phone to Emily's ear, and I could see by the way her eyes darted around that she was listening."

She stared at the photograph on the piano. "I told Sue about Emily's new residence, and how close that is to here, and how she'd be there in just a week or so. I told her things would be better for Emily than they'd been in Wassaic. But I didn't tell her any of my worries about Emily's move. And I stopped myself from begging her to visit."

In the short silence that followed I watched Mrs. Benedict's face puff, as though tears had come not only to her eyes, but, held back, had swollen the tissue of her cheeks as well.

"I suppose I could have tried to forget Emily, to put her out of my life the way Sue seems to have, but that's one of the hard things about growing old. You begin to realize that they can throw you away when they don't need you any more. You're disposable, really." She straightened Sue's photograph so it faced straight out into the room. "Only I'm not disposable to Emily."

With Emily's suitcase in my trunk, we began the drive back to Wassaic. We drove through the short blocks that were Mrs. Benedict's rural town, and as we passed the small tobacco store, with its old-fashioned gold-lettered sign, I glanced at the apartment above it. Then I saw the street sign for Park Street. I remembered that Emily's social worker kept referring to the residence as "the Park Street house." I made a quick right turn.

A painter's van was parked in front of a large, one-story brick house that stood on a sizable lot, as though it had once been someone's grand gesture, an attempt to gussy up a neighborhood of frame houses. A long wheelchair ramp of thick planks and sturdy railings had been built to the front door. Emily held my wrist as we walked up the ramp.

"This is where you're going to live, Babes," I whispered.

Inside, the walls were light yellow, the trim a gleaming white, and it smelled of fresh paint. Everything looked new and in perfect order. There were comfortable couches and easy chairs, end tables and lamps and all the things normal living rooms have. "Go ahead and look around," the painter said, and disappeared.

Sliding glass doors led from the dining room onto the deck. In Juniper there was a courtyard, but no staff to supervise both outside and inside. There could be no wandering from one place to the other. Sliding glass doors and four staff for ten residents would mean more freedom for Emily.

We went into a bedroom; Emily felt secure enough to let go of my wrist. I looked out the window, and there was the street, with cars moving along it, and an occasional pedestrian on the sidewalk. In spring there would be bicycles, and kids on skateboards; if Emily lived in this room she could watch them.

Mrs. Benedict had said she was still concerned about having Emily so close. She was worried that Emily would see her driving by. I thought of the times I'd scurried past her dayroom, hoping she wouldn't be looking at the door. I thought of the whispered conversations in the halls when I feared she'd hear my voice. I also remembered the odd pleasure I'd had being in Juniper when I couldn't see her, just knowing she was in the same building. Mrs. Benedict would work it out.

I sat on the bed and imagined the room with bright posters, a bedside lamp, country curtains. "It's a nice room, isn't it Emily?" I asked absently.

For an answer Emily rolled the shade up and down.

The kitchen was large, with an oval table big enough for a group of staff and clients to make cookies, or peel potatoes, or eat a cozy breakfast. There were drop cloths on the counters, and the painter balanced on a ladder, putting the last coat of varnish on cabinet doors.

"Some big house, huh?" he asked. "Can you imagine one family living in this? That was it. Guy used to own a couple of gas stations. Now I hear they're planning to put retarded kids in here."

Retarded kids. There are activist groups trying to change the structure of labels: They feel the order of words changes our perceptions; so "retarded kids" becomes "kids who are retarded," giving emphasis to the idea that they are kids first, and putting the distance of two words before retarded.

"I guess that's one of them," the painter continued, gesturing at Emily with his brush.

I nodded warily. This was Emily in the outside world. This was Emily taken from the shelter of the institution, exposed to the judgments of the community. This was the legacy of Patsy Boggs.

"Well, don't worry about a thing, kid. We're going to fix this place up real nice for you."

7

"What a beautiful house Emily's going to live in," Vera said, her round face transparent with admiration. "We took her and the other four kids from Wassaic who are moving there for an open house today, and everything really went well. The place is gorgeous. The furniture is so nice you'd think it was a private home. I guess that's the point of a community residence. And I can't believe the staffing ratio. Four staff for eleven kids! That's fantastic. Here we're one to six at best.

"Emily was a little overwhelmed by all the strange people

at first—the house was packed—but she got over that and started looking around. The guy who runs it showed me where her room's going to be, overlooking the street.

"And you should have seen her when we stopped for lunch on the way home. I was so proud of her. We went to a Burger King and I ordered up a Whopper for her. The other kids had to have theirs cut into pieces and eat it with a fork, but I just cut Emily's in half, and let her go to it. I mean, I've had catsup and mayonnaise down me a dozen times, but she ate her Whopper perfectly."

Emily reacted to this tale of her accomplishments by gripping my wrist. She looked at me with a tender, interior smile that had nothing to do with me, as though she were tapping a new source of pleasure.

A scarlet coat hung in her closet, Mrs. Benedict's Christmas replacement for the torn, raggedy one. I wrapped a purple wool scarf around her neck, and put a knit cap on her head, but she pulled it off. She giggled as I tugged on a pair of stiff nylon mittens, and giggled harder as I solemnly explained how she had to hold her thumb separately.

Outside, the sidewalks were slick with slush, and wet flurries drifted through the damp air. We walked down the Juniper steps and there was Sam. A frozen, searching expression came over Emily as she used all her resources to link this person from her past to this moment. Then it clicked, and she took her hand from my wrist and grabbed on to Sam's. "She certainly changes allegiance fast, doesn't she?" Sam chortled back over his shoulder.

"I think it's great—and very encouraging—what curiosity and interest Emily has in other people," Sam said after dinner. "I mean she's only seen me a dozen times in her life, and look how willing she was to be with me on our walk. She'll respond to anyone who'll come forward to her."

I sat in the rocker by the fire after Sam had gone to bed. It was late but I couldn't stop thinking about Emily. Staff people had cautioned me: Things were not as they should be in the community—some houses were not well run, some of the programs were shabby. But I'd seen for myself how Emily bloomed under attention and respect. It had to be an improved situation. She would be well cared for, given a greater sense of freedom and love.

Though I was tired, I knew I would sleep little that night. Taking a flashlight, I left the comfort of the house and went to my studio. Every crack in my darkroom had been sealed, pin holes covered with black electrical tape, the door edged in weather stripping. Even so, I felt safest working with film at night, when there was no chance a stray stab of light could fog it. Each night for the past year I had unloaded exposed film and reloaded fresh film for the next day's shooting at Wassaic.

I turned out the overhead bulb and was plunged from light to dark. In total darkness everything has to be in its exact place. On my worktable was an empty film box, and next to that a pile of film holders. I felt for the top of the stack, picked up the first one, turned the lock, and pulled out the first dark slide. I removed the 4 × 5 film, careful to touch only the edges. In the silver halide of that emulsion was a latent image of Emily, waiting to be released by developer and made permanent in fixer. I turned the film holder over, withdrew the other dark slide, took out another piece of film, and added it to the holding box. I took out piece after piece of Emily.

Sam's car wouldn't start, mine had a flat tire, and I was late on Emily's last morning in Wassaic. Her last morning.

My coat brought cold into the steamy Juniper corridor; an hour ago the thermometer read twelve below zero. In the bathroom, Louisa sat naked on the toilet. June and Wonder Woman waited in their room for showers, still in their pajamas. Carrie babbled on and on.

Emily sat on her bed with her shirt drawn up and the doctor's round stethoscope disk pressed to her chest. So it was really going to happen. This was the final medical check before she transferred out.

Her hands groped for me. Her face was alert, expectant.

"The night shift got her dressed this morning," Vera said coming from the bathroom, "but look what they put on her. These clothes are raggedy. I'm going to get her into something decent."

"Is she ready?" asked a social worker, also bringing in cold air. "We've got the van outside and we're ready to go when you are."

"Almost ready," Vera called, as she peeled off the faded clothes. She took off Emily's underpants too, as though she wanted Emily to make a thoroughly clean beginning.

Emily had entered puberty. She had small new breasts and a faint down of pubic hair.

I felt the same ambivalence about Emily's growth as I did toward the growth of my own children. Each month Max inched closer to my height. That morning, as he brushed his teeth, I had come up behind him and looked at us both in the bathroom mirror. Our eyes were level. "Don't grow any more," I wailed, perhaps only half joking. His eyes met mine in the mirror; they were serious. "I can't wait to grow up," he said.

Perhaps Emily felt the same way.

Vera dressed her, and full of false cheer, I made a few photographs. "Hey Emily! You're going to your new house today. Give me a smile, that's it!" But when Vera went for Emily's new shoes, I put down my camera and sat on the bed. I looked down at the thin, bare feet on the floor of Juniper hall, and when I looked at Emily's face, her lips were trembling.

She understood exactly what was going to happen. There was no fooling her with my business-as-usual blither. Emily knew she was leaving Wassaic forever today. I saw it in her excitement and in her fear. Her hands trembled too, and when I took them both in mine she let me hold them, while her blue eyes searched my face for truth and reassurance. We were alone. I could talk to her.

I told her it was going to be all right. Sometimes it would seem hard—she'd be lonesome for her teacher or Vera or me, but there would be new people who'd love her and care for her. Her grandmother would be nearby—she'd see her more than she ever had before.

Her eyes never left me; she seemed to understand every word, the trembling stopped.

"Here are the shoes," Vera said coming back with new brown leather loafers. Emily stood, pretty in her plaid skirt and blue sweater. Vera held out her new red jacket. I wiggled on her mittens, feeling for the thumb she flattened against her palm. "I'm going to miss her," Vera said quietly as she gave a final tug on the parka zipper.

Emily clutched my wrist as we opened the door to the outside. The social workers had packed her clothes in one box, her charts and records in another, both piled on a steel cart. They rolled it down the ramp while Emily and I followed. She limped toward the van.

"One last photograph, Emily," I asked, and she stopped, still against the back of the van, waiting patiently while I fumbled to bring her into focus. Her face was serious, trying to please me, but she could barely contain her excitement for the adventure she knew was coming, as though electricity buzzed through her body telling her to *get on with it*; yet she stood there patiently trying to do this thing she knew was important to me.

The flash dismissed her into the van. I saw the seat belt go on. I heard her low excited hum, her sound of freedom. Tears gathered in my throat. The door slammed shut. I rubbed a circle of frost from the window and tapped on it to bring her back to me just one more time. But Emily looked straight ahead.

In layers of warm clothes topped by the crocheted hat Martha made me years ago, I went cross-country skiing on the old railroad bed above our house. Katrina was away at school; I missed her solid figure in front of me, plugged in to rock-and-roll on her Walkman, bobbing as she glided. Martha wasn't skiing this winter, for in three months her baby would be born. Only the dog cheered me up, yelping and leaping in a canine hornpipe. Emily's name adjusted to the rhythm of my skis. I headed off the railroad bed and up the old logging trail.

When I had gone back into Juniper after Emily left, I couldn't stop the tears that jumped down my cheeks. "I'm happy for her, Vera," I said. "I really am."

"Could have fooled me, crying like you are," Vera said, and patted my shoulder. Then she said something that nagged me as I skied through the bottleneck of tall brush to the open meadow. "Guess we won't be seeing you any more now that Emily's gone." Did I respond? I don't think so, because it seemed true. The project was almost over, the photographs made, and the person who most firmly anchored my heart to Wassaic had left.

I skied to the top of a rise in the meadow and looked down on large, white-patched fields. In the distance were misty hills, the pink of fading light shimmering above them. A tissue moon had risen and hung in the sky with a curved sharp top and a bottom like torn paper. I remembered Vera asking me last year, when I began, if I was only going to photograph the pretty ones. I took the hill pushing off hard with my poles, crouched to give me speed. At the bottom I slowed in the new snow, then turned into the old apple orchard. An ancient tree had fallen, its branches dark and defeated against the snow, the only change since last year.

Today five people had left the institution. Fifteen hundred remained.

Afterword

Vera had been right. When my time at Wassaic was over, I visited sporadically for another year, but felt ill at ease without my camera, and uncomfortable with not having a role. I still spent time in Ward C, and though I became especially fond of Wonder Woman, Emily's absence was tangible. Gradually I stopped going to Wassaic. I cannot say that without feeling sadness.

Mrs. Benedict has called me occasionally to give me news of Emily. Emily's weekdays are structured by programming, as they were in Wassaic, though she now attends a "day treatment center" in a converted grocery store, rather than the basement school of Juniper Hall. Several times a week she visits her grandmother for a few hours. She "plays" the piano, and Mrs. Benedict reports she can now find middle C. When her grandmother takes her back to the Park Street residence, there are no tears. Mrs. Benedict looks forward to the birthday parties and parent suppers the staff gives;

recently they celebrated both Mother's Day and Father's Day. "Because I'm a grandparent, I was invited to both!" she said.

I planned several times to see Emily myself, but each time something went wrong: once she was ill, once we had an ice storm, another time Mrs. Benedict had an unexpected overnight visitor. And so it was two years before I saw Emily again. I felt nervous, for Mrs. Benedict had told me she had changed a great deal.

"Why, look Emily, it's Rebecca. Do you remember her?" she asked, holding Emily's shoulders. I ducked my head to put my face in the line of her downward gaze. She didn't focus, and she didn't seem to care who I was, as she tugged on her grandmother's arm.

I studied her. She had lost her scrawniness. She was now a slender young woman, in a plaid skirt that sported a large, chocolate ice cream stain at the hem. Her features had become more definite, her body more womanly. At last she looked up at me, and after long seconds her memory and eyes seemed to engage: very deliberately she reached for my wrist. We were together again.

I could see not only physical changes in Emily, but emotional growth as well. She took me from room to room of her grandmother's house with confidence, as though she were showing me around. As Mrs. Benedict and I talked, she sat quietly on the porch swing, self-contained in a way she'd not been at Wassaic. An overlay of anxiety seemed to have been dissolved. Although her mental age was said to be under three, in many ways Emily had, at the age of fourteen, passed out of a long infancy.

Although I went to Wassaic on brief errands many times over the years, it was not until 1987, four years after I had begun photographing, that I returned specifically to find the people I had photographed. It was spring, and when I drove up the long road to the top of the hill, dogwood were in bloom. An overnight rain had caused the dandelions to bolt, and a field of them stood ready for me to pick and blow in Emily's face. The cement on many of the buildings had been painted to decrease the severity gray concrete imposes, but their size and number again overwhelmed me. The place looked better and yet more horrifying than ever.

The central hall of Butternut Learning still had a sweetish, fecal smell. When I asked if Sherry was teaching in the same room, an aide said, "Oh, she left years ago. Packed up her kids and moved to another state. Someone told me she works in a prison there." When I asked after other staff and clients, I received occasional information, but more often a puzzled headshake.

I found Gregory's residential building and heard his growling, whining voice as I walked down the corridor toward his room. He still needed an aide one-on-one. There were large bruises on his wrists and ankles. The aide told me that Gregory had returned the day before from a three-week hospital stay in a nearby medical center where he'd had to be restrained the entire time. "But we're not allowed to do that here, you know," the aide said, running after Gregory who had just escaped from the room.

John Doe Number 11's condition had not improved. He continued to assault both clients and staff from the confines of his wheelchair, recently biting the head of an aide as she bent over to adjust his shoes. Another aide, who had developed the same sort of paternal fondness for him that Clay had felt, said that John—Delmar Tate—was happiest after dinner, when a group of clients were taken for "music appreciation." They would listen to rock tapes, clap or dance, and John Doe would beat his hands on the side of his wheelchair. But, as Elaine's music therapy had abruptly ended, so the music group was going to stop soon, "because the aides are getting sick of it and so are the clients."

I especially wanted to see the women who had been my friends and Christmas dinner guests. Two of them had been transferred to different buildings. Rhoda Alexius had been transferred to a mental hospital.

Once again it was Emma's birthday. Though she had to be propped up in her wheelchair, she looked glorious in a dress of spring flowers, and glowed with the happiness of the occasion. She wore two new bracelets given to her by the aide who brushed her hair; when the client coordinator came by to give her a gift—an up-to-date, yellow radio cassette player—Emma was thrilled. I was without a present for her, but Emma cheerfully told me she wanted Bing Crosby and Dean Martin tapes. "Who?" the aide screeched. "What about Madonna and Bruce Springsteen?" Emma told me she was still waiting for a community placement.

Gertrude Healey's health was fragile and, like many octogenarians, her memory of recent events was slipping. She couldn't remember my name, asking me to repeat it half a dozen times, but did recall our Christmas dinner and most clearly remembered her years on Randall's Island, more than fifty years ago. Her teacher said she had been upset by the death of clients younger than she, but in the last few months had talked about her own death with calm acceptance. Gertrude was charming and graceful, signaling when she'd had enough of me by asking that I return to visit her again.

Tillie was the hardest of all to see, for we had maintained a relationship after I had left Wassaic; I had brought her home several times. But the more relaxed she had felt with us, the harder it was for her to leave. The last time she came, she began weeping as soon as she arrived because six hours later she would have to go back to Wassaic. I was ashamed by my own reaction, which had been to make excuses for not having her over again. "I thought you were sick, or moved away!" she cried when I came in her room. We sat on the couch, TV blaring a few inches from our ears. She told me her mother was now too old to bring her home, and begged me to take her out, even for one day. "You can't imagine how lonely I am on Saturday and Sunday."

Finally, I talked to Hollis W. Shaw, director of Wassaic, who had made it possible for me to photograph there in the first place. Although he was in Albany as a deputy commissioner in the Office of Mental Retardation during the year I was there, he had now returned to Wassaic. Plaques decorated his office walls, commemorating his continued adherence to his college precept that each person has a responsibility to improve the human condition. Several African carvings on bookcases reflected not only his artistic taste, but also his Afro-American heritage.

Hollis Shaw is a tall man with grey hair turned white in front, which matches a trim mustache and contrasts with his brown skin. Often, when puzzling over a question, he takes off his glasses, as though allowing the external world to blur while he looks for clarity inside. He believes that institutions such as Wassaic should not exist; that as long as a handicapped person is alive, he or she has the right to be placed in the community. "I used to think that breathing should be the only criterion for placement, but now we have a client on a respirator living successfully in the community," he told me. He has envisioned community residences as stepping stones, not ends in themselves, and has cautioned against accepting stepping stones without imagining something better. The solution would be "family care"—families who would be willing to take in one or two clients for remuneration—which would produce rewarding jobs for thousands of people who chose to work at home, would be an enormous saving for the taxpayer, and would establish the stable environment clients need in order to make progress. He pointed out that the family is still the primary source of our ideas and values, and institutional life, even on a small scale, can not provide constant exposure to a role model. How, he asked, can anyone find a person to emulate when six different care-takers are rotated through a week?

I left Wassaic filled with new ideas and conflicting emotions, as I had so many times before, and went home. That night I called all three of my children on the phone.

Wynne, whose law school experience has included volunteer work in prisons, was studying for final exams. He is achieving his goals with confidence, and I know he values his considerable intellectual gifts in an unselfconscious way.

Katrina is now in college. For her high school graduation present I had made a book of photographs from her childhood; in one picture, she and Tillie are baking cookies in our kitchen. Perhaps because of her exposure to Wassaic, she spent part of a summer in Spain as a volunteer in a hospital for quadriplegics.

Max is a senior in high school. He's a photographer and an actor, a smart, articulate, and sensitive young man. Now that he's older, he's been able to set aside his fear of retarded people. More and more I understand that my anger towards him during the Wassaic year stood for a part of me I could not bear to examine. This becomes acutely evident when I look at my reluctance to be near Tillie's pain.

With all three children, I have learned to relish their talents and respect their differences.

Sam continues to work at Wassaic, planning for a declining

population and involving the community in designing proposals to utilize the institution's buildings as they become vacated. His increasing commitment to deinstitutionalization and to architecture that fosters a high quality of life for all disabled people, is an ongoing source of inspiration.

The photographs I took have been printed and edited, and are, at last, ready for exhibition. When I show them to people, I try to stifle my inclination to gloss over, with stories and anecdotes, the upset I know they feel. Some react with compassion and concern, while others cannot bear to look. Because I've seen their reaction mirrored in my own life and family, I no longer feel judgmental, but feel instead a re-dedication to make visible those we have "put away."

Millerton, NY
March 1988

Acknowledgments

I must begin by thanking those who cannot be named. I am deeply grateful to the residents of Wassaic Developmental Center for allowing me into their lives. Their contributions are the core of this book, and the lessons they taught me will remain with me always. I am grateful as well to the dozens of staff members who were friendly, helpful, and patient, answering my many questions without reserve.

Many people believed in this book and helped it inch forward to completion, all of whom I owe great thanks. Hollis W. Shaw, director of Wassaic, encouraged me to explore the institution freely and has consistently aided me in every way. It is enlightened thinking like his that will enrich and protect the lives of retarded men and women. The Dutchess County Arts Council saw the artistic value of this undertaking, and through Barbara Upton-Horvath of Rehabilitation Programs, Inc., helped me obtain the New York State Council on the Arts decentralization grant in photography that launched this project.

I am especially grateful to Honor Moore for her continued support and friendship. She read this manuscript many times, and her insightful criticism was crucial in its development. Honor's dedication to honesty and belief that women have been too long silenced led her to begin the workshop Women Writing/Women Telling in 1979. It was through those summer workshops that I gained the courage to use words. Some of the workshop participants continued to meet year-round, and many of them contributed to this manuscript, especially Jean Sands, Courtney Svalstedt, and Francine Clark. Sondra Zeidenstein, another workshop member, has given me strength and encouragement during the years it took to write this book.

Christopher Hewat read the manuscript when it was over twice its present length, and proved once again his value as a friend and artist. Henrietta Cosentino also helped with early revisions, and I owe her not only thanks for her sharp editorial skills, but gratitude for her continuing presence in my life. Kim Chernin spent the winter of 1982 in this part of the world, and provided inspiration by sharing her own work, as well as structural suggestions as I wrote the first draft. Carol Green has supported me with her large heart and personal example of serenity, courage, and wisdom. Michael Hoffman made himself continually available, and offered advice on the photographs. Tom Cole generously took time from his own work to read and comment on the manuscript, as did Victoria Rue, Marnie Pillsbury, and Victoria Munroe. I gained much from Ann Arensberg's thoughtful reading and continue to be deeply grateful for her advice and good humor. Hampton Howard's considerable efforts in my behalf came just at the right time; his friendship has been invaluable. I am also grateful to Wendy St. John and Christopher St. John for their contribution. The final draft was written during a fellowship at Blue Mountain Center, a haven for artists that reflects the social concerns of its director, Harriet Barlow. To her, and to Kay Burnette, Jill Medvedow, Gordon Adams, and Sam Sills, I give my special thanks.

Wendy Weil, my literary agent, has sustained me with her faith and guidance. Mary Cunnane, my editor at Norton, has been all I could ask for—advising me, probing with the right questions, yet giving me responsibility for my own words. Margie Brassil's copy editing greatly improved this manuscript. Renee Schwartz provided excellent legal counsel.

Three women—Martha Zimiles, Jennifer Almquist, and Lucy Hackney allowed me to use their personal experiences of motherhood, for which I am very grateful. Patricia Egan, my aunt, not only gave me editorial advice, but helped me live this book by befriending both Emily and Tillie. My father, Gene Starkloff, contributed his candor and I thank him. Thanks also to my sister, Kathleen, for being who she is. Finally, I hope the role of Sam and my children is visible on every page. Their love is my rock, and their generosity in allowing me to expose their feeling is a gift beyond words.

Further Reading

The following books have been useful to me as background and research material. Some of them have given me visual information, some have given historical context, others have broadened my perspective on different disabling conditions. Although not intended as a scholarly bibliography, I hope this list will provide readers with resources for their own explorations.

Apgar, Virginia, M.D., and Beck, Joan. *Is My Baby All Right?* New York: Simon & Schuster, 1972.

Baroff, George S. *Mental Retardation: Nature, Cause, and Management.* Washington, D.C.: Hemisphere Publishing Corporation, 1976.

Blatt, Burton. *Christmas in Purgatory: A Photographic Essay on Mental Retardation.* Newton, MA: Allyn & Bacon, 1967.

Blatt, Burton. *Souls in Extremis.* Newton, MA: Allyn & Bacon, 1973.

Bosworth, Patricia. *Diane Arbus.* New York: Alfred A. Knopf, 1984.

Campling, Jo, ed. *Images of Ourselves: Women with Disabilities Talking.* London: Routledge & Kegan Paul, 1981.

Collins, Patricia. *"Your Daughter Is Brain Damaged": A Mother's Story*. New York: Dutton, 1980.

Dass, Ram, and Gorman, Paul. *How Can I Help? Stories and Reflections on Service*. New York: Alfred A. Knopf, 1985.

Diane Arbus: An Aperture Monograph. Millerton, NY: Aperture, 1972.

Dickerson, Martha Ufford. *Our Four Boys*. Syracuse, NY: Syracuse University Press, 1978.

Dix, Dorothea. *On Behalf of the Insane Poor*. Salem, MA: Arno Press & the New York Times, 1971.

Edgerton, Robert B. *The Cloak of Competence: Stigma in the Lives of the Mentally Retarded*. Berkeley: University of California Press, 1967.

Farber, Bernard. *Mental Retardation: Its Social Context and Social Consequences*. Boston: Houghton Mifflin, 1968.

Foucault, Michel. *Madness and Civilization: A History of Insanity in the Age of Reason*. New York: Random House, 1965.

Gilman, Sander L. *The Face of Madness: Hugh W. Diamond and the Origin of Psychiatric Photography*. Secaucus, NJ: Citadel Press, 1976.

Goddard, H. *Feeble Mindedness—Its Causes and Consequences*. New York: Macmillan, 1914.

Goddard, H. *The Kallikak Family*. New York: Macmillan, 1931.

Goffman, Eric. *Asylums: Essays on the Social Situation of Mental Patients and Other Inmates*. Garden City, NY: Doubleday, 1961.

Goffman, Eric. *Stigma: Notes on the Management of Spoiled Identity*. Englewood Cliffs, NJ: Prentice Hall, 1963.

Greenfeld, Josh. *A Child Called Noah: A Family Journey*. New York: Henry Holt, 1972.

Greenfeld, Josh. *A Client Called Noah*. New York: Henry Holt, 1987.

Greenfeld, Josh. *A Place For Noah*. New York: Henry Holt, 1978.

Hurley, R. *Poverty and Mental Retardation: A Casual Relationship*. New York: Vintage Books, 1969.

Laing, R. D. *Wisdom, Madness, and Folly*. London: Macmillan, 1985.

Lyon, Jeff. *Playing God in the Nursery*. New York: W. W. Norton, 1985.

Maddow, Ben. *Let Truth Be the Prejudice. W. Eugene Smith: His Life and Photographs*. New York: Aperture, 1985.

Nolan, Christopher. *Under the Eye of the Clock*. New York: St. Martin's Press, 1987.

O'Conner, Gail, and Meyers, C. Edward. *Home Is a Good Place*. Washington, D.C.: American Association on Mental Deficiency, 1976.

Ornstein, Robert, and Thompson, Richard F. *The Amazing Brain*. Boston: Houghton Mifflin, 1984.

Pastor-Bolnick, Jamie. *Winnie: "My Life In the Institution."* New York: St. Martin's/Marek, 1985.

Pietzner, Cornelius M. *Village Life: The Camphill Communities*. Salzburg, Austria: Neugebauer Press, 1986.

Reed, Elizabeth W. *Mental Retardation: A Family Study*. Philadelphia: Saunders, 1965.

Rivera, Geraldo. *Willowbrook: A Report on How It Is and Why It Got That Way*. New York: Vintage Books, 1972.

Rosen, Marvin, and Clark, Gerald R., eds. *The History of Mental Retardation: Collected Papers*. 2 volumes. Baltimore: University Park Press, 1976.

Rothman, Barbara Katz. *The Tentative Pregnancy: Prenatal Diagnosis and the Future of Motherhood*. New York: Viking, 1986.

Rothman, David J. *Conscience and Convenience: The Asylum and Its Alternative in Progressive America*. Boston: Little, Brown, 1980.

Rothman, David J. and Sheila M. *The Willowbrook Wars: A Decade of Struggle for Social Justice*. New York: Harper & Row, 1984.

Rubin, Alan, M. D. *Handbook of Congenital Malformations*. Philadelphia: Saunders, 1969.

Russ, Martin. *Half Moon Haven*. New York: Holt, Rinehart and Winston, 1959.

Sacks, Oliver. *The Man Who Mistook His Wife for a Hat*. New York: Simon & Schuster, 1986.

Saxton, Marsha, and Howe, Florence, eds. *With Wings: An Anthology of Literature by and about Women with Disabilities*. New York: The Feminist Press, 1987.

Scheerenberger, R. C. *A History of Mental Retardation: A Quarter Century of Promise*. Baltimore: Brookes Publishing, 1987.

Simons, Robin. *After the Tears: Parents Talk About Raising a Child With a Disability*. Denver: Children's Museum of Denver, 1985.

Tractenberg, Alan. *America and Lewis Hine: Photographs 1904–1940*. Millerton, NY: Aperture, 1977.

Vail, D. J. *Dehumanization and the Institutional Career*. Springfield, IL: Charles C. Thomas, 1966.

Wolfensberger, Wolf. *The Origin & Nature of Our Institutional Models*. Syracuse, NY: Human Policy Press, 1975.